Family Finance 2012

A guide to making

and saving money

Colm Rapple

With many thanks to the efficient and informed sub-editors Nuala and Simone and to all who have helped over the years with information and advice.

ISBN: 978-0-9553982-5-4

Published by Squirrel Press

Cover designed by Karen Doyle

Cartoon by John Brennan

Printed in Ireland by Brunswick Press, Dublin

Contents

1. Budget 2012 and beyond 5
2. Managing your cash flows 19
    Flexible friends if used sensibly. 26
    Managing holiday money 37
3. Getting the most from your savings 43
    Secure investments 51
    Direct stock market investment 60
    Investment funds 63
    Investing a lump sum — some options . . . 71
4. Life insurance — for peace of mind 79
5. Borrowing — it can often make sense 98
    Tackling debt problems 112
6. Putting a roof over your head. 118
    Mortgage and rent tax relief 129
7. Inheritance, probate and making a will 134
8. Enforcing your rights as worker and citizen. . . . 144
9. Insuring your home and possessions 163
10. Planning for your retirement 174
11. Using your rights as a consumer. 193
12. Social Welfare — the basics 214
13. Guide to the tax system 230
    Budget changes 2012 231
    PAYE guide 233
    Self-employed income 260
    Working outside Ireland. 268
    Capital Gains Tax 271
    Inheritance and gift taxes 274
14. Reducing your tax liability. 279
    Employing your child or spouse 280
    Tax and marriage 285
    Share incentives 290
    Tax breaks for relatives and carers 297
Your guide to a quick and easy money makeover   301
    Worksheets for your makeover 318
Appendix 1. Summary of tax rates 330
Appendix 2. Civil service mileage rates 338
Appendix 3. Social welfare benefits 340
Index   342

1 Budget 2012 and beyond

The Irish economy started to grow again in 2011 and the growth rate is expected to accelerate in the years ahead. Each year we'll be creating more economic wealth than we did in the previous year. Initially all of the increase will be used to reduce our debts so that the amount available for consumption will continue to decrease. Personal spending is expected to decline by 1.3% in 2012 after a drop of 2.5% in 2011. It's expected to level off in 2013 and then start to rise slowly from 2014 onwards. We're unlikely to feel much better off, however, because the Government intends to continue cutting its spending on day-to-day services by about 2.2% a year, at least until 2015. But the tide has turned. Employment is expected to stabilise in 2012 and grow in 2013 with the number out of work slowly declining.

The impositions of the 2012 Budget have been widely spread and the individual impacts may be small, but the overall burden on many families will be significant. Basic income tax credits, rates and bands remained unchanged but many of the other changes have an impact on individual incomes — in a few cases for the better but mostly for the worse.

But everyone, even those who get a small boost to their incomes, face higher taxes on their spending. No-one can

Budget changes that you may need to take

☐ <u>DIRT</u> is being increased from January 1, 2012 to 30% on most deposit income and 33% on longer-term deposits and investment funds. This increases the relative attractiveness of tax-free savings options such as An Post Savings Certs particularly as deposit rates will come under downward pressure as the euro crisis recedes. See page 54.

☐ <u>Mortgage interest relief</u> is being increased to 30% for first-time buyers who bought between January 1, 2004 and December 31, 2008. A couple can get that relief on a maximum of €20,000 interest a year up until 2017. Those buying during 2012 are to continue to get tax relief at 25%. While the relief will continue up to and including 2017 for those already in the system, it will not be available for those buying after December 31, 2012 — at least that's the intention as stated in the 2012 Budget. See page 129.

☐ <u>Pension contributions</u> will continue to qualify for relief at the claimant's top rate of tax. It had been intended to reduce the maximum relief to 34% in 2012, 27% in 2013 and 20% in 2014. It continues to be attractive for top-rate taxpayers to use pension funds to save for retirement. Future changes have not been ruled out. There is a commitment in the EU/IMF Programme to reduce the maximum relief to the standard rate and it is recognised that some changes are inevitable and likely to be introduced in 2013. For top-rate taxpayers who want to save for retirement there may be an advantage in front loading pension contribution. See Chapter 10 starting on page 174.

☐ <u>Capital Gains Tax and Capital Acquisitions Tax</u> rates were increased from 25% to 30% with effect from December 6, 2011. From the same date, the tax-free threshold for transfers from parents to children was reduced significantly from €332,084 to €250,000 but there was no change in the other thresholds. Although expected, no change was made to the Capital Acquisitions Tax relief on the passing of farm and business assets which for tax purposes are valued at only one-tenth of their real value. Neither was there any mention of a curtailment of the Capital Gains Tax relief on the gifting of house sites to children. With further tax increases inevitable in 2013 and 2014 these may be targeted in future Budgets. See page 274.

into account in your financial planning

☐ <u>Approved Retirement Fund</u> (ARF) withdrawals are liable for tax and irrespective of the amount withdrawn, tax is applied to a minimum of 5% of the funds value. That rate is being increased to 6% from the end of 2012 for funds worth in excess of €2 million. From that date too, this imputed withdrawal provision will apply to vested Personal Retirement Savings Accounts, which are PRSAs from which a tax-free lump sum has already been taken. See page 191.

☐ <u>The Universal Social Charge</u> rates bands are unchanged but those with incomes of less than €10,036 a year will be exempt. The exemption limit was €4,004 in 2011. Those with earnings in excess of the exemption limit are liable for USC on all of their income.

☐ <u>PRSI</u> relief on employee contributions to pension funds no longer applies from January 1, 2012. In 2011, employers paid only 50% of their standard PRSI liabilities on such contributions. From 2013, PRSI is to be applied to rental, investment and other forms of income that have been escaping the net.

☐ <u>The Household Charge</u> of €100 applies to most private dwellings. The owner, rather than tenant, is liable for the charge. Those in receipt of Mortgage Interest Supplement or living in certain designated unfinished estates are exempt.

☐ <u>The Enterprise and Investment Incentive</u> was approved by the EU before the Budget as a replacement for the Business Expansion Scheme. It greatly extends the range of businesses that can benefit, and increases the maximum amount of qualifying finance. It provides tax relief for those willing to invest equity capital in start-up ventures. See page 293.

☐ <u>The Carbon Tax</u> increase from €15 to €20 per tonne applied to motor fuels from December 7, 2011, to heating oils and LPG from May 2012 and not to solid fuels which remain liable to the tax at €15 a tonne.

☐ <u>Stamp Duty</u> on commercial property transfers was reduced to a flat rate of 2% from December 7, 2011. As a further incentive to property investment a Capital Gains Tax concession is to apply to properties bought between December 7, 2011 and the end of 2013. If the property is held for at least seven years, no Capital Gains Tax will apply to any gains made during that seven years.

avoid the increase in the standard rate of VAT from 21% to 23%. Many of the items subject to the standard rate are essentials rather than luxuries.

Then there is the new €100 Household Charge, motor tax, the carbon tax and increased excise duty on tobacco. Some can be avoided, most can't. The net impact will vary from individual to individual and won't depend to any great extent on relative income. High earners will, in many cases, bear a smaller proportionate burden than poorer families, particularly those families impacted by some of the changes in social welfare benefits. The basic rates of benefit remain unchanged but restriction on some payments result in a significant drop in income for some individuals (see page 215).

Not many people will be able to buck the trend but with some skilful management the impact can be reduced. It's a matter of making the most of what you have and managing your income and assets to best effect, taking account of changes in the economic outlook and in the tax and social welfare systems. That involves gathering as much information as possible, considering the options and drawing up a plan.

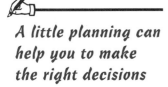

A little planning can help you to make the right decisions

It's all a matter of planning. There are no easy solutions that can be applied to all people in all circumstances. But you stand a better chance of making the best decisions if you first take the time to set objectives and gather as much information as you can. You need to review your personal finances in as much detail as you can. The more work you put into it, the better chance you have of making the right decisions. Past decisions need to be revised in the light of changed circumstances. Financial objectives may remain the same but the ways of achieving them have changed. The impact of the recession hasn't been confined to incomes. There has also been a sharp fall in asset values. The value of what we own has gone down: property, shares and pension funds. For many, that fall is reflected solely in figures on a sheet of paper and will only be translated into actual cash losses if, and when, the asset is sold. The losses are real enough. If your house has fallen in value, you certainly feel less wealthy. The feeling will be even more acute if your savings and investments have fallen in value and more acute still if it's your pension fund.

Financial objectives are likely to be the same at any time in the financial cycle. Most people want to maximise both their income and the value of their assets. The objectives may remain the same but not the best ways of pursuing them. Attitudes to risk also change as confidence ebbs and flows.

So how best to prepare for the upturn while surviving the downturn? The Money Makeover section starting on page 301 outlines how you should go about setting goals, assessing where you are and how best to set a route to where you want to be. It's worth going through in some detail and then repeating the exercise as frequently as possible as the financial climate and your circumstances change. Short-term objectives, in particular, may change. The following are some of the factors to take into account. You'll find others throughout the book.

Some factors to consider when preparing your personal budget

■ Savings

You may want to keep more money easily accessible in emergency funds during the downturn but less as the upturn takes hold. But make sure you get the best return. The best rate available on demand deposits in December 2011 was 300 times higher than the worse rate. But both the best and the worst enjoyed the same Government guarantees. With DIRT increased to 30%, tax free options have got more attractive. See page 51.

■ Getting back to work

Getting back to work is a top priority for all too many people and it needs to be seen as a full-time job in itself. It's not a topic that this book purports to cover in any great detail but there are some suggestions later in this chapter.

■ Investments

Investment values have fallen sharply from their peak and most people are, understandably, more risk adverse now than they ever were before. But there must come a point at which the risk of making fresh investments will outweigh the risk of a double-dip recession. It won't be the same for everyone. It depends on an individual's personal risk profile. It's as well to know what that is and to keep an eye out for opportunities.

■ Pensions

If money is really scarce it may be sensible to postpone funding your pension. But by doing so you may be foregoing an opportunity to invest at or close to the bottom. You should also consider tax relief changes. See chapter 10, page 174.

■ Mortgage difficulties

Those with mortgage difficulties need to assess their options and check on their rights. Repayments have to be met but there are ways of reducing the burden. It may be possible to extend the term of the loan, switch to an interest-only mortgage or, in exceptional cases, it may be possible to postpone repayments entirely and have the interest rolled up and added to the loan. See page 114 for advice on tackling mortgage arrears.

Borrowers finding it difficult to meet mortgage repayments or rent may qualify for State assistance provided they are in receipt of a social welfare or HSE benefit. Application for this supplementary benefit is made to the Community Welfare Officer who can be contacted through your local HSE office.

If you are still in a job and your mortgage is well covered by the value of your property, you are the kind of borrower that many lenders are looking for. You may be able to negotiate a cut in your interest rate or switch to a cheaper option.

■ Life insurance

There may be scope to freeze, or even dispense with, some life insurance policies. Care is obviously needed but it's worthwhile reviewing your needs and cover.

■ Get a tax rebate

Claiming a tax rebate can provide a once-off income boost. See page 254.

■ Shop around for house/car insurance

Increased competition has made it essential to shop around for the best deal. Substantial savings can be made without suffering any loss of cover. It's best to do the legwork yourself on the internet or telephone. Don't assume that a renewal quote is the best deal available from your insurer. You're likely to be offered a better deal by pretending to be a new customer.

- ### Cancel unnecessary, bad value policies
  You need house insurance. The impact of losing your home, however small the risk of it actually happening, is too great a risk to take, even when money is tight. But you could survive if you lost your mobile phone or your credit card. So do you need insurance? See page 170.

Budgeting

Knowing exactly where your money is coming from and how it is spent is essential to your decision making whether or not you have taken a drop in income. You can use the worksheets starting on page 318, a spread sheet or the back of an envelope. However you do it, the more information you collect the better.

There is no single way to balance a household budget. It depends on the individual as much as it depends on circumstances. Some can get by with penny-pinching over a wide range of spending items. Others feel happier zoning in on a few big items of spending and targeting those. There are no right or wrong answers. If you have to cut back, the decision on where and how is very much a personal one. But the more information you have the more likely you are to take the most appropriate decision.

It's good business practice to use recessions to cut out the fat that has accumulated during good years to create a slimmer, more efficient organisation. A similar approach can be taken with your personal finances. It can ease the problem of surviving the downturn and/or create additional savings that can be used to invest or to capitalise on buying opportunities that arise during the upturn. You'll find suggestions on how to save or make money throughout the book.

Managing your assets

Asset values have fallen sharply during the recession and most will rise in value again. Property values will rise again.

Even some bank shares will recover some of their value. Very few will be able to claim that they bought at the very bottom of the dip and those that do will have done so more by luck than design. Continued uncertainty causes volatility and the more aggressive risk-takers can make, or lose, fortunes on the swings and roundabouts. Others are content to wait and see. The best approach, of course, lies somewhere between the wheeling and dealing of the speculator and the 'do nothing' approach of the conservative. Doing nothing may be the right approach is some circumstances. It may be the only thing to do with regard to your home. But it's very wrong to hold onto an asset simply, or mainly, because you don't want to crystallise a loss.

If you like your home and have no inclination to move, then its market value is of little concern, even if it has fallen to less than you actually paid for it or is worth less than the outstanding mortgage. Difficulties might arise if you have to sell, or if, because of a drop in income you find it hard to meet the repayments. But if you are not in that position, then there is little point in worrying about it.

The price you paid for an asset has no bearing on its current value or on whether or not you should sell it

Okay, so it's annoying to realise that your new neighbour has now bought an identical house to yours at a lower price than you paid. But there is nothing you can do about it. It happens, and on the basis of past trends, house prices will eventually rise again, maybe sooner rather than later, and you'll be sitting on paper profits again.

If you have to, or want to, sell to move house, don't get hung up on the fact that you may be taking a capital loss on the sale. The price you paid for the house is immaterial. It only exists in your mind. It's the current value that counts and the price you paid for the house has no bearing on that. It should not enter the decision-making process at all. That may be easier said than done.

Nobody likes incurring a capital loss. But the price you paid for any asset has no bearing at all on its current value. That's true for all assets although it is all too often not recognised by those who invest in shares. What's important is not the past but the future prospects. The question to ask is whether your money is better invested where it currently is, or alternatively invested somewhere else. At any point in time your investment is worth whatever it will sell for. If you had the money would you invest it back in that share, or is there another investment outlet offering better future prospects? That's the question that investors should constantly be asking themselves.

Shares have an objective underlying value. It's the net present value of the future flow of earnings. But, of course, there are different views of what that earnings flow will be. Some investors will base their decisions simply on the prospects for future earnings. But others will base their decision on how they believe other investors will react, not to the actual reality but rather to market sentiment i.e. what other people think. They are not interested in the future flow of earnings because they are only gambling on making a capital gain by buying cheap and selling dear in the very short-term. Market sentiment can be very fickle reflecting mainly emotion and a herd instinct, all of which adds to the volatility of stock market values.

All of those factors have to be taken into account when buying or selling shares. They are just as relevant during a boom as they are during a downturn. The one factor that shouldn't be taken into account is the price at which shares were originally bought. But at the same time, there is no harm in being aware that other people may be inclined, rather illogically, to take original purchase prices into account. It can result in people holding onto shares in the vain hope of an upturn, long after they should have sold.

Getting back to work

Most people generate the bulk of their income from work. Nothing reduces income quite so sharply and significantly as having one's job made redundant. The inevitable drop in income creates financial difficulties that can only be solved by cutting back on spending. Balancing the budget involves all of the actions outlined above. The financial review and budgeting process applies equally whether you are in a job or unemployed, have suffered a drop in income or not. But maximising your income crucially involves keeping your job, preparing yourself for a better job as the opportunities arise during the upturn, and/or getting yourself back into the labour force after a job loss.

Of those the most urgent is obviously getting yourself back into a job when the old one has been made redundant. An important first step is to recognise that it is not you who is redundant, but rather the old job that has outlived its usefulness. So do not go around saying, or even thinking, that you have been made redundant — put it the other way, my job was made redundant. That should put you in the right frame of mind for the difficult tasks that lie ahead.

Much of what needs to be done to get back into a job can also usefully be employed by those in jobs to enhance their future employment prospects. Redundancy can be seen as an opportunity. For many it has been the spur to shake off inertia, recognise their potential and put that potential to use. Employment growth will lag behind the upturn in economic output. But some businesses — they tend to be the better ones — start hiring in advance of their needs while they have the widest choice of applicants. The upturn brings with it opportunities to get, and to switch, jobs. To achieve your ambitions on the jobs front, however, you need to work at it, look on it as a job in itself. Just as in the Money Makeover outlined above you need to:

- Establish your goals — what job do you ideally want?

- Set out the skills that you have. Not just the ones that you are currently using but all of the skills you have acquired. There is no need to be modest.

- Outline your strengths and weaknesses. Once again there is no need to be modest but be realistic.

- Discover what attributes are needed for that ideal job. It may be your current job as it evolves to meet changes or it may be a new job. What are the relevant employers looking for? Do some research. Talk to someone who is in or close to your ideal job.

- Get qualified for the job. Upgrade your skills. Get training. Get relevant work experience by taking casual, freelance or even voluntary work.

- Start applying for jobs.

- Keep your CV short and concise.

- List what you are doing, what you have achieved, what you can offer and what you are looking for.

- Summarise all important information on a single page and keep the whole CV to no more than 2 or 3 pages.

- Tailor the CV for each job.

- Do your homework on the potential employer.

- Put yourself in the interviewer's shoes. What is he or she looking for? Don't be afraid to ask.

- Be specific. Not "I'm well capable of doing that" but rather "I did that in my last job" or "I have had training in that".

Get a copy of the excellent "Working for Work" published by the Irish National Organisation of the Unemployed (INOU). It's free. You can download it from www.inou.ie/workingforwork or get it from INOU, 8 North Richmond Street, Dublin 1. Tel: 01-8560088.

If you are working at least 19 hours a week on a low income and have a dependent child or children you may be entitled to Family Income Supplement. It can be a valuable benefit for those on short time or who are considering whether some part-time work is a worthwhile option. See page 220 for full details.

Job Assist tax relief

More than half of the 300,000 plus registered as jobless in Ireland at the end of 2011 have been out of work for a year or more. The long-term unemployed can find it hard to get back into the active labour force. They can get disheartened, tired of trying, and employers sometimes view them with suspicion. But there are tax incentives that can more than offset those perceived disadvantages.

Employers who hire someone who has been out of work for more than a year can write off double their wage costs as a taxable expense, while the employee gets extra tax allowances. Both concessions continue for up to three years.

These incentives are provided under the Revenue Job Assist scheme that has been in existence for many years but isn't publicised as much as it might. It provides a major incentive for employers to take on extra workers and can help potential employees to make the transition from dependence on benefits to gainful employment.

There are generous tax reliefs for employers who take on someone who are been out of work for a year or more and also tax relief for the employee

To qualify, the employee must have been continuously unemployed for a period of at least 12 months prior to taking up the job. Up to 15 days of incidental employment are ignored. They must also have been in receipt of one of the following social welfare payments: Jobseeker's Benefit or Allowance, One-parent Family Payment, Disability Allowance, Blind Person's Pension, Illness Benefit or Invalidity Pension.

Periods on FÁS (SOLAS) courses and training schemes are counted so long as the person was previously on one of the relevant social welfare benefits.

The job must be for a minimum of 30 hours a week and be capable of lasting at least a year. No more than 75% of the income must be commission based, the previous holder of the job must not have been unfairly dismissed and there must have been no redundancies in the company during the previous 26 weeks.

If those conditions are satisfied, the employee is entitled to an additional tax allowance of €3,810 in the first year in addition to €1,270 for each dependant child. These are tax allowances rather than credits so they are granted at the worker's top rate of tax. That provides an added incentive to those who can command sufficient pay to push them into the top rate tax net.

The personal allowance is worth €762 in saved tax for those paying tax at 20% and €1,562 for those paying tax at 41%. The child allowance is worth either €254 or €561 in saved tax and it's granted for each qualifying child.

The personal allowance drops by a third to €2,540 in the second year and by a further third to €1,270 in the third year. The child allowance goes down to €850 in year two and €425 in year three.

The initial claim can be delayed until the year after starting in the job. For instance, someone starting work towards the end of the year can delay the initial claim for extra allowances until the following year. Once claimed it continues for three years so long as the worker stays in either that job or another job.

In addition to these tax benefits, the employees also maintain entitlement to any secondary benefits they were entitled to while out of work subject to some income conditions. These include rent/mortgage subsidy, fuel allowance. If they have a medical card, they keep it for three years from the date of taking up the job.

These incentives for employees may encourage employers to offer lower wages although that's not the idea since they benefit from very generous tax incentives of their own.

They are allowed to claim extra tax deductions in respect of any qualifying employee that they have taken on. They can deduct from their taxable income, double the wages paid and also double the employer's PRSI paid in respect of that employee. That can greatly reduce the net cost of taking on an extra worker.

Since July 2011 the lower rate of employer PRSI has been halved for all jobs that pay up to €356 per week.

There was another scheme that was due to end on December 31, 2011, under which employers did not have to pay their share of PRSI for certain employees for 12 months. It was open to employers who created new and additional jobs. Those who created a new job at any time since January 1, 2010 might still qualify for the exemption. Towards the end of 2011 it was unclear if the scheme would be extended.

The rules were similar to those applying to the Revenue Job Assist scheme but with slight differences. The worker needed only to have been drawing a Jobseeker's Benefit or Allowance, Disability Allowance or One-parent Family Payment for six months rather than 12. Alternatively they can have been on a FÁS/SOLAS course for three months.

Workers on Job Assist also retain entitlement to some social welfare benefits including rent subsidy, fuel allowance and medical card

The job had to be a new and additional one but needs to last only six months. The purpose of the scheme was to support job creation and counter the drift of people into long-term unemployment and welfare dependency.

More information on the Employer Job (PRSI) Incentive Scheme can be obtained from Department of Social Protection, Floor 2, Shannon Lodge, Carrick-on-Shannon, Co. Leitrim. Locall: 1890 927 999.

Information and applications forms for the Revenue Job Assist Scheme can be obtained from any Revenue office.

2 Managing your cash flows

The Irish banking system is in a state of flux. There are fewer banks offering day-to-day banking services. There are also fewer deposit takers. Anglo Irish Bank and Irish Nationwide Building Society ceased operations during 2011. Halifax and Postbank closed in 2010. Anglo's deposits were transferred to AIB while Irish Nationwide's were transferred to Permanent TSB. The EBS is being acquired by AIB but will continue to operate as a separate entity. National Irish Bank's cash services are contracted out to An Post. The bank still provides ATM services while lodgements and withdrawals can be made at post offices throughout the country. The trend is towards fewer banks offering fewer cash services. With less competition it is likely that the cost of banking will increase. More so than ever before, customers will need to keep informed and be willing to switch if they want the best value.

It is possible to exist without a bank account but it has become increasingly difficult. Most income gets spent before the next pay day, but during those few days or weeks that it is yours, it needs to be kept safe, easily accessible and in a form that enables bills to be paid with the minimum of cost and inconvenience. We still have a preference for cash in Ireland but that's waning and increasingly money is being transferred electronically from one account to another. It's a trend that the Government has sought to accelerate at the behest of the banks by imposing an extra stamp duty on cheques while the banks have ended, from the beginning of 2012, the cheque guarantee scheme under which cheques up to €130 in value could be accepted with minimal risk. In addition to any transaction charges imposed by the bank, there is an additional stamp duty of 50c on each cheque or other bill of exchange.

The majority of people need a place to lodge money and/or have their wages paid into. They need to be able to withdraw it when needed and to pay bills with the minimum of fuss and inconvenience. For most people the ideal arrangement is to have income paid directly into a bank that provides them with ready access to a good network of ATMs and the facility to make electronic payments directly from that account.

This type of money transfer service is best provided by what is known as a current account. That used to be synonymous with a cheque book account but that's no longer the case. The cheque book is being slowly, but inevitably, superseded by debit cards and electronic transfers. Most banks offer a similar range of services and there may be little difference in terms of convenience given that most ATMs accept all cards and you may seldom have to visit your bank branch. But there can be significant differences in cost and quality of service, so it pays to shop around when opening a new account or when reviewing your existing account, as you should do from time to time. There is less competition but you should be able to get an account that:

- imposes no transaction charges;

- offers access to low-cost loans and/or overdrafts; and

- pays interest on credit balances in some circumstances.

Mind you, you may not want all those features. Transaction charges won't break you although they can be as high as 30c a time and are best avoided. You may never want to borrow and you should always shop around even if your existing bank claims to offer the best rates. If you never have much money in your current account, then any interest payments are bound to be small. And if you are into electronic banking, it's very easy to switch spare money out of your

Joint accounts and inheritance

☐ There are many reasons for opening a joint bank, building society or post office account. People sharing living expenses may find it the easiest way to operate. Elderly people sometimes open joint accounts with a relative or friend to ease access to their money. They can give the other person the right to withdraw money but they can also retain that right themselves. It may be intended that the money will automatically pass to the survivor but that is not always the case. A court decreed in 1932 that the money in such an account should pass into the estate of the deceased person to be divided up in accordance with the terms of any will or, where there was no will, the division laid down by the courts or the Succession Act.

The precedent created by this judgment was effectively overturned by a Supreme Court ruling on a new case. It concerned an elderly woman who opened a joint account with a niece. She clearly wanted her niece to inherit the money after her death but also wished to retain sole access to the account during her own lifetime. Both aunt and niece were in the bank when the account was opened. Both signed the documentation. The account was made payable to the aunt or to the 'survivor'. In other words, only the aunt could withdraw money during her lifetime but it was her clear intention that after her death her niece should have access to the money.

After her death, other claimants to her estate took a case against both the niece and the bank and a lower court found in their favour citing the 1932 case. That decision was appealed to the Supreme Court which found in favour of the niece. But the judgment does not give an automatic right of ownership to the survivor. There should be no problem, of course, where account holders have each contributed to the account but where only one has contributed, the other or others, will gain ownership only where there was a clear indication that this was the deceased person's intention. It is best to make the intention clear in writing. Whatever about the actual ownership of the account, money in a joint account may be liable to Capital Acquisitions Tax in the hands of the survivor — see page 274 for more details. Ownership, of course, is different to access. A surviving spouse doesn't require tax clearance to access an account held jointly with the deceased partner. In other cases, formal tax clearance from the Revenue is required if the account has more than €50,000 in it.

current account and into a high interest deposit account with another bank or with your existing bank.

The following are some of the packages available to new customers at the end of 2011. Existing customers may be on different, often more costly, accounts that are no longer being marketed.

- **Ulster Bank** charges no transaction fees or maintenance charges.

- **Bank of Ireland** customers can qualify for free banking by keeping a minimum of €3,000 in their account or, alternatively having €3,000 lodged to the account during each three-month period and also making at least nine payments from the account using the Bank's phone or online service. Otherwise there is a fee of 28c per transaction. Customers can alternatively opt to pay €11.40 a quarter for up to 90 transactions. If used in full that works out at 12.7c per transaction.

- **AIB** provides free banking services to customers who, during each three month charging period, make at least one purchase using an AIB debit card and make one payment using its phone or online service. Those who don't qualify for free banking pay a fee of €4.50 a quarter and 20c per transaction.

- **EBS** charges 30c on every debit card and ATM transaction on its Money Manager Account. The first five withdrawals in branch or from an ATM are free if €1,500 is lodged to the account each month or if a minimum balance of €500 is maintained in the account.

- **Permanent TSB** has no transaction charges on its current account. Its €12 a quarter maintenance fee can be avoided if at least €3,000 is lodged to the account each quarter, at least 18 card purchases are made and at least one payment, or funds transfer, is made using the online banking service.

- **National Irish Bank**, whose branches no longer handle cash, has three personal current account packages. There are no transaction charges on any of them, and no maintenance charge on its standard "Easy Customer Package". There are maintenance charges on the other two, an annual fee of €75 on its Easy Plus package, and a fee of €125 a year on its Prestige account. In return for those charges the customer get a 1% return on credit balance in an Easy Plus Account and 1.75% on balance in a Prestige account. Earning interest on credit balances may be worthwhile for anyone who keeps large sums of money in a current account. But with electronic banking it's very easy to switch money out of a current into an interest bearing deposit account and many offer rates well in excess of 1.75%. Account holders also qualify for credit cards carrying the same interest rate as applies to overdrafts. But lower rate cards are available from Bank of Ireland and AIB.

It's not too difficult to switch banks if you think it worthwhile, but first check if your existing bank can offer you something better than the account you have. The banks have adopted a voluntary code under which customers or potential customers are provided with "switching packs" that outline, in simple language, the process of switching, who is responsible for what, how long it will take and what the customer has to do. There is a commitment to have the new account up and running within 10 days and all standing orders etc. transferred from the old account within seven days after that.

If you are liable for charges on your existing account and can't be bothered switching, there are other things that you can do to reduce your costs. Paying a bill by credit card costs nothing, for instance, provided the balance is paid off in full each month. That is the only sensible way to use a credit card. Paying the same bill by cheque can cost over €1.40 made up of as much as 30c to the bank, 50c in stamp duty and 55c in postage. Even without bank charges it costs over a euro, a cost that can be avoided by paying electronically. Many utility bills can be paid without charge at post offices or at PostPoint facilities in retail outlets. An Post's BillPay is also available on the internet at BillPay.ie.

In all these examples, the savings are small enough but you may be able to save significant amounts by ensuring that you don't keep too much money in your current account. It makes sense to transfer any spare money out to a deposit account. Internet and telephone banking have made it easy

Use online banking to speedily switch spare money out of current accounts into high interest accounts

to switch money between accounts. If you can access your current account online, it only takes a few key strokes to organise an electronic transfer of funds out of your account into another either with your own bank or with another financial institution. You usually have to set up the account details in advance but that's a once-off chore that shouldn't take more than a few minutes. Inertia is the enemy. But don't simply complain about the banks. Do something. Shift any spare money you have to where it can make the best possible return. There may be no interest paid on money left in your current account while you can earn over 3% on money in a deposit account.

Credit Unions

Credit unions are co-operative, non-profit making, ventures established within a community covering perhaps a locality or a workplace. Through that community, all the members enjoy what is known as a "common bond". Their basic role is to encourage saving and provide loans but they are greatly expanding the range of financial services that they provide. In addition to being a home for savings and a source of loans, many credit unions operate budget accounts which provide for the payment of regular bills. Members may also have access to group rate medical health insurance premiums which can offer a 10% discount on individual rates and increasingly credit unions are providing a wider range of financial services.

Credit unions are self-help non-profit making organisations

The dividends paid on share accounts vary from credit union to credit union. Members have the option of having DIRT deducted at source, or of declaring their own interest for tax purposes. Credit unions, in common with other deposit takers, can offer all of their deposit accounts on a DIRT-free basis to eligible savers who are over 65 or permanently incapacitated and not liable for tax.

A major benefit, of course, is the access to loans at reasonable rates of interest compared particularly to the often more expensive finance houses — see chapter 5. The maximum rate of interest that credit unions can charge is 12.6% APR but it can be less. Some also pay year-end rebates out of whatever surplus is available. But there is less scope for this in the current climate. Loan protection insurance providing for the repayment of the loan in the event of death or permanent disability is included. Limits may apply to the size of the loan and the cover is curtailed for the over 60s and not available for the over 70s.

Another built-in insurance provides for the payment of a benefit to a member's estate in the event of death. In the case of a member aged under 55, the benefit is equal to the amount on deposit or in shares at the time of death. The benefit is lower for those over 55 and in the case of the over 70s, limited to savings made before reaching that age. Security also varies from one credit union to another.

Depositors are insured against loss resulting from fraud on the part of officials, and the credit unions are included in the Government's guarantee scheme covering deposits up to €100,000. There is also an internal savings protection scheme with cover of up to €12,700 for each individual.

Flexible friends, if used sensibly

Plastic money is steadily replacing cash as the premier method of payment. It has a lot going for it. For many purposes, plastic money is safer and more convenient than cash and it comes in a wide range of different forms. There are credit cards, charge cards, debit cards, and ATM cards, and that doesn't exhaust the possibilities. There is a range of variants within most of those categories.

As the range of options has extended, so too has the competition and the need for the consumer to understand the pros and cons, the costs and benefits. The options can be confusing by times. All forms of plastic money can be used to advantage but, without care, most can prove costly in one way or another. The first step towards avoiding the pitfalls is to understand how the types of card differ. You can save money by knowing what you need and by shopping around.

Plastic money

The more popular forms of plastic money include:

- **Credit cards** such as Mastercard and Visa give you instant access to credit. You can make a purchase or pay a bill and not have to part with any cash for almost two months. You get a statement each month and can either pay it off in full to avoid interest charges or spread the payments over a period, effectively taking a loan.

- **Charge cards** issued by American Express and Diners Club as well as by Mastercard and Visa, offer the same facilities as credit cards — usually with a wider range of extra benefits — but you are expected to pay the bill in full each month.

- **Debit cards** such as Laser card and the Visa debit card operate like an electronic cheque book. They allow the holder to make payments from their own bank or building society account. The card is used to make payments just as a cheque would.

- **ATM or cash dispenser** facilities are generally included on a debit card. From January 1, 2012 banks no longer provide cheque guarantee facilities.

Those are the basic forms of plastic money. Within each type there can be a wide variation. So let's have a look at each option in some more detail.

Credit cards

A credit card can be a true flexible friend if used sensibly. It need cost you no more than the annual €30 stamp duty if you pay in full each month and only use the card to make purchases. For that you can get up to 56 days free credit between the time you make a purchase and actually pay the bill. Your card provides a free and flexible way of paying bills by phone, post or over the internet and saves you having to carry around too much cash. But if you don't pay in full each month, run over your credit limit, miss payments, or use your card to withdraw cash, the costs can mount up and your flexible friend can become expensive.

Towards the end of 2011, personal card holders had credit card debt of €2.6 billion. That was down 8% on the end-2010 figure. Monthly repayments, at €765 million were running about €16 million ahead of credit card spending.

All too often consumers take whatever card is offered by their bank or alternatively make the choice on the basis of a seemingly low-interest rate or a short-lived interest free period on the balance transferred from another card. But the choice needs to be made on the basis of all the factors involved, not just one.

The following are some of the factors that need to be considered. They can all significantly affect the cost:

- What interest rate is charged on cash withdrawals?

- Does the interest apply from the date of the cash withdrawal even if the total balance is paid in full and on time?

- If a part payment is made, is it used to reduce that portion of the debt bearing the highest interest or the lowest interest?

- What charges are imposed for cash withdrawals, late payments or exceeding the credit limit?

Credit cards can be an expensive way to borrow money particularly when used for cash withdrawals. Partial repayments are, in some cases, used to pay off the lower interest debt on purchases while interest may continue to be charged for years on a cash withdrawal at 26% or more

The weight that you give to each of those factors depends on how you intend to use the card. If you are never going to run into debt, for instance, you don't have to worry about the rate of interest. Unfortunately no single card ranks number one on all of those criteria but some cards rank very well on most of them.

While you can get details of credit card interest rates and charges on itsyourmoney.ie, the National Consumer Agency's website, it unfortunately doesn't contain details of a large range of cards issued by banks in the past. They are no longer being marketed but many people still have them and are not being told by their issuers that there are better value alternatives available. Don't assume that your card from a particular issuer is the one currently being marketed.

There are pluses and minuses with all cards. Pay in full each month and make no cash withdrawals and a card need cost you no more than the annual stamp duty and for that you get up to 52 days free credit depending on when you make your purchases. If payment is not made in full and on time, interest is usually charged from the date of the transactions and, in the case of AIB and MBNA, interest continues to be charged on the carried forward portion of the debt even if the account is cleared in full and on time the following month.

AIB's "click" card and Bank of Ireland's "Clear" card offer the lowest rates of interest on purchases. AIB charges 13.6% and Bank of Ireland charges 13.8%. Those are comparable rates that include the stamp duty in the cost. AIB is the better option. It scores in other ways too. Neither bank charges any interest on cash withdrawals if the total debt is paid in full, and on time, but if there is only a partial payment AIB uses it to reduce the higher interest debt arising from cash withdrawals first whereas Bank of Ireland does the opposite, reducing the lowest interest debt on pur-

Buying on the internet without a credit card

☐ It is possible to buy on the internet without using a credit card. If you don't have a credit card or if you are simply fearful of sending your card details over the web you can instead make use of a prepaid virtual Visa card. One such card is issued by 3V. Blank cards are available at participating local convenience stores showing a Payzone logo. You can also order one online at 3V.ie. At that stage you pay nothing. The next step is to register your card and personal details with 3V. Once the card has been registered you can load it with up to €350 at one of the participating stores. You get a voucher with a 16-digit number which can then be used in the same way as a credit card number. Security details including a PIN and expiry date are emailed to you or can be obtained over the phone. A flat charge is levied for each top-up of more than €20. It's €2.50 for amounts between €30 and €100 and €5 for amounts over €100. Funds left on the card can be redeemed for a flat charge of €5. A commission of 1.75% is charged on non-euro transactions.

Skrill, which formally went under the name Moneybookers, offers a pre-paid MasterCard. Ryanair doesn't charge its €6 administrative charge on Irish bookings made using this card a concession usually only allowed in Britain for those using Ryanair's own pre-paid MasterCard. It also offers a secure way of paying for online purchases but there is, of course, a cost involved. There is a €10 annual charge while ATM withdrawals cost a flat €1.80. You can top up your pre-payment free by bank transfer or Laser card.

Details at http://g.moneybookers.com/mastercard/ie/

chases. It represents a major difference for those who use their credit cards for cash withdrawals and who don't pay in full each month.

For example, let's suppose that you run up a credit card bill of €1,000 over the course of a month by making a cash withdrawal of €200 and making purchases totalling €800. The interest rate on the cash withdrawal will be far higher than that charged on the purchases. If you have an AIB card and make a partial payment of say €200, it will be used to pay off the cash withdrawal debt so your ongoing debt will be only subject to the lower interest rate. That may seem like a small enough concession, but it's a concession that many other card issuers don't give. With the Bank of Ireland cards any partial payment is used first to reduce the amount owing as a result of purchases and only when that is completely clear is there any reduction in the amount owing as a result of cash withdrawals – the amount bearing an interest rate of 26%.

The extra cost can be very significant. If the card is constantly in use and constantly in debt, the repayments may never be enough to make inroads into the cash withdrawal debt. It could go on for years or decades. MBNA, which issues cards in its own name and for many other issuers including EBS, uses the same system as Bank of Ireland. It's even worse because it starts charging interest from the date of the cash withdrawal.

There is clearly a need to be careful. The unfair imposition can be completely avoided, of course, by simply not making any cash withdrawals. That's true for all credit cards. With the exception of National Irish Bank, the interest rate charged on cash withdrawals is higher than that charged on purchases and most charge an administrative fee of 1.5% of the withdrawal subject to a minimum of €2.54.

More onerous are the fees that card issuers charge for late payment or going over a credit limit. Most charge between €7 and €8.50 for a late payment or for going over your credit limit but MBNA and its associated card issuers charge a whopping €15.24 for a late payment and €12.70 for going over a credit limit.

These charges can all too easily be incurred by simply forgetting to make a payment or by miscalculating a credit limit but they can be avoided with a bit of care. None of the MBNA cards could, in any case, be considered a best buy. That accolade has to go to AIB for its "click" card. The interest rate on purchases is one of the lowest available and it doesn't impose unfair rules for the allocation of partial repayments. But, as with all cards, cash withdrawals should be avoided.

INTRODUCTORY OFFERS

A number of card issuers offer low rates of interest for new customers transferring balances from their existing cards. The low rates only last for a limited time, of course, but can provide a significant saving. But don't forget that it may get clawed back in the long run, of course, if you transfer into an account with a higher interest rate — unless, of course, you switch again but you need to be very organised and committed to do that.

- PermanentTSB and Tesco Personal Finance charges no interest on transferred balances for six months.

- EBS also offers a 10-month interest holiday on transferred balances.

- MBNA, offers a similar 10-month interest rate holiday for transferred balances on its "platinum" account while charging a rate of 1.9% for six months on its Standard card.

Some issuers offer up to a six-month interest holiday on new purchases made with the card.

Credit cards can be usefully employed as a means of sending money to family members abroad or vice versa. The parents of a child studying away from home, for instance, can get an extra card on their Visa or Mastercard account and give it to the child. The parents can lodge money into the account and the child can draw it out through a local bank cash machine. It is completely secure although the cash withdrawal will usually be subject to a fee of 1.5%.

Do not be tempted to make a habit of postponing payment of the accounts beyond the due date. If you find yourself permanently in debt to the credit card company, you could save money by getting a bank or credit union loan at a lower rate of interest and paying off the credit card. If you have built up a credit card debt already, or intend making a big purchase, shop around for the cheapest personal loan. It's a far cheaper option than borrowing on the credit card.

This simply means using the card whose bill you received last. If you just tend to forget to pay off your credit card bill, you should consider signing a direct debit form. That allows the credit card company to take either the full payment or a minimum payment from your account. So the payment is made automatically. It's a good idea if you intend making the full payment each time.

Opting to make partial payments is, in effect, accepting that

It is well worth having at least one credit card. It can be worthwhile having two and alternating their use to get the longest possible period of free credit.

you are going to remain constantly in debt to the credit card company. And given the interest rates charged, that's not a good idea.

Charge cards

The front runners in this area are American Express and Diners Club although both Mastercard and Visa also issue charge cards. Charge cards have particular attractions for individuals who are high spenders or who do a fair amount of travel. Mastercard and Visa can be used at a far greater number of outlets worldwide but, if the quantity of outlets accepting charge cards is smaller, the quality is better and the big spender will possibly find a charge card accepted in most of the outlets he or she will want to frequent.

Charge cards have another advantage. It is possible to use them as super cheque guarantee cards to get cash from one's own account incurring no interest if there is a credit balance in your account and only the relevant bank rate if there is not.

Like credit cards, the charge cards offer some free insurance cover when you buy your travel tickets with the card — a point sometimes forgotten by the holders. Indeed the charge cards are more generous in this regard. Charge cards are, however, not free. In addition to the €30 stamp duty there is an annual subscription — it depends on the card. An American Express standard Green card is €47 a year while a Gold card costs €100 and a Platinum card costs €550. There is a basic Blue card with no annual fee. Diners Club charges €48 a year. Both American Express and Diners Club provide cash withdrawal facilities too. In addition to its cheque guarantee facility, American Express cards can be used at cash dispensers worldwide.

Debit cards

A debit card is, in essence, an electronic cheque book with an endless number of cheques. They are issued by banks and building societies. The most common debit card in Ireland is Laser but a number of banks now offer Visa debit cards that are accepted worldwide where ever Visa credit cards are accepted. Unlike a credit card, the transactions on a debit card are charged directly to the holder's own bank account. Some banks issue debit cards in addition to a chequebook, others issue them instead of a chequebook.

There is an annual €2.50 annual stamp duty on debit cards. The same duty applies to single purpose ATM cards while the duty is €5 on combined Laser/ATM cards.

You use a debit card as you would a chequebook. Payments made with a debit card are debited to the holder's account in exactly the same way as a payment made by cheque or a withdrawal from an ATM. The money may come out of your account a bit quicker but transaction charges are lower — there's no stamp duty compared with the 50c applied to each cheque. In general, the same sort of rules apply to the use of debit cards as to the use of a cheque-book. You should have the money in your account or an overdraft permission. If you run up an unapproved overdraft you'll be liable for heavy charges. They were outlined in the previous section.

The shops accepting the card are charged about 15c per Laser transaction by the operators of the system while Visa charges up to 1.5% of the transaction value — that amount varies from shop to shop and from issuer to issuer but it is paid by the retailer not the consumer. With most of the banks the charge for a debit card transaction is similar to that imposed on a transaction at an ATM. Where charges are applicable they are added to the customer's current account in the normal way. But they are also waived in the normal way if the customer qualifies for 'free banking'. In any case, it is cheaper to use a debit card than pay by cheque.

The main advantage of having a debit card is that you don't have to carry cash around. For those liable for bank charges, a debit card is cheaper than writing a cheque for single transactions. But someone out on a mini spending spree could save money by withdrawing cash from an ATM. An ATM withdrawal only attracts a single charge while there would be a separate charge for each debit card transaction. In some outlets, shoppers are able to draw out up to €100 in cash in addition to paying for their purchases. The mechanics of using a debit card are similar to using a credit card. You have

For those who travel a lot, the cost of getting a charge card or two is relatively small given the flexibility and security provided

There's an annual stamp duty of €2.50 a year on ATM and debit cards

Plastic money — some rules to follow

- ☐ Do not draw money on your credit card except in an emergency or unless you have already lodged money to the account so that it is in credit. The charges can be high and interest may start accruing immediately.

- ☐ The accounts of charge cards like American Express and Diners Club must be paid in full each month. Otherwise penal charges are imposed.

- ☐ Store cards are best avoided since they discourage shopping around, encourage overspending, and some charge hefty rates of interest.

- ☐ Do not keep constantly in debt to the credit card company. The interest rates are too high. There are much cheaper ways of borrowing.

- ☐ Make sure that you are given back your own card and not a fake or out-of-date one.

- ☐ Never reveal your PIN to anyone. Never leave your cards in your car. And don't leave them in a coat on the back of a chair in a restaurant or even at work.

- ☐ Be careful when keying your PIN into a cash machine that you are not been watched either by someone close by or by a camera.

- ☐ Keep a couple of separate notes of your card numbers and the phone numbers of the relevant companies so that you can act quickly if they are lost or stolen.

- ☐ If you want to be sure of paying off your monthly statement in full and on time, arrange to do it by direct debit.

- ☐ Don't let your card out of your sight. It takes only seconds to scan it.

- ☐ Do not forget that most cards provide extra benefits such as travel insurance. Read the leaflets carefully and know what you are entitled to.

- ☐ If you are making a large purchase and have the cash, see what sort of a discount you can get by offering it as an alternative to a credit card. Remember that the shop has to pay the card company a commission of up to 6%.

- ☐ When buying over the phone, or on the internet, be careful to deal only with reputable firms.

- ☐ Always check your bills.

it swiped and then key in your pin. The charge is then made to your bank account, a process that may take a couple of days but don't rely on it.

Some of these are operated by the stores themselves but most are now operated for them by finance houses. There are a number of different types of account. There are monthly accounts which are like charge cards. The amount due has to be paid each month and no interest is charged. It is obviously a worthwhile facility to have if you do a lot of shopping in one store or with the one group.

Then there are budget accounts. The store generally sets a maximum credit limit calculated as a multiple of the minimum monthly payment. It may be 20 times so that if you are prepared to pay €100 a month, the limit is set at €2,000. The interest rate is usually quite high — about the same as on a credit card. The credit limit remains set so that the customer can continue to buy more goods as the amount due goes down.

There are other accounts which are like a Mastercard or Visa account. They are known as option accounts and allow the customer to pay off in full at the end of each month — incurring no interest — or else make a minimum repayment and incur the interest. There is usually no charge for getting a card — other than the interest. Store cards encourage you to shop in that particular store or group and not to shop around for the best price.

A budget account may be worthwhile to cover the cost of a major purchase but not if the money could be borrowed from one of the larger banks instead. An overdraft or term loan would cost far less in interest charged. In general, the advice must be to steer clear of store cards. Mastercard or Visa provide similar benefits in most cases without the need to confine your shopping in one store.

There are exceptions. Monthly cards are cost free and you can benefit from promotions which stores sometimes put on for card holders — special sales and pre-Christmas openings for instance.

ATM cards

All the major banks and the building societies have their own ATM cards and they all use different names. With AIB it is Banklink while Bank of Ireland has PASS; Ulster Bank has ServiceTill and NIB has Autobank. All of the bank systems are interlinked so it is possible to use most, but not all, bank cards in any of the other banks' machines. On the basis of the queues, it seems that many people don't realise this. It is, of course, necessary to have an account with one of the institutions concerned and to either have some money in it or else have permission to overdraw. The machine is simply an automated teller and the transactions are just computerised versions of what was, and still is, done at the bank counter. Most of the machines operate on a round-the-clock basis providing the most flexible way of getting ready access to cash.

Managing your holiday money

Foreign holidays may be viewed as being a little unpatriotic in times of recession and, undoubtedly, holidaying at home provides a very real, if small, boost to the economy. But there must be intangible benefits to be gained from even a short respite from the domestic climate of doom, gloom and uncertain weather. Euro 2012 and the Olympic Games will be viewed by many as an opportunity not to be missed. But, overall, there may be fewer people venturing abroad during 2012 and, those who do, may have less to spend. All the more reason, then, to manage the available funds to good effect. Within the eurozone, where most people holiday, there is little by way of extra managing to do.

Under EU regulations, bank charges for credit card or ATM transactions can't be any higher than they are on similar transactions at home. There may be restrictions on the use of some cards and there's a need to watch out for extra ATM charges that some independent ATM providers charge in other countries, but for the most part the money transactions are exactly the same as at home.

Outside the eurozone, however, the charges can mount up. There are currency exchange rates that can vary from day to day and from one bank or bureau de change to another. This applies not only to the purchase of currency but also to credit or debit card transactions and withdrawals from ATMs. A commission of 1% to 1.5% is usually charged on currency purchase, while a fee of up to 3.5% may apply to card transactions. There is often a minimum fee, so that small transactions can be particularly expensive. By taking a little care you can save yourself a lot of money.

The eurozone comprises 17 countries: Austria, Belgium, Cyprus, Estonia, Finland, France, Germany, Greece, Ireland, Italy, Luxembourg, Malta, Netherlands, Portugal, Slovakia, Slovenia and Spain. The euro is also the currency of choice in Andorra, Kosova, Monaco, Montenegro, San Marino and the Vatican. The EU countries remaining outside the eurozone are Bulgaria, Czech Republic,

Denmark, Hungary, Latvia, Lithuania, Poland, Romania, Sweden and Britain.

So what's the best way to carry money abroad? Like most money problems there is no single correct answer. There are two basic options: cash and plastic. The best solution usually contains elements of both with an ever-increasing emphasis on plastic cards for all areas except the particularly financially underdeveloped. In making your choice you have to consider convenience, security and cost. Let's have a look at the options in some more detail.

Cash

Cash is the most readily acceptable form of money. Local cash is always acceptable but some other currencies, such as the US dollar, sterling and euro, are also widely accepted in many popular holiday resorts. The euro has become acceptable in many non-eurozone holiday destinations. In some developing countries, there may be advantages in having a recognisable currency like dollars or euro. But be careful of carrying high value notes, particularly US dollars, which have a bad reputation in some countries as potential forgeries.

The simplest thing, of course, if you are holidaying outside the eurozone is to change all your holiday money into local cash before you leave Ireland. You can shop around for the best exchange rate and incur only one set of commission charges. The only drawback is the risk — and it is a major one. Cash is too easily lost. But it is advisable to have some local cash to take with you — if only for incidental expenses when you arrive and maybe to carry you though a weekend if you arrive on a Friday night or Saturday morning.

Credit cards

Credit cards such as Mastercard and Visa and charge cards such as American Express and Diners can all be used abroad. Not all outlets accept them, of course. So in some countries - and particularly in the more remote areas - they cannot be relied upon. But they are, at the very least, a very useful standby and in the more popular holiday resorts they may cover most requirements, although they would always need to be supplemented with some local cash. If you have put your credit card account into credit, most issuers charge nothing for euro cash withdrawals from ATMs. The exceptions are MBNA, Ulster Bank and EBS on its members' card.

The cost of purchases outside the eurozone is translated into euro at the exchange rate on the day the item is debited to the credit card account. The exchange rate may include some hidden charges but may be no worse than you would get from buying foreign currency. Most banks also charge a transaction fee of 1.75% but Ulster Bank charges 2% while MBNA and EBS, on its members' card, charge 2.65%. These charges also apply to cash withdrawals from ATMs outside the eurozone and are in addition to the standard cash advance fees. That can push the cost to over 4% with some cards while 3.25% is fairly typical. So using your credit card to withdraw cash is best avoided except in emergencies particularly outside the eurozone.

If you need to withdraw cash outside the eurozone, use a debit card rather than a credit card and if possible make large withdrawals rather than many small ones

Debit cards

Debit cards are convenient and cheap to use in the eurozone. They include Laser and the Visa debit card. Not all Laser cards can be used abroad but those which carry the Maestro, Cirrus, or LINK logo on them can. Within the eurozone debit cards are used in exactly the same way as at home in outlets or ATM machines. The charges are the same as if you were using them in Ireland. Outside of the eurozone extra charges apply. There's a hidden charge within the foreign exchange rate applied and some banks apply transaction charges up to 1.75%. Minimum charges generally apply and are higher for cash withdrawals.

Bank ATM cards

Very often your Laser card is combined with a bank ATM card but there are stand-alone ATM cards that can be used to make cash withdrawals from ATM machines abroad if they carry the Cirrus, Maestro, Visa Plus or LINK logos. LINK is a British network and it is usually cheaper to withdraw money from one of its machines than other independent ones. As with the other cards, there are no extra charges for withdrawing money within the eurozone. The same charges apply that would apply in Ireland. Depending on the card, the charge can vary from nothing to as much as 34c. Outside the eurozone, the usual foreign exchange costs are incurred together with transaction fees of up to 3.5%. Some ATM providers abroad also add their own charges and while these should be outlined on the screen before you withdraw your cash the notice is easily missed.

Travel Insurance

Travel insurance can provide a real benefit in the form of peace of mind even if you never have to make a claim. But be sure to read the fine print and know exactly what you are covered for and what you have to do to make a claim. It's usually necessary to report any loss to the local police, for instance, and to make the claim within a fixed time period. There are a wide range of policies available and the cover varies greatly, as does the cost. Travel agents normally offer insurance with their holidays and may charge an extra fee — perhaps €10 — if it is not taken out. But it can still be worthwhile shopping around. It is not too difficult to save €10 on a holiday insurance premium and still get wider cover. Don't forget that you may already have insurance cover for some risks. You may have items like jewellery, cameras, etc. covered for 'all risks' both inside and outside your home on your existing household policy.

It's worth shopping around for travel insurance

People who travel a lot should consider taking out an annual policy rather than one for each trip. There's certainly a saving to be made if you make three or more trips a year. You may want cover for the potential loss of having to cancel a holiday should a close relative die. This cover is usually fairly restrictive. You also need cover for medical expenses. Quinn Healthcare, VHI and AvivaHealth provide some cover but not enough. Some insurers give discounts to people with medical insurance. VHI has its own separate travel insurance product. You can save money on travel insurance by shopping around. If you have access to the internet you should check out Getcover.com; Justcover.ie; Ryanair.com; Blueinsurance.ie; Chill.ie, VHI.ie, Aerlingus.com, 123.ie

Your holiday finance checklist

A bit of advance planning can help you avoid some unpleasant financial surprises while on holiday. The following are some pointers:

☐ Increase your credit limit just in case you need it — unless, of course, that might prove too much of a temptation to overspend.

☐ Check that the magnetic strip is in good order.

☐ Get additional cards for your partner.

☐ Get a PIN number to use for withdrawing cash if you don't already have it. If you haven't lodged money to your account in advance, it can be an expensive way of getting cash but useful in an emergency.

☐ Check out the Cirrus, Visa Plus, or Maestro facilities that may be bundled with your bank card. Get the information on how to use them and where they can be used.

☐ Make a note of all your card numbers and details of where you have to ring to report their loss. Keep a couple of copies so that you can report any loss quickly.

☐ If you're going to an EU country, make sure to get a European Health Insurance Card from your local Health Board. This electronic card which is about the size of a credit card may eventually contain medical details such as blood type. It replaces the old form E111 and ensures that you get the same sort of free medical insurance as the locals in whatever EU country you go to. Once you get the card, it will last for years but it may take a few weeks to get, so apply to the local area Health Service Executive a few weeks before you first need it. You can get an application form from your local citizens' information or health centre.

☐ If you have medical insurance, check what cover it provides when abroad and make a note of any special contact telephone numbers. It's not an alternative to travel insurance but it is a very useful addition.

☐ Don't forget to take out some form of travel insurance. The insurance offered by the travel agency may not be the cheapest or best. It can be worthwhile getting your insurance elsewhere even if the travel agent charges you a small fee for allowing you to do so.
Read the section on page 40.

and AIB either in branch, or if you get it online you qualify for a 10% discount. It's also worth checking your union or staff association which may have negotiated a special group deal. There is a wide variation between the cheapest and the dearest but the choice shouldn't be made solely on price. The dearest is not necessarily the best. It may not provide the best cover and the rules and exemptions may not be the least onerous. So in making your choice don't simply look at the price. Price is, of course, important but you should look at the cover you are getting and read the fine print.

Don't expect insurance companies to automatically accept your word. You must substantiate a claim

Having taken out a policy there may be very little you can do if you subsequently find out that a certain risk isn't covered. It's no wonder that disputes arise over whether or not the conditions outlined in the fine print have been met. Knowing what these conditions are and then complying with them can be of prime importance.

One case considered by the Insurance Ombudsman concerned a traveller who, on arrival at Dublin Airport, discovered that two of his suitcases had been damaged. The damage didn't seem to be too great so he didn't report it to anyone at the airport. He subsequently discovered that some items were missing from his luggage. Six weeks later, he submitted a claim form to his insurance company. It refused to meet the claim.

The problem was that the policy document required claimants to have obtained a police report within 24 hours of discovering any loss relating to personal baggage and to have obtained a *'Property Irregularity Report'* from the airline involved. Neither of these conditions had been met. The Ombudsman ruled in favour of the insurance company.

She also found in favour of the insurance company in a dispute over whether a sum of money could be deemed to be 'unattended' when left in the claimant's holiday apartment. An 'unattended clause' is common in travel insurance policies and its meaning is frequently being disputed. The Ombudsman referred to a British court judgement which suggested that an item was unattended if there was no-one in a position to observe any attempt to interfere with it and close enough to have a reasonable prospect of preventing any such interference.

> *Foul cankering rust the hidden treasure frets.*
> *But gold that's put to use more gold begets — Shakespeare*

3 Getting the most from your savings

People save more during recessions. While some have to dip into their savings to survive or to maintain their living standards in the face of falling incomes, others adopt a precautionary approach, cut back on spending and save more in anticipation of worse to come. That's not just an economist's model. It is borne out by facts. The trend has been very evident in Ireland over recent years. Not only do people save more during recessions but they are also likely to prefer less risky options — cash and deposits rather than asset-backed investments such as shares and property.

Deposits have the added advantage of being Government guaranteed and there is no reason to doubt the soundness of the guarantees. Maintaining trust in the banking system is essential to the economic recovery that is of every bit as important to those we owe money to as it is to ourselves. In due course, the economic recovery will be firmly enough established to improve the attractions of the asset backed investments. To maximise returns coming out of a recession requires constant vigilance and a willingness to take some risk. That means a willingness to accept that asset values can go down as well as up and it's not for everyone.

There is no clear-cut distinction between the concept of savings and investments and no generally accepted definitions. But the term 'savings' is often taken to apply to assets such as bank accounts that can easily be converted into cash without risk of loss. Everything else that can be expected to yield a financial return, by way of income or capital gain, can be considered an investment. That includes property, shares, investment funds, pension funds, and business assets.

At its simplest, saving may only involve holding onto some money to meet the occasional expense that arises less regularly than pay days — a holiday, the car or house insurance, even the ESB, gas or heating bills. But that type of saving has more to do with managing your cash flows— a topic dealt with in the last chapter. The sums involved are generally small and the money is only being kept for relatively short periods so the main considerations are convenience and ease of access. But when larger sums of money are being put away for longer periods, different factors come into play — most importantly the rate of return and the risk involved.

In general, the greater the expected rate of return, the greater the risk. The return on a bank deposit is more secure than an investment in shares which may fall in value. So where should you save or invest?

Your choice of investment outlet depends on a wide range of factors. First you have to decide:

- **YOUR OBJECTIVES:** What is the investment for? Is it to be a contingency fund providing security for the future or is it money earmarked for a specific purpose: to provide a regular income, to pay the deposit on a house, to fund the children's education, or for retirement. Some investments are particularly suited to specific objectives.

- **YOUR TIME FRAME:** When do you expect to realise the investment? Your objectives may dictate the answer. In general the longer the investment term, the greater the potential return.

- **YOUR NEED FOR ACCESS:** Is there a possibility that you'll need to convert some or all of your investment into cash at short notice? Most medium and longer term investments impose penalties on early encashments. Such penalties are not a worry if you definitely won't need access to your money. Otherwise you have to decide whether to keep some funds readily accessible in short-term outlets or take the chance of incurring the penalties.

- **YOUR RETURN/RISK BALANCE:** There is usually a trade-off between the two. Risk may be measured in terms of volatility i.e. the extent to which the value of an investment moves up and down. The greater the volatility of an equity fund, for instance, the greater the potential returns but also the greater the chance of loss. There is no objective measure of how much risk a person should take. It depends partly on personal make-up and partly on circumstances.

  Attitudes to risk vary greatly. There is nothing intrinsically wrong with being a risk-taker or with being risk-averse. The important thing is for the investor to recognise the degree of risk appropriate to his or her personality and to avoid overstepping the mark.

  Circumstances may dictate an even tighter limit on the degree of risk to be taken. A pensioner investing his or her life savings, for instance, may need to keep a risk-taking personality in check. Equally, an overly risk-averse individual might benefit from a cool assessment of his or her fears. But in all cases, both personal make-up and circumstances need to be taken into account and potential returns balanced against possible personal anguish.

- **THE COSTS:** While it costs nothing to put money on deposit, most other investments involve some charges. Charges reduce your net return and need to be taken into account when deciding not only between alternative investments but also between advisers. Stockbrokers vary in their commission rates. Investment fund managers differ in their initial charges and annual management fees. There may also be a choice between indirectly paying a broker's commission or paying a fee to a fee-based adviser and getting the commission yourself. While tax cannot properly be regarded as a cost, it has much the same effect and should be taken into account particularly when comparing investments taxed in different ways.

Getting the best from advisers

- Buying financial services is fraught with danger. Taking out the wrong insurance policy or making the wrong investment can prove very expensive and wrong does not necessarily mean bad. There are policies and investments which, while excellent in some circumstances, may be disastrous in others. Professional advice can be well worthwhile but only if it is knowledgeable and soundly based. You can access a list of registered advisers at http://registers.financialregulator.ie/ or check if an adviser has met minimum competency requirements at www.qfaboard.ie/register, phone (01) 4553018. But being 'competent' is no guarantee that the advice is always the best. It's all too easy for an adviser or a salesperson to err through ignorance or a lack of concern for a client's real needs or by not knowing enough about the range of products available. That's true whether you pay by way of a fee or by way of commission. You need to check around before choosing an adviser and then compare the costs. The Financial Regulator provides authorisation for three types of financial adviser.

- AUTHORISED ADVISERS are independent of the banks, insurance companies and other financial institutions that supply investment and insurance products. They are expected to trawl the market to find the best option for you.

- MULTI-AGENCY INTERMEDIARIES can only offer you products for which they hold agencies. They must hold agencies for at least two product providers.

- SINGLE-AGENCY INTERMEDIARIES only hold an agency for one supplier. They are sometimes known as tied agents.

In all cases, your adviser should ask you a lot of questions. To give adequate advice, a financial adviser needs to know something of your other savings, income and responsibilities, tax situation, attitude to risk etc. You need to ask some questions too, making sure that you understand the answers.

- What do I need?

- How is the product going to supply that need?

- Why this product rather than something else?

The answers to some of these questions should be evident from documentation that advisers are required to give to clients. For instance they have to complete a 'fact find' outlining your financial situation, your objectives and →

your attitude to risk. They also have to supply you with details of their terms of business. But you should keep those "what, how and why" questions firmly in mind. The "what" question is one to ask yourself. Supermarkets try to encourage impulse buying. You can guard against it by making a shopping list and sticking to it. The same is true in the financial area. It's up to you to decide what you want. Don't let the adviser decide for you. He or she may make suggestions but make sure that you make the decisions.

Before you take any advice, decide what you want yourself — if only in very broad terms, such as "I need to save for the children's education" or "I need insurance cover". Then try to go a bit further than that. If the product is insurance what cover do you need? Do you need it on yourself or your spouse or both? Try to put broad figures on your needs. Are you willing to take a risk with your savings? How much can you afford to save? Jot down your answers. Use it as a check list to see if the salesman or adviser has got you to deviate from your original objectives. If so, did he give adequate reasons why you should?

The other "how and why" questions are asked of the salesman or the adviser. How is that particular product going to satisfy your particular needs and most important, why that product rather than something else? And that includes the most important question of why one company's products rather than another's. Do not be afraid to keep asking why or how and make sure you understand the answers. Ask about alternatives. You can be sure that there are alternatives even if you don't know what they are. The salesman or adviser should know what they are and be able to justify the alternative he has chosen for you. Has he or she taken all the alternatives into account? Do you need to do some shopping around yourself?

And remember that if you don't understand it, it is not your fault. A salesman or adviser who understands a product should be able to explain it in simple, easily understood, language. If he or she is calling to your home it can do no harm taking out your recorder explaining that you are a bit muddle headed and would like to go over the detail later. That should at least stop excessive claims. Don't forget that your professional adviser is getting paid for his time and expertise either by way of fee or commission. There is no need to feel guilty about asking questions and getting answers before you decide. See page 93 for details of the information that must be given with life insurance and investment products.

Read the following sections for more details on these various investment options

There is no single option that is best for everyone. It all depends on individual circumstances and the factors outlined above. But there are some general rules of thumb that one can follow in making a decision. Even with a decline in the rate of inflation, the return on deposits and similar safe investments, such as the post office schemes, are still below the rate needed simply to ensure that a nest egg keeps pace with rising prices and retains its purchasing power.

Those willing to take some risk can hope for better returns and there is a range of options open to them. The amount of risk varies and is usually unpredictable as the stock market slide of recent years proves. There are investment products that guarantee at least a return of the initial investment — so that the worst that can happen is that you'll get your money back. But such guarantees come at a cost in terms of potential return. Others guarantee a minimum rate of return with the chance of something better. But most investment products offer no guarantees. There is the hope of a good return but also the risk of losing part, or even all, of the initial investment. The following are some of the options which are outlined in more detail in the sections that follow:

Using spare money to pay off debt can yield a very high return although it may not always make sense to pay off a mortgage

- <u>Paying off debt</u> yields a very high and certain return. Invest €1,000 at the best deposit rate available and you earn just over €22 a year after DIRT tax. Invest the same money in paying off a bank term loan — carrying an interest rate of 10% — and your gain is €100 a year. It makes sense to pay off the loan. Paying off the loan does reduce your flexibility but that's not a problem if you are in a job and are fairly sure of being able to borrow again if you need to.

  Mortgages are the exception. The interest rate is low and some of the interest may be eligible for tax relief. The true cost of a mortgage at 3.5% may be as low as 2.8% after tax relief at 20% or only 2.45% if you are a first time buyer entitled to tax relief at 25%. The cost is higher, of course, if all the interest doesn't qualify for tax relief. Taking the example above the gain from paying €1,000 off such a mortgage is €28 a year. That's less than the tax free €35 to be earned on €1,000 in An Post Saving Certs or the €29 that could be earned net on a good one year fixed deposit account late in 2011. So from a financial point of view there is not a lot to be gained from paying off the mortgage.

If you once pay off the mortgage, it's not so easy to borrow again at such a favourable rate. It is, of course, possible to get a top-up mortgage but it may not be eligible for tax relief. And there'll be set up costs. Assuming a mortgage rate of 4%, a married couple who qualify as a first-time buyer can get tax relief on a mortgage of up to about €500,000 while a single borrower gets relief on a mortgage up to €250,000. There is no tax relief on the portions of the loans above those levels. The limits are lower for non first-time buyers. See page 129 for more details of mortgage tax relief.

■ **Deposit accounts** with banks, building societies and credit unions — rates vary greatly depending on the institution, the amount involved and the period of notice required. **See page 51.**

■ **An Post** Saving Bonds and Certs are an attractive option, particularly for those who are liable for DIRT and can afford to leave their money untouched for a few years. Money can be withdrawn on demand but the money must be left for a few years to gain the best return. The newer Solidarity Bonds are less attractive because the best annual returns come towards the end of the term and those who have to withdraw their money early get a poor return. **See page 54.**

■ **Investment funds** offer a wide range of options. Some guarantee a return of capital while others make no guarantees, the return depending solely on the performance of the underlying investments which can range from very high risk to very low risk. **See page 63**.

■ **Direct stock exchange investment** carries a high degree of risk in the short term. As was very evident in recent years, share prices can be very volatile, even the shares of what may seem to be the most secure of companies. Those with a relatively small amount to invest can't spread the risk adequately over a number of shares and the cost of dealing in small lots of shares can be very high. **See page 60.**

- **Investments under certain tax incentive schemes** such as the Employment and Investment Incentive which has replaced BES, and Film Relief offer the chance of good returns but not without risk. **See page 293.**

- **Property investment** can yield good returns but not always, as those who bought at inflated prices during the boom years know only too well. Direct property investments involve high initial costs so that only very large investors can afford to spread the risk among a range of properties. It can also be difficult to convert an investment speedily back into cash. One of the attractions is, or was, the fact that you can, or could, more easily gear up your own resources with borrowings. But that's a major drawback during a recession when property values fall.

Those are some of the options. The choice depends very much on the individual and on his or her particular needs. As stressed above, it depends on attitudes to risk and on what is required from the investment. There is no single best option. It all depends on individual circumstances and objectives. And, of course, the relative attractiveness of different options can change with time.

Secure investments

No investment is entirely secure but putting your money on deposit with a financial institution is almost risk free. That's true even in the current uncertain financial climate because of the Government guarantees. They provide about as much security as it is possible to get. Even in an economic meltdown one of the last things that a Government would want, and one of the last things that any external creditor would demand, would be the destruction of confidence in the country's banking system. Trust in the banking system is essential to the maintenance of the economic activity that underwrites the country's debts.

There are other options where the loss of your capital is equally unlikely. Investors may look for two levels of security. The most basic is an assurance that the capital invested will be returned either on demand or at some specific time in the future. That is all some secure investments promise. The other level of security involves the rate of return.

A fixed term bank deposit offers a fixed rate of interest so the investor can expect to get not only the capital back but also a specified return on that capital. With other investments, such as demand deposit accounts or tracker bonds, the rate of return may depend on circumstances.

There tends to be a trade off between security and rate of return. It's not always the case, but very often the more security built into an investment, the lower the potential return. The following are some of the options open to those who want to limit their risk.

Deposit accounts

Banks, building societies and credit unions all pay interest on deposits. The rates may vary with the size of the deposit and with the length of notice required to withdraw the money. They also vary from institution to institution and, of course, over time. There are rates fixed for a set time and variable rates that can be changed from day to day without notice. In general the longer the term and the larger the amount, the higher the rate of interest but that is not always the case. Sometimes higher rates are offered on smaller deposits in an effort to attract smaller depositors while better rates are sometimes offered on demand deposits than on fixed-term deposits. The rates on demand deposits can, of course, be varied without notice at the discretion of the institution.

It's important to shop around, not only when you are initially putting the money on deposit but regularly thereafter to ensure that you are still getting the best rate available. The interest rates on offer change frequently so you may need to switch your money regularly to ensure the best return. An up-to-date list of most available deposit rates can be assessed on the National Consumer Agency's website Itsyourmoney.ie.

The Government guarantees, see page 53, apply equally to all the institutions covered so a deposit with one is as safe as a deposit with another. The guarantee that covers deposits irrespective of size, is due to end at the end of 2012 unless extended but the more general guarantee that covers deposits up to €100,000 per person per institution has no end-date. But competition for deposits is intense although it hasn't resulted in a convergence of the rates on offer.

At the end of 2011, it was possible to get as little as 0.01% or more than 3% on a demand deposit . That's the difference between earning €1 or €300 plus a year on a deposit of €10,000.

Regular saver accounts

A number of banks offer higher rates on regular savings accounts than on standard variable rate deposits but there are limits to the amount that can be invested and usually restrictions on withdrawals. They have been used as a marketing ploy and since the rates are generally not fixed, it is very important to occasionally check what the current rate is. It's all too easy to open an account offering a high rate and find that it has been significantly reduced. While rates of 7% were on offer in the past, at the end of 2011 the best rate available was 5%.

Deposit guarantee — who's covered

The most wide-ranging is the Government Guarantee Scheme which guarantees depositors against loss on deposits without any upper limit. It runs until December 31, 2012 and may be extended beyond that. Some foreign-based institutions are covered by guarantees operating in their home countries.

☐ The Irish Government Guarantee

All deposits in the following institutions are covered by this guarantee.

AIB,   Bank of Ireland,
EBS Building Society,   ICS Building Society,
Permanent TSB,

Deposits with Irish Nationwide were transferred to Permanent TSB and deposits with Anglo Irish transferred to AIB on July 1, 2011.

☐ Irish Deposit Guarantee Scheme

All the institutions listed above are also covered by this guarantee which protects 100% of deposits up to a maximum of €100,000. The following institutions are also covered in addition to many other financial institutions registered with the Financial Regulator.

ACC Bank,   Credit Unions,
IIB Bank plc (KBC Bank Ireland), Ulster Bank,
Pfizer International Europe,   National Irish Bank,
Northern Rock deposits are being transferred to Permanent TSB

☐ British Compensation Scheme

This provides full cover for deposits of up to £100,000 sterling per person. The following banks operating in Ireland are covered.

Investec Bank plc,   Leeds Building Society,
Nationwide Building Society UK,   Northern Rock.

☐ Dutch Guarantee Scheme

Full cover for deposits of up €100,000 per person. It covers

Rabodirect.

☐ Danish Guarantee Scheme

It covers deposits up to €100,000 per person. It covers

Danske Bank (trading as National Irish Bank).

Credit unions

Many credit unions pay dividends on members' shares. They are not strictly deposit accounts and the rate is not fixed in advance. The rate is agreed by members each year on the basis of performance. While they don't have to make a profit, credit unions have to be mindful of the margins between the rate they charge on borrowings and the return they provide for their saver/shareholders. They are covered by both Government guarantees on deposits.

DIRT

DIRT is levied at 30% on most deposit interest paid or credited after January 1, 2012. It was 27% during 2011. No further tax is due on deposit interest even if the recipient is liable to pay a higher rate of income tax. People who are not liable for income tax and who are either over 65 years of age or permanently incapacitated can claim back the tax or alternatively have the interest paid or credited to their accounts tax free once they verify to the deposit taker that they are over 65, or permanently incapacitated, and not liable for tax. In the case of a married couple, it is sufficient for either partner to be over 65 years of age. This facility is available on any deposit account. Get in touch with whoever holds your deposit and make the necessary declaration.

A claim for repayment of DIRT is made on a simple form that you can get in any tax office, at larger post offices or from wherever you have your savings. You also need a certificate from the bank or building society giving details of the DIRT stopped. Fill out the form, attach the certificate, and send it off to the tax office — the address is on the form. You can make claims going back four years — up to December 31, 2011 you can make a claim for 2007 but in 2012 you can only go back as far as 2008.

An Post investments

Postbank, the joint venture between An Post and Fortis Bank closed in 2010 but An Post itself still offers its long established range of medium to long term investment products. These include Instalment Savings, Saving Certificates, Savings Bonds and the newer four and 10-year Solidarity bonds that were launched during 2010.

The basic An Post deposit account paying 1% gross is not attractive although there is a lot of money earning just that amount and many of the depositors don't require immediate access to their money. By switching to a Deposit Plus account that requires one month's notice of withdrawal, they could treble their rate of return to 3% gross.

Both of those deposit accounts are subject to DIRT as is some of the return from the Solidarity Bonds. There is no tax on the returns earned on Savings Certificates, Savings Bonds and Instalment Savings.

- **Savings bonds** are a three year investment with guaranteed returns each year. It is possible to withdraw money at any time without penalty other than the fact that no interest is payable if the money is withdrawn during the first year. The rates of return are as follows: money left in for one year - 2.2%; two years - 5.2% (which is 2.6% a year) and three years - 10% (which is 3.23% a year). That three year return is equivalent to a gross return, before DIRT (at 30%), of 4.6% a year.

- **Saving certificates** offer a tax free return of 3.53% a year if held for five years and six months. That's equivalent to 5% gross. An initial investment of €1,000 grows to be €1,210 over that period. With the interest only added in every six months, it is important - if you have to cash in - to do it as soon as possible after a six-monthly anniversary. That way you lose the least amount of interest. But ideally you should stay the course because the best returns come in the latter years.

- **Instalment savings** are primarily aimed at those savers who can save a fixed amount each month for a year. As a scheme for encouraging savings it's great and the returns are not bad considering that only relatively small sums are being deposited. The saver - who must be over seven years of age - agrees to save a stated amount each month for 12 consecutive months. The minimum monthly saving is €25 and the maximum €500. At the

The Instalment Savings Scheme is an option for those wanting to save a fixed amount regularly each month end of the 12-month period, the total amount saved is left on deposit. If the savings are left for five years after the initial year's saving period you are guaranteed your money back plus 20% - that works out at only 3.37% a year. But that is tax-free. You'd need to earn a gross 4.8% before DIRT at 30% to get that after tax.

In general the Solidarity Bonds are not as attractive as their older cousins, Savings Bonds and Certs.

- **Solidarity bonds** There are both four and 10-year versions. In both cases the bulk of the return comes towards the end of the term so they are not as attractive as Savings Bonds and Certs for anyone who might have to make an early withdrawal. The way the return is calculated on the 10 year bond is particularly complicated and given the current uncertainties in the financial markets, the term is very long.

It offers a reasonable return at the end of seven years but anyone forced to cash in during the first five years gets a very low return. On the plus side is the fact that investors know exactly what return they can expect to get but it's impossible to know in advance how the promised rates will compare with general market rates on bank deposits. In the current uncertain climate, it's impossible to forecast what the banks will be paying for deposits in a year's time, yet alone in 2022.

It's also impossible to predict inflation over such a long period. Even before the recent downturn in prices we had got used to low inflation. But who can be sure that there will not be a return to the double-digit inflation experienced in the past. It's not thought likely but neither was the banking crisis. But the Bond does offer a guaranteed fixed return for those who want to put money away for the longer term, like the idea of having access to it should an emergency arise but are fairly confident that it can be left for the full 10 year term.

At the end of 10 years, a €1,000 invested in a Bond will have grown to €1,500. A very small proportion of that return will be liable for DIRT leaving a net return of €475 on the initial €1,000 investment. That's equivalent to an average return of 3.9% a year. You'd have to earn a gross return of 5.6% a year on a bank deposit to get 3.9% after tax.

The return is made up of an annual 1% that is taxable and applied only to the original sum invested. In addition to that 1%, a tax-free bonus of 10% is paid if the bond is cashed in during the sixth or seventh year. A tax-free bonus of 22% is paid on bonds cashed in during the eighth, ninth or 10th year and a bonus of 40% if cashed in when the Bond matures at the end of the 10th year. These represent annual percentage rates after tax as follows for bonds cashed in at the end of the various years.

1 to 4	0.7%	8	3.1%
5	2.6%	9	2.8%
6	2.3%	10	3.9%
7	3.5%		

For any period less than five-and-a-half years, An Post Savings Bonds or Savings Certs offer a better deal and they may offer a better return over longer periods if the current rates are still available when the three-year Savings Bonds or the five-and-a-half years Savings Certs mature.

The four year Solidarity Bond pays 1% a year which is taxable and an 11% tax free bonus at the end of the term. So the return is very low if the bond is cashed in before maturity but works out at an annual average of 3.31% net. That's only marginally better than the average 3.23% paid over three years on Savings Bonds, far from enough to offset the much smaller penalties, in terms of lost interest, that apply to early encashment of Savings Bonds.

Tracker bonds

Tracker bonds is a loose term that covers various forms of fixed-term investments generally over three to six years. There is a range of different options. Most offer a guarantee that the investor will at least get his or her money back at the end of the agreed period. Some offer a minimum return on top of that basic guarantee. The maximum possible return is usually based on the performance of some stock exchange index or mix of indices. For instance the return may be linked to the performance of the FTSE100 index of British stock market prices. So, for example, a person making an investment of €2,000 might be guaranteed the return of that money at the end of six years. That's the worst outcome.

There may also be a guarantee, for example, that the value of the bond will rise by half of any increase in the FTSE100 index. So if the index happened to go up by 60% over the period then the return would be 30% of €2,000. The investor would get back €2,600 less tax at 28%. In most cases, there is a cap on the maximum return just as there is a floor under the potential loss.

The guarantees are usually underwritten by a bank or banks and may not be worth anything in the unlikely event of a bank failure.

Bonds are opened for investment from time to time. They usually have fixed starting and maturity dates. They must be viewed as fixed-term investments since there can be heavy penalties for withdrawing money too soon.

Income from annuities

An annuity is a way of using a lump sum to provide an income for life. It was the traditional way of providing an income during retirement mainly because it was the only option open to those with personal pension money to invest. But that is no longer the case for the self-employed, directors of family firms, and those not in company pension schemes. But while individuals with personal pension funds to invest are no longer required to purchase an annuity, they are still there as an option – an option that may be attractive to some.

Annuities may have an appeal to anyone with limited capital that they want to spread out as income over the post-retirement years. The basic idea behind an annuity is that in return for a lump sum investment it provides a guaranteed income until death. There are also annuities suitable for couples. Known as **'joint survivor annuities'** they are taken out on the joint lives of the couple. On the death of one, the income continues at a reduced rate until the death of the other. The rate of return on joint survivor annuities is, of course, lower than on a single life annuity — about 20% less in the case of a husband aged 65 whose wife is 61 when the annuity is taken out. This 20% reduction also assumes that the income is halved on the death of one partner.

Around that central idea there are a fair number of options. In all cases, the income is guaranteed for an uncertain period. The assurance companies that sell annuities do not know when the person is going to die. But they have an idea of the average life expectancy of annuity purchasers. In money terms those who live longer get a very good return while those who die younger do not. But in all cases there is the security of knowing that the income will continue until death.

When interest rates are low, annuity rates are also low. In 2011 one company was quoting that a man aged 65 would require about €100,000 to buy an income of €4,700 a year for life with half that income carrying on to his widow, as-suming she was aged five years younger than he. But annuity rates can change from day to day and from company to company so it is important to shop around. You can do it very easily by phone.

The initial payment would be smaller if the income is to sub-sequently rise with inflation. The standard annuity usually provides for the first income payment to be made six months after the annuity is purchased. Thereafter the pay-ments are made at six monthly intervals. It is usual to guar-antee that the annuity will be paid for at least five years even if the purchaser dies during that time.

It may be possible for those in bad health to get better annuity rates

People with medical conditions that are likely to shorten their life span can, in some cases, get higher returns than those in good health. Most companies refuse to take medical history into account even though they would make sure to do so when quoting life insurance premiums. Some compa-nies may, however, offer what is known as **'impaired life annuities'**. If appropriate, it is worth searching them out. The annuity rates can be significantly higher.

Direct stock market investment

With its main provisions well flagged in advance, the 2012 Budget has little impact on investors in Irish shares who, at the time, were more concerned with developments in Brussels. The day after the Budget the ISEQ index of Irish share values closed at 2755 down 73% on the peak of 10041 reached on February 2, 2007 after a long upward trend that started early in 2003. At the top, Irish shares were valued at a total of €150.8 billion and most of the losses since were in bank shares. The bottom was reached on March 3, 2009 with the index down at 1,880. Since then there has been some recovery but it has by no means been constant or marked.

The small investor may be better spreading the risk by investing in shares indirectly through a managed fund

Investors have lost heavily. Most of them own their shares indirectly though pension and other investment funds. The fund managers will have been selling and buying, making or losing money in the process. Even in a recession, it is possible to make significant returns on investments by buying in the troughs and selling on the peaks. But it needs a large degree of luck. No-one can now doubt the truth of the old adage that share values can go down as well as up. The message has been brought home with a vengeance. The impact has been traumatic for many, although some are gambling on the up and down swings while others are simply waiting to buy in when the inevitable upswing is more firmly established.

It is hard to believe at the moment but shares tend to out-perform other investments over the longer term. But, in the short-term, the downturns can be very sharp. The shorter the term of any investment the greater the risk of incurring losses rather than making gains. There can be no certainty. Even when the market is tending upwards there will always be some shares moving in the opposite direction and the general upward trend can always be punctuated with sharp downturns of uncertain duration.

Irish investors are not, of course, restricted to investing on the Irish stock exchange but few markets have escaped the recent downturn. There is no additional foreign exchange risk when investing within the eurozone. But non-euro shares have to be bought in foreign currency and there is always the risk that the euro will devalue against that currency.

Whatever the prospects, small investors must always be particularly wary of investing in shares. They cannot spread their money over a wide range of shares in order to spread the risk and they must realise that share values can go down as well as up. But for those willing to take a gamble, there may be money to be made providing they realise and accept that there can be no certainty.

It can be argued that the small investor is better advised to invest indirectly through an investment fund. These are considered in the next section. By investing in a fund rather than directly in individual shares, the investor gets the benefit of skilled management and also gets to spread the risk to a far greater degree than would be feasible by investing in individual shares.

A knowledgeable, or lucky, individual can always hope to do better than a fund manager, of course, and he or she might be able to do just that. But it does require time and knowledge, not only of how the stock market works – that's the easy bit – but also an insight into how economic trends are going to impact on sectors and individual companies. You'll need to be able to pick the winners and the losers or, at least, some of them.

Investing in a company on the stock exchange gives you a part ownership in the company concerned. The return on this part ownership depends on the performance of the company, so together with the prospect of a high return, goes the risk of no return. The degree of risk varies with the type of share and with the company.

There are debentures and preference shares which carry a fixed rate of interest and have first claim on a company's profits, and then there are ordinary shares, which are the real ownership shares, and carry with them full risks of ownership and the full prospects. If the company makes no profits, they get no dividend; if it prospers, they get all the cream.

Investing on the stock exchange requires time and a bit of dedication. If you don't have both and still want to invest on the stock market then indirect investment through an investment fund is possibly the best option. An alternative is an investment club where a small number of individuals share their expertise and money to invest

How to buy shares

Given the costs involved it doesn't make sense to invest very small amounts. Brokers who don't offer any advice and simply execute your order charge the lowest commission. Brokers who offer advice typically charge up to 1.65% on deals up to €15,000 with a minimum of between €60 and €70. There is also a Government stamp duty of 1% on all purchases of Irish shares, 0.5% on British shares.

Transaction costs can be kept to the minimum by dealing in shares online through the internet. Goodbody Stockbrokers, a member of the Fexco group offer such services. You have to register and keep a minimum amount of money in a special account with Goodbody. With AIB, which previously owned Goodbody and uses it to provide stockbroking services, you can use your current bank account. A commission of 1.25% is charged on the first €25,000 and 0.5% on anything above that. There is a minimum commission of €32 per trade. There is also a €26 annual registration charge and a charge of €13 if you withdraw a share holding from the service and a final charge of €40 if and when you close the account. Davy Stockbrokers also offers an online service. There is a twice yearly account maintenance charge of €40 while commission is charged at the rate of 0.75% on the first €25,000 and at 0.5% above that.

Online services include access to information and research but not individual advice. Even brokers who offer advice don't keep a permanent eye on your investments, unless you pay them to. They issue regular newsletters with buy and sell recommendations and prepare detailed reports on selected companies but it's not a personalised service. It's up to the investor to keep an eye on the market and his or her own portfolio of shares.

A list of stockbrokers may be obtained from The Chief Executive, Irish Stock Exchange, Anglesea Street, Dublin 2. Phone (01) 6174200.

Investment funds

Not everyone has the time, knowledge or skill to manage direct investments on the stock market or in commodities or property and while such investments are currently out of favour with most investors, there is no doubt that, in the long run, investment in real assets should provide a far better return that simply putting money on deposit. But the long run describes an average over a long period during which values have fluctuated up and down. Some investments fell far short of the average and the total market in shares or property can sometimes fall significantly.

To get the best return, and avoid loss, it is essential to actively manage the investment, not simply trying to invest at what you hope might be a low point with the hope of selling at the top. The bottom and top is not the same for all investments and prospects are constantly changing. So too is the market sentiment, which may not be based on reality but does determine the current value of investments. One way of getting the benefit of some active management and of spreading the risk over a range of investments is to invest indirectly through an investment fund. There is a wide range of funds to choose from. Most allow for lump sum investments and some accept regular savings.

All investment funds have one thing in common. They are pooled investments. Each individual investor's money is pooled with that of other investors and professional managers manage the whole fund on their behalf. They have to be paid, of course, and the companies they work for have to make a profit, so there are charges involved. They can amount to a few percentage points a year so that in order for you to get any real return, the underlying investments need to be growing by an average of up to 4% or more a year.

In some cases charges can take up to four percentage points of the annual return on an investment

So in picking an investment fund it is essential to not only consider the prospects for your preferred class of investment but, also, how much of your fund is going to go in management charges each year. Remember those management charges apply even when the fund has declined in value. And it is not only the annual management charge that you need to take account of. The cost of investing through an investment fund may include all or some of the following:

- **Allocation rate:** This is the proportion of your initial investment that actually goes into the fund. In some cases it may actually be over 100%, particularly if you are making a large investment. But, more often, it is less than 100% although usually not less than 98%. Anything below 100% is effectively an initial set-up charge. Allocation rates can often be improved through negotiation. Brokers may get better rates than are available to investors going directly to the company offering the investment fund.

- **Bid offer spread:** Units in an investment fund are sold at the offer price and bought back at the bid price and there can be a difference of up to 5% between the two. Invest €10,000 in a fund with a bid offer spread of 5% and it is effectively worth €9,500 if you wanted to cash it in. Not all funds impose a bid offer spread.

- **Early encashment charge**: With some funds there is no bid offer spread and with others it may be described as an encashment charge that reduces over time. For instance there may be a charge of 5% on any encashment made in the first year reducing to 1% in year five and nothing thereafter.

- **Annual management fee:** Practically all funds impose management charges that may vary from 0.75% of the fund value to 2%. The fine print may include provision for allowing an increase in such fees in certain conditions.

- **Administrative charges:** Such charges may be imposed on regular income payments from an investment, or for switching from one fund to another.

- **Other charges:** If you make your investment through an intermediary, you may be charged for them keeping a watching brief on your investment and advising when switching might be advantageous. The charge can be as high as 2% a year.

Costs are very important but equally important, of course, is the choice of investment. In all cases, the investor should be looking to the medium or long term in order to achieve a sufficient return to offset the costs and ensure some levelling out of the ups and downs. Investors should be prepared to leave their lump sum investments for at least five years while regular savers should be thinking in terms of at least 10 years. There are various different types of investment funds and within each type there is a wide range of funds offering varying degrees of risk. Funds can be categorised within the following types:

- Unit funds

- With-profit funds

- Tracker bonds

Unit funds

The term "unit funds" covers a multitude. They are operated by banks, insurance companies and other financial institutions. Investors' money is pooled and managed on their behalf by professional fund managers. There is every conceivable type of fund. You can choose to have your money invested in almost any category of shares in a range of markets. So you can have all your money invested on the Japanese or Australian stock exchange or you can choose a wider option.

There are also funds invested entirely in property and others invested solely in Government funds. You take your pick and usually you can switch to a different fund operated by the same company if and when you like. There may be some cost involved but usually some switching is allowed without any charge.

Each investor is allocated so many units in the total fund. Their value changes daily or weekly as the value of the underlying investments change. With most funds the movement can be down as well as up but some funds put a floor under your potential losses by guaranteeing a minimum return.

The returns are liable to a 33% income tax stopped at source similar to the way DIRT is stopped on deposit interest. The various types of unit funds are called different names by dif-

How to pick an investment fund

There are four factors to consider in choosing a fund.

☐ What is the money invested in and how risky are those underlying investments? A wide spread provides some protection against major or rapid downturn in value but greater returns may be obtainable from specialised investments in a single sector if it happens to do well. Your best choice depends on your attitude to risk and your personal circumstances.

☐ What does it cost you to invest? There may be a 5% upfront charge in the form of a spread between the offer price at which you buy the units in the fund and the bid price at which the fund managers will buy back the units if you wanted to immediately cash them in. Some of that cost may be covered by a greater allocation of units given to larger investors or by way of special inducement. But some fund managers impose no upfront charges — the bid and offer prices are the same. All funds will charge an annual management charge, usually at least 1% but sometimes significantly higher.

☐ Are there any guarantees? Most investment funds simply rise or fall in line with the underlying investments but some funds do provide guarantees to investors. Such guarantees will always lower the potential rate of return but for those adverse to risk they may offer the certainty of at least getting the initial capital back at a fixed time in the future. You should be very clear about what guarantee you are getting.

☐ Can you switch funds without cost? Most fund managers allow you to switch between different funds at least once a year without cost.

ferent companies and the same name may, in some cases, mean different things. The following are some of the terms with a brief explanation of what they usually mean.

■ Unit-linked funds: These are insurance-linked unit investments. The life insurance element is usually very small but it allows for the fund to be set up under life insurance legislation. If it's included, you pay for it, so if you don't need it choose a non-insurance linked option. Different companies call their funds by different names.

- Unit trusts: These are unit funds set up under a trust deed. From the point of view of the investor, there is little difference between unit trusts and unit-linked funds. The differences have more to do with how they are set up and administered.

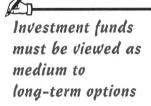

Investment funds must be viewed as medium to long-term options

- Managed funds: These are unit funds with a mix of investments. The term is usually applied to funds carrying a medium degree of risk because they have a wide spread of investments but there is no strict definition and the term could equally apply to a fund invested in a mix of riskier investments. But, in effect, all funds are managed although some more actively than others.

- Absolute return funds: Actively managed funds that invest in a wide range of assets including hedge funds and derivatives that allow the managers to bet on future trends thereby opening the potential for making money even when investment values are falling.

- Specialised funds: While a managed fund usually offers a spread of investments over a range of sectors, the specialised fund targets a particular sector, country or investment area. The investor is putting all of his or her eggs into the one basket. If the chosen investment area does well, then the returns will reflect that.

- Indexed funds: A fund managed in such a way that its performance matches the ups and downs of a stock market index or group of indices. It doesn't have to be as actively managed as other funds so management charges are sometimes lower. The managers don't try to outperform general stock market trends but they shouldn't underperform either.

- Consensus funds: A variant of indexed funds which are managed to at least match the average performance of other funds.

- Tracker bonds: These are a form of guaranteed investment fund. There is usually a commitment to return at least the initial investment at the end of a specified period, often five or six years. In addition, they provide a return based on the performance of some stock market index or group of indices. For example, a bond might guarantee to refund at least the initial capital at the end of five years and 11 months and to give a return equal to 70% of any rise in the FTSE index. Tracker bonds are dealt with in greater detail on page 57.

With-profit funds

With-profit funds are offered by insurance companies. In many respects they are the same as a managed fund with some exposure to the stock market but they differ from other funds in that the returns are averaged out over time by balancing the good times with the bad. How that balance between the good and bad years is achieved is determined internally by the company's actuary. The return comes by way of annual bonuses declared each year and a 'terminal' bonus at the end of the agreed term of the investment. That final bonus can be significant if the fund has done well but there is no certainty. Returns have been disappointing in recent years and these funds are now rarely actively marketed.

Returns on with-profit funds have been disappointing in recent years and these funds are now rarely actively marketed

Some bonds offer a guarantee that if you cash them in at fixed dates in the future — for instance after five, seven or 10 years — you'll get at least your capital back. Others guarantee both your initial capital plus any bonuses already declared. But in all cases the guarantees operate at fixed times. Early encashment may involve fixed penalties and companies reserve the right to impose additional penalties known as "market value adjustments" in the event of a significant market downturn. That can impact on final payouts as well as early encashments. Entry charges, allocation rates, management charges and early encashment penalties vary from company to company. It's hard to make overall comparisons since the company that's good on one of those elements may be bad on another.

The set penalties for early encashment also vary greatly. Very often there is a penalty of 5% on encashment during the first year phasing out in later years with no penalty after the fifth year. Companies operating a 5% bid/offer generally impose no early encashment penalty since it is already built into the initial charge. With most companies, it is possible to take an income from the bond by way of regular withdrawals on a monthly, quarterly, six-monthly or annual basis. The withdrawals, of course, should not exceed the likely annual bonus rate otherwise the initial investment is been eaten into.

Which is best for you?

The type of investment you choose depends very much on your own circumstances and attitude to risk. Specialised unit-linked investments offer the best chance of high return, but there is a risk that it will not materialise. If, for instance, the fund is invested in equities, the amount eventually paid out will depend on the state of the stock market at the time of the payment. And who is to say what market conditions will be like in 10 years time. With-profit policies offer a chance of participating in the insurance company's own profit and usually once bonuses are declared, they can't be taken back. The risk is less than with unit-linked funds but the returns can be very disappointing and have been in recent years. But past performance is not a good guide to future prospects. The sophisticated investor will also want to look at the mix of investments within each fund. This can vary greatly from one fund to another. Charges can have a major impact on the actual returns you get so it's essential to consider those in detail.

With all of these investments it is important to take a medium to long-term outlook. It can be costly to withdraw too early. The cost of switching from one fund to another depends on the set-up costs involved. Most companies allow investors to switch without cost from one fund to another within their own stable – usually at least once a year. The switching option doesn't arise with tracker bonds or with-profit funds.

Normally with unit funds, any income earned on the fund is reinvested to the benefit of the investors – although there are provisions in some plans for the investor to get a regular income. This is arranged, however, by the sale of units and there is no guarantee that the remaining units will continue to be worth as much as the initial investment. In other words, the income could, in some cases, be paid out of capital. There is no single answer to the question 'which is best?' It all depends on the individual, his or her personal

Charges can have a major impact of the actual returns you get so it's essential to consider those in detail.

circumstances and attitude to risk. Before seeking advice or making a decision, ask yourself what you are investing for, how much risk are you willing to take, and what are the chances of you needing speedy access to your money. Having the answers to those questions in your head will help you to make the right decision.

Investor Compensation Scheme

The money invested in most investment funds is covered by the underlying assets which are effectively owned by the investors, not by the fund managers or the promoters. In addition life insurance companies have to maintain substantial reserves. Other investment firms are covered by the Investor Compensation Scheme which protects investors but only to 90% of the amount due subject to a maximum pay-out per individual of €20,000. It's not much so it is important to be aware of what category your investment falls into. Money invested in a life assurance company's investment fund should never be worth less than the value of the underlying assets. That's not going to be affected no matter what happens to the insurance company itself. Guarantees given in respect of returns, such as those on tracker bonds, are only as good as the company, usually a bank, that has underwritten them. But the risk of a bank failure is relatively small.

At the greatest risk is money invested with other investment firms including investments in transit from investment intermediaries to the funds of insurance companies. Making out the cheques for such investments directly to the insurance company provides an additional safeguard.

Investing a lump sum

Y ou may come into a lump sum by way of an inheritance, a maturing investment, the sale of some assets, a redundancy, or a lucky win. Alternatively you may have accumulated a lump sum over time. It may be spread over a range of saving outlets but combined, it makes up a lump sum. Whether it's a new lump sum or one that you have had for a long time, you should be continuously examining your options. That's the ideal but at the very least you should do so occasionally. The following options are not listed in any particular order of preference, risk or likely return. The mechanics of some of them such as stock market investment, bank deposits and pensions are dealt with in more detail elsewhere in the book. Here they are listed in brief with an outline of the pros and cons.

Clear some debts

R educing your debt can provide a far better return than simply putting the money on deposit. Paying off a loan on which the interest rate is 10% gives the same return as putting the money on deposit at 10%. The big drawback is that it reduces your future financial flexibility. If, having paid off the loan, you need money again, you may find it difficult, expensive or both to borrow again. Much depends on the type of loan.

It generally makes good sense to pay off credit card debt. Used sensibly, credit cards are truly flexible friends but that means totally avoiding interest charges by paying the full amount due each month. But most people pay interest at some time or other and the rate can be over 20%. You'd need to be getting 28.6% before DIRT tax to end up with 20% net. So paying off the loan, that is costing you 20%, provides you with the same financial gain as investing money at 28.6%. That's not a bad return.

The same sort of argument applies to personal loans. The interest rate is likely to be lower so the saving is that much less. Make sure, of course, that there are no penalties for early repayment. Such penalties may apply to loans issued at a fixed rate of interest or to some finance company or hire purchase loans. But with most personal loans, interest is charged on a daily basis. The interest charges stop clocking up as soon as you make your payment.

The benefits of paying off a mortgage are not as clear cut as paying off credit card debt or personal loans mainly because the interest rate is lower and may even qualify for tax relief. Let's suppose you have a mortgage at 3.5%. If you reduce it by €10,000 your interest charges will be reduced by €350 a year. Assuming you are getting tax relief on that at the standard rate your net saving is €280. If alternatively you put the €10,000 on deposit you could earn about as much, or more, even after paying DIRT tax. Even if you are not eligible for tax relief, the saving compared with keeping the money in An Post Savings Bonds, for instance, is very small.

Pros

☐ Paying off debt can provide a very good financial return many times better than putting the money on deposit.

☐ There's a great psychological satisfaction in paying off or even reducing a mortgage. It's hard to put a money value on that but it can be worth a lot.

Cons

☐ Having cleared off the credit card debt, you may be tempted to run it up again but that's only a drawback if you give into the temptation.

☐ Make sure that there are no penalties for early repayments.

☐ If, having used spare money to reduce your mortgage, you find yourself in a position of having to borrow again, the new loan is likely to be more expensive. Depending on your circumstances you may have to take out a new mortgage, pay set-up costs and not get the benefit of tax relief or at worse have to rely on a much more expensive personal loan.

Spend the money on education

Many studies have shown that investing in education yields a very high return both to the individual and to the community. The return to the individual can come by way of extra earning power over a lifetime and increased job security. That return can be measured very easily in cash terms. But education can also provide less tangible returns. It can give you a greater degree of choice in picking a career and allow you to enjoy a broader and more satisfying lifestyle. Learning to appreciate art, literature or music may not put any money in your pocket but it can nonetheless yield a very rich return.

There is a very wide range of educational courses to choose from. You need to be clear in your objectives. If you want to increase your earning power you need to acquire knowledge and skills that are in demand and will remain so. But pick a course that suits your ability and will retain your interest. It can be costly in terms of wasted money and time to drop out of a course.

Pros

☐ Education can yield a very good return in terms of money and satisfaction and the benefits can last a lifetime.

Cons

- ☐ Money only buys you the teaching. The learning you have to do yourself and it takes time and effort.

- ☐ You generally need to pay up front and you may have wasted both time and money if you drop out.

Spend it on home improvements

A conservatory, an extension or an attic conversion can greatly improve your quality of life if they satisfy your needs. Only you can put a value on the enjoyment you may get from summer days spent in a conservatory and likewise with regard to the extra living space provided by say a kitchen extension or an extra room in the attic. If you are going to remain living in your home, that's what you should be considering and it's a very personal decision. But if you envisage yourself as being on a property ladder moving ever onwards and upwards you'll need to be more concerned with whether or not the home 'improvement' actually adds value to your home in the eyes of a potential buyer.

Even if you are staying in the home, that is of some importance but it's a lot more so if you are planning to sell in the not too distant future. So what adds value to a home? Estate agents will tell you that a conservatory won't add much, if any, value to a property if it is poorly built or obviously only of use during a few warm days in summer. They are keener on extensions which if well designed, they say, can add significantly to the value of a property. But you need to see your house through the eyes of potential buyers. Families with young children might prefer a garden to an extension.

Pros

- ☐ Could greatly improve your quality of life if you need and will enjoy the extra space.

- ☐ May add value to your property but the emphasis is on 'may'.

- ☐ Building costs are currently at a low if you shop around.

Cons

- ☐ A badly designed or badly built extension won't increase the value of your property. It could even reduce it.

- ☐ There is no direct financial return until you sell the house and, even then, the actual value added by home improvements is uncertain.

Put it on deposit

Deposit accounts are about the safest place to keep your money. But you can't always expect to get a good return. At the end of 2011, it was possible to get a real return that would at least ensure that the purchasing power of your savings were maintained and even enhanced. But at other times, the purchasing power of your lump sum may be steadily eroded as a result of price inflation. There is always a wide difference between the best and worse rates on offer. It pays to shop around and to regularly review the rates available.

Pros

- ☐ **Your investment is about as safe as it can be thanks to Government guarantees.**

- ☐ **You can get a return that will maintain the purchasing power of your nest egg.**

- ☐ **If you need it, demand accounts give you ready access to your money.**

Cons

- ☐ **Those willing to take some risk can hope for better returns.**

- ☐ **Getting the best rate requires some care and a willingness to shop around.**

Invest in a pension fund

This used to be a very attractive option for those liable for tax at the top rate and the proposal to progressively reduce the maximum tax relief to 20% by 2014 has been shelved. The relief from PRSI income levies has already been abolished but tax relief at 41% is still available and will continue to apply to contributions made in 2012. Have a read of Chapter 10 on page 174 before making any decisions. Great care must, of course, be taken in your choice of fund, and on the costs involved. If you are in an occupational fund these matters may be outside your control although check that your representatives on the board of trustees are keeping an eye on such matters.

Pros

- ☐ **If you are a top-rate taxpayer, the State will add €41 for every €59 you contribute. The eventual pension may be taxable but that's a long time away and you may not be paying tax at the top rate in retirement.**

- A quarter of the fund built up by additional voluntary contributions to an occupational pension or by contributions to a PRSI or personal pension plan, can be taken as a tax-free lump sum on retirement subject to a maximum of €200,000.

Cons

- Your money can't be accessed until you retire and there may, in some cases, be limitations on your access after that.

Put the money into an investment fund

This is an option for those who want to invest their money for the medium to long term. It's an alternative to putting money into a pension fund where it would have to stay until retirement or of using the money to invest directly in property or on the stock market. Investment funds provide professional management and a better spread of risk.

All investment funds have one thing in common. They are pooled investments. Each individual investor's money is pooled with that of other investors and professionals manage the whole fund on their behalf. To pay for those services, there is always an annual management charge and there may also be a set-up charge. With some sums, an immediate 5% of your investment goes in set-up charges and then up to 2% is taken off each year as a management charge. But there are funds which impose no initial charge and levy, only 1% a year management fee and that's what you should be looking for. See page 63.

There are also guaranteed bonds and tracker bonds giving guarantees of at least getting your money back after perhaps five years while offering the chance of some return linked to stock market performance. But in return for the guarantee, you have to accept some limitation on the return you can hope for. Make sure that you know exactly what you are being guaranteed, who is providing the guarantee and how any return is to be calculated. With most funds, the value of your stake depends on the performance of the underlying investments. Values can fall just as easily as they rise. So in choosing a fund you need to consider, not only the set-up and ongoing management charges, but also how the money is to be invested and the outlook for those particular investments. You may also consider the past performance of the fund managers involved but don't forget that past performance is not necessarily a good guide to future prospects.

In summary — look on investment funds as at least a medium term investment. Try not to pay any set-up charges and no more than 1% annual management charge. Make sure you know what the fund invests in and be aware of the risks involved.

Pros

- Investment funds give you an opportunity to spread your risks and get professional management.

- ☐ There's the potential to get a better return than you would by keeping the money on deposit.

Cons

- ☐ Set-up and management charges can be high if you don't shop around for the best deals.

- ☐ With most funds, values can move down as well as up so you can lose and lose significantly.

Buy shares through the Stock Exchange

Direct stock market investment is one of the options open to those who have no immediate need for a lump sum, don't want to spend it and would prefer to put it aside earning them a return. It's also an option for someone who wants to gamble on the ups and downs of the market. It's not, of course, a risk-free option. Trends over the past couple of years amply confirm that. Share prices can be very volatile although, in the long run, the potential is good. Shares tend to outperform other investments over the longer term, but there can be no certainty, and losses can be substantial in the short term or if you have bought at, or near, a peak and have to sell at, or close to, the bottom of the cycle.

Even when the market is tending upwards, there will always be some shares moving in the opposite direction an upward trend can always be punctuated with sharp downturns of uncertain duration. All share markets experience the same sort of swings and some shares, of course, experience a greater degree of volatility than others. Investments outside the eurozone carry an additional foreign exchange risk.

The shares have to be bought in foreign currency and there is always the risk that the euro will devalue against that currency. To invest directly in shares you need some knowledge, some luck and a willingness to maintain an active interest in your investments. Investing small sums can be expensive because of minimum dealing charges but you could split €20,000 between a few different shares without incurring unduly onerous charges particularly if you make your own choices and don't look for any advice from the broker. The choice is endless. At one end of the scale you can go for a high dividend income with limited potential for major capital gain. At the other end there are speculative shares offering no dividends but the chance of a sharp increase in value, if all goes well. See page 60.

Pros

- ☐ Shares in general have tended to provide good returns over the longer term. But like all averages that doesn't necessarily hold true for specific shares at specific times as has been obvious in recent times.

- By investing directly you are in control. You pick the shares and can buy and sell as you see fit.

Cons

- Share prices can just as easily move down as up. The movements can be quite sharp at times.

- Dealing charges can make small transactions quite expensive and can be a disincentive to spreading the risk over a number of shares.

Use your lump sum to start a business

A small lump sum may not be sufficient to finance the start up of a business but it could be a start. There are other sources of finance available including grants and tax rebates. Those on PAYE who leave their jobs to start up a business on their own can (subject to terms and conditions) claim a rebate of all the income tax they paid over the previous six years.

The type of business that qualifies has been greatly extended in the new Enterprise and Investment Incentive (EII) that replaced the Business Expansion Scheme in late 2011. There has also been an increase in the maximum qualifying investment. The rebate is limited, of course, by the amount of tax you actually paid over the six years. The new incentive is to continue at least until the end of 2012. See page 293.

If you meet the requirements you can make a back-claim for tax relief extending over the past six years on up to a maximum of €600,000 invested in the new business. At 41%, that gives you a maximum rebate of €246,000. In essence that means that you can get back all of the tax you paid on up to €100,000 of income in each of those years. If you've paid tax on that amount each year at the top rate of 41% you are eligible for a rebate of €41,000 (41% of €100,000) for each year. The basic requirement is that the would-be entrepreneur is setting up a new business and leaving a PAYE job. The incentive isn't available to an existing businessman moving into a new venture and each claimant must own at least 15% of the shares in the venture.

But apart from the finance, starting and running a business requires skills, creativity and determination which not everyone has.

Pros

- Being your own boss can be very satisfying even if you have to work harder.

- Few people manage to become really wealthy on their wages.

Cons

- ☐ Starting a business is hard work and there can be no certainty of success.

- ☐ A worker in a larger firm can be more secure than the owner/manager of a small firm.

Buy a new car

A significant proportion of the wealth generated by the Celtic Tiger was spent on buying cars. They satisfy two distinct needs. A car provides transport but it can also satisfy some less tangible needs to show off and boost the owner's status. If you are thinking of buying a car to gratify those latter needs then only you can judge whether or not you are getting good value. You'll possibly get most satisfaction from a new car, big or sporty. But if you simply need the car to get you from one place to another, then it makes a lot more financial sense to buy second-hand. The greatest single cost of motoring is depreciation. A car can drop in value by 25% in the first year and by a further 15% the following year. After the first couple of years the car depreciates at a somewhat slower pace, possibly about 10% a year. You can avoid the heavy initial depreciation cost by buying second-hand. If you take a little care, the gain is unlikely to be offset by additional repair costs.

Pros

- ☐ There's an opportunity to show off, turn heads and maybe boost your status among some. If the existing car is getting past its best, you may actually save some money by cutting down on maintenance costs.

Cons

- ☐ The benefits may not justify the heavy costs involved particularly if 'new' means a really new car and not a second-hand one.

4 Life insurance — for peace of mind

Life insurance is primarily about providing financial cover for dependants in the event of premature death although the general term may also be applied to products providing benefits in the event of illness or disability. The need for life insurance varies from individual to individual and it changes over time. Obviously the more cover you have the better, but there is a cost involved. Choices have to be made and they usually involve large sums of money.

Insurance products are sometimes made unduly complicated. Policies are often composed of different elements in a unique package that is impossible to compare from a cost point of view with even a broadly similar product from another insurance company. It is not uncommon for companies to combine insurance policies with savings plans but it is important for the buyer to separate the twin objectives of protection for dependants and saving for the future. Be sure of what you need and what you are buying.

Apart from death, suffering an illness, accident or disability can also have a major financial impact in terms of lost income and expense. Hopefully you'll avoid all three but you can never be sure. Insurance can provide the peace of mind of knowing that if the worse does happen the impact will, at least, be eased by some financial benefits. Such peace of mind comes at a price in terms of premiums and only you can decide if the benefit is worth the cost.

- **Assess your needs, ideally within the context of a general financial review,**

- **prioritise them,**

- **take into account any cover you have,**

- **make decisions on what additional cover you want,**

- **take advice.**

It is important to assess the cover you already have. In particular you should take into account any cover you have as a member of a pension scheme. Most occupational pension schemes provide benefits for your dependants should you die before retiring and many include insurance that guarantees a continuing income should you be unable to work because of an illness, accident or disability.

The provision of protection for family and other dependants is the first and primary role of life assurance. An essential part of any family finance plan must be the protection of one's dependants against the financial loss which inevitably results from the death of a bread winner.

One thinks usually of the death of the husband in this regard, and the loss of income which will result. But the early death of a wife, even if she is not an income earner, can also impose a financial burden on a widower trying to keep a family together. Life assurance offers a way of easing these financial burdens caused by death. But many life assurance policies involve more than basic life insurance. They combine cover for dependants in the event of death with a way of saving for the future — for retirement, educating the children, or even marriage. Most assurance policies satisfy both needs to some extent. Some are aimed more at protection while others are aimed more at saving. Some only offer protection with no monetary return if the insured person lives beyond a certain age.

It is important for people taking out the insurance to be clear on what they need from the policy and to keep the dis-

Even a small monthly premium represents a significant cost when payable over a long period. So it makes sense to take your time considering exactly what you need and how best to satisfy those needs at the lowest possible cost tinction between protection and saving in mind. The insurance industry is pledged to emphasise the differences, in response to the complaints over a lack of clarity in the past, but it is no harm to keep it uppermost in one's mind. Let's first have a look at the type of policies generally available, and then examine how they can be used to satisfy the average family's needs.

There are four basic types of life assurance:

- term or temporary insurance,

- whole of life assurance,

- endowment assurance, and

- disability and illness insurance.

Term insurance

A man aged 30 can ensure that his dependants receive €200,000 if he dies within the next 10 years at a premium cost of about €14 a month. Taking a similar policy out at age 50 would cost about €47 a month. But quotes can vary greatly from one company to another so it's important to shop around. You can get an independent broker to do it for you but he or she may not always offer the cheapest option. Some insurance companies don't deal through brokers. It's as well to supplement a broker's efforts by shopping around yourself.

This type of insurance is called term insurance and all too little of it is sold. In Ireland, we tend to spend a lot on life insurance compared to our counterparts in other countries but we favour savings-type policies which are really geared towards saving for the future and which only pay out a relatively small amount in the event of early death.

Term insurance pays out nothing if the insured person lives for the set term of years. Suppose like our example above, you are 30 years of age and take out a 10-year policy. If you live until you are 40, the policy ends and you get nothing back. But it is not a complete loss. Indeed it is no loss. What you have bought during the 10 years is peace of mind: the

It is important when buying life insurance to distinguish between protection and saving for the future

knowledge that should you die your dependants will be provided with some financial resources.

That peace of mind is worth buying. Not everyone needs term insurance. But there are a lot of people who need it and do not have it. If you are in a company pension scheme, you are possibly fairly well covered for life insurance within the scheme. But it is worth checking out how high the cover is and considering whether or not you should take out a little more.

Then what about insurance on the stay-at-home spouse. The financial cost of keeping a family together following the death of a wife and mother can be substantial. A lump sum would certainly make living more bearable. One recent survey indicated that full-time house parents spend an average of 86 hours a week on household tasks including childcare, preparation of meals, general cleaning duties etc. If the minimum wage was applied, the weekly cost would be over €744 a week without building in any provision for overtime rates. According to another study it could cost €60,000 a year to outsource the household tasks of the typical homemaker.

Term insurance may also be important for people who lose their jobs. The loss of the job may also mean the loss of the insurance cover provided within a pension scheme. In some cases, employers will keep the insurance cover in place for a short time, or it may be possible for the redundant worker to keep up the payments himself. There are a wide range of term insurance options to choose from.

You can pick the number of years and the size of the cover. The older the person is when the policy is taken out, the higher the premiums. Term insurance is the cheapest way of providing real financial protection for dependants and it is the first type of policy young parents on slender means should consider. Within this general category there are a number of different possibilities.

Level Term: In this case the sum insured remains fixed for the term of the policy. If the person insured survives the term no payment is made by the insurance company. If he or she dies during the term, then the sum insured is paid out. Even if there is no pay-out, and hopefully that will be the case, the policy offers value for money in the peace of mind it provides.

Convertible Term: This provides the same basic insurance cover as level term assurance, but there is an option to convert the policy into another type. Usually the assurance company allows conversion at any time during the life of the policy and agrees not to require any further medical test or proof of good health. The policy into which you convert will operate from the date of conversion and will be at the normal premium rates applied to such policies given the insured person's age at the time of conversion.

A convertible term assurance policy need not cost much more than a level term policy — particularly if it is a relatively long term policy. Unless your means are very slender and unlikely to improve over time, convertible term assurance makes much more sense than level term. It provides flexibility in the future when life cover may be less important.

Decreasing Term: This type of policy is often referred to as a mortgage protection policy since they are often taken out for this purpose. The life cover gradually decreases over the term of the policy. For instance, a policy may provide initial cover of €100,000 declining over 20 years. If the insured person dies in the first year his family would get the full €100,000, but by year 10 it has reduced to €79,500 and in the last year the cover is only €12,000.

This, of course, is an ideal way of providing for the repayment of a house mortgage in the event of death. The sum owed to the bank or building society is decreasing year by year as repayments are made and the sum payable by the insurance company will more or less keep pace. Some decreasing term policies simply guarantee to pay off the mortgage in the event of death — less any arrears — provided interest rates remain within set limits.

Banks and building societies make it a condition of granting a mortgage that the borrower takes out a mortgage protection policy but you don't have to take out the policy with the lender's own insurance company. It is, however, often cheaper and easier to do so since the premium can be col-

It could cost at least €744 a week to employ someone to carry out the duties of a house parent on the minimum wage of €8.65 an hour with no extra overtime rates

Mortgage protection policies are an example of term insurance lected with the repayments and some lenders make it expensive to switch by imposing an additional fee on borrowers who take out the insurance elsewhere.

Family Income Benefits: This is another type of term insurance which provides, instead of a lump sum, a regular income for the family or dependants. For example, the policy on a married man might provide for the payment of €10,000 a year every year between his death and the end of a 20 year term. The payment made by the insurance company would not be liable to income tax.

Whole of life assurance

Term assurance is pure protection. There is no element of saving since no payments are made if the insured person survives the term. With whole of life assurance there is an element of saving, although it is saving for your dependants after your death. The insurance company undertakes to pay the agreed sum — plus bonuses if you go for a with-profits policy — whenever you die. So unlike term assurance, the payment is made at some time.

Obviously the premiums payable for a given life cover are higher in this case than on a similar term assurance. You can opt to pay premiums up to your death or else elect to stop paying premiums at a certain age. For most people, whose incomes fall after retirement at 65, it is a good idea to have premium payments stopping then. In some cases, the premiums are reviewed every so often, maybe every 10 years. Whole of life policies are often included in combined hybrid policies offered by insurance companies — see below. Special whole of life policies are used to provide for the payment of inheritance tax.

Endowment assurance

With endowment policies the saving element is uppermost. Pure life insurance is often kept to the minimum. The actual sum payable on death is relatively small compared with a term or whole life assurance carrying the same premium. They are best viewed as a method of saving or investing and for this reason have been dealt with in chapter 3 on investment.

Combined insurance plans

Most insurance companies offer life insurance plans which may have elements of all the above. They are difficult to understand and it's practically impossible to compare one plan with another. They usually include some life cover and some element of saving although the saving is often geared towards building up a fund out of which future premiums may be paid. As the insured person gets older, the cost of the life insurance portion of the plan rises so less of each premium is going into the investment fund.

At some stage the cost of the ongoing life insurance exceeds the premium and the accumulated savings start to be drawn down. If, and when, all of the savings are used up, the insured person has the options of paying more, accepting reduced cover or ending the policy. The advantage of these plans is that they are flexible and they may be less costly than other options over the longer term. But the premium for a set amount of life cover will be higher in the earlier years than an equivalent term policy. A typical policy works something like this.

The life cover is provided by way of a whole of life policy with premiums rising periodically as the insured person gets older. The cover is effectively renewed from time to time with a guarantee that the cost will not be affected by any medical condition that has arisen in the meanwhile. It will rise but only to the rate payable by a healthy person at that age. That guarantee continues for whatever term you pick. The longer the term, the higher the insurance cost.

In the initial years, the premium payable is higher than the cost of the insurance and the surplus after charges is put into a fund. In due course the cost of the insurance exceeds the premium that is being paid. At that stage the insurance company taps into the investment fund. How long the fund can continue to pay the ever-increasing cost of the life cover depends on the investment return. In addition to life cover, most plans will also allow you to add in other types of cover such as serious illness and income continuance. The

Beware of insurance policies that mix cover with savings in a way that's not totally clear to you

one-stop-shop aspect of a plan can be appealing but each element of the plan should be assessed as to:

- whether you actually need it, and

- whether there are better stand-alone alternatives.

The comments made with regard to endowment policies also apply. Putting money into an investment fund to pay future life insurance premiums can make sense but it does involve two different decisions. It may not make sense to save for the future if you are in debt or saving to buy a house and what you really want is the maximum life cover at the lowest possible cost.

Income protection insurance

Disability benefits are often included in company pension schemes. About three-quarters of all private pension schemes provide for income continuance where a member is unable to continue working due to disability or long-term illness.

For those who are not covered through a company scheme there is always the option of providing the cover through what are known as Permanent Health, Income Continuance or Income Protection policies.

Self-employed people can be particularly vulnerable to loss of income in the event of illness or disability. As with all insurance, it is well worthwhile shopping around or getting a broker to do it for you. It is important to compare not only the price but also the extent of the cover and, most importantly, what is **not** covered.

As an example of the type of cost involved, one company is quoting a premium of €38 a month to insure a man aged 30 for €317 a week while he is unable, because of illness or disability, to work at his usual job. The premium goes up to €60 for a man aged 40. No benefits are paid for the first 13 weeks of illness unless the claimant is hospitalised.

While tax relief on life assurance policies has been abolished it is still allowed in full on the premiums paid for this type of policy up to a limit of 10% of income. So the true cost can be reduced by almost half for a top rate taxpayer. Any benefits received, however, are taxable if the recipient is liable for tax.

Serious illness insurance

We usually think of disability arising as a result of an accident but, of course, it can also arise as a result of serious illness. And serious illness can put many strains on a family's finances. Over the past couple of years, the insurance companies have been vying with one another in devising ever more elaborate policies providing lump sums in the event of the insured person suffering a serious or critical illness. Payment is usually only made if the person survives for 14 days after being diagnosed as suffering from one of a stated list of illnesses. Not all illnesses are covered so it is important to read the fine print.

This type of policy should not be seen as an alternative to medical insurance, such as Aviva, Quinn Healthcare or VHI insurance plans that are designed to cover the cost of medical care. Neither is it an alternative to permanent health insurance designed to pay an income if you are unable to work because of an illness or disability. It is not really an alternative to basic life assurance either.

But it does pay out a lump sum which may be used for any purpose. It may help to pay medical expenses or to supplement income. But there is no need to show that the medical expenses have been incurred or that you have lost income. The claim is allowed provided you have suffered one of the designated illnesses and survived for more than 14 days. The vast bulk of claims in Ireland are made in respect of people suffering from cancer followed by heart problems and multiple sclerosis.

Critical illness insurance is not really an alternative to medical insurance like Aviva, Quinn Healthcare or VHI

With some policies, premium levels are fixed and guaranteed for the term of the policy. With others, the premium is reviewed from time to time and you may be called upon to increase the premium or else accept a reduction in the level of cover. With this second type of policy, part of each premium is invested and the policy may build up a surrender value. The level of future premiums, after an initial fixed period, depends on the performance of the investment fund.

Bad value loan insurance

☐ Lenders often sell payment protection insurance alongside their loans but it is generally as much a protection for themselves as it is for the borrower. Indeed it is worth a lot more to the lender. If a sister company isn't providing the insurance, the lender is at least earning commission. Payment protection insurance is very profitable. It is designed to provide cover should you have difficulty in meeting the loan repayments as a result of illness, disability or simply losing your job.

Many people have benefited from such insurance in recent times as jobs were lost but this type of policy may be unnecessary for those in secure jobs with good sick pay schemes. Of course, no job is totally secure in the current climate but, in many instances, the worst outcome is likely to be redundancy with some lump sum compensation. It's nice to have insurance if you have to make a claim. But against that security you have to weigh the cost.

To take out the insurance all you have to do is tick a box on the application form or simply nod yes when asked by the salesman filling out the loan form on your behalf. Even if you get around to reading the fine print you may still find it very difficult to work out the true cost in terms of euro and cent. But be assured that this type of insurance is not cheap.

For instance, the payment protection cover offered by credit card companies typically costs about 60 cent a month for every €100 outstanding. At first glance that seems to be a very small amount. But 60 cent a month adds up to €7.20 a year. Since that is on every €100 outstanding it's the same as paying an additional 7.2% on your debt. The benefit is usually no more than a phased reduction in the debt over 12 months if the cardholder is disabled or loses his or her job.

It's hard to get figures in Ireland because of the way the official statistics are compiled but in Britain it is estimated that only 15% to 20% of the premium income from such policies is paid out in claims. The survey also found disturbingly high levels of commission being paid particularly in small and medium-sized retail outlets when about 40% of the firms visited were considered to be offering a level of incentive to sales staff that could encourage the mis-selling of policies. The commission payable was as high as 80%.

There is heavy competition among the companies so it is well worthwhile shopping around for the widest cover at the cheapest price if you feel that you need this cover.

Products are changing. But by way of illustration, a man of 45 should be able to get cover for €64,000 in respect of serious illness or total permanent disability for a monthly premium of about €34 but some companies quote premiums as high as €60 a month. Premiums depend on a range of factors including gender.

Conditions vary from policy to policy so you can't compare on a strictly like-with-like basis. You can shop around, however, by yourself or through a broker. A good broker should be able to justify his or her recommendation. Just ask, why this product rather than another and make sure you get a credible answer.

You should also ask how many quotes the broker sought and for a list of the companies he approached. Most brokers only have agencies for a limited number of companies and may not seek quotes from others. It's always well worthwhile to do a little shopping around on your own behalf.

What to choose

No family should be without some form of life assurance. As mentioned in the introduction to this chapter the early death of husband or wife can impose severe financial burdens on the surviving spouse. And for a relatively small sum, life assurance can provide you with some protection and a certain amount of peace of mind.

Remember, that even if you live to pay all the premiums on a term assurance, and therefore get no monetary gain, you have still got a return in the peace of mind you have enjoyed over the years knowing that your family had some protection against the financial loss they would have suffered through your early death. It is important, however, to get the right type of assurance that is geared to your own particular circumstances. There can be no hard and fast rules. Every family's circumstances are different, but here are some guidelines to follow. Protection is obviously the first consid-

Life assurance is primarily concerned with providing protection for your family and dependants in the event of early death eration. And a newly-married couple on a tight budget can get this through term assurance. Unless their budget is extremely tight, convertible term assurance offers the best bet providing the flexibility to convert into other types of assurance as the family circumstances, and possibly budget, improve.

So the first policy should be a convertible term assurance providing a lump sum on the death of either spouse but particularly on the death of the principal earner or, alternatively, the guarantee of a regular income over a set number of years. This basic cover may well be provided as part of an occupational pension scheme. In that case, term insurance may not be needed.

Life insurance needs change over time but the basic need is for protection rather than saving for the future

First check if there is adequate cover through an occupational pension scheme. If not, then term assurance is the cheapest way to get protection. A 25-year-old might take a policy over a 25 year term — by the end of which the need for cover may have declined as children mature. If money is really tight, a shorter term policy can provide similar cover at a lower premium.

If a house is being purchased on a mortgage the lender will undoubtedly require a mortgage protection policy. For a very low premium this will provide enough funds to pay off the mortgage should the breadwinner or, in most cases now, either spouse die within the set term. Basically it is a declining balance term assurance i.e. the amount paid out on death goes down each year in line with the reduced indebtedness to the provider of the mortgage. It is also possible to get a term assurance to cover the full value of the house without any decline in the amount payable on death, but this is more expensive.

Even if both spouses are not earning it is important to consider having insurance on both. A mortgage protection policy will usually be on the joint lives ensuring that the mortgage is paid off in the event of either dying. But even with the mortgage paid off, a surviving spouse with children can be burdened with a lot of additional expense while at the same time the family may have lost the earnings of the deceased spouse. Few people think of the costs imposed on a family by the untimely death of a parent even if he or she was not wage-earning. The surviving spouse who wishes to keep the family together might need to employ a housekeeper and will certainly face some extra expense in looking after the children.

One approach is to combine a mortgage protection policy on the joint lives of the spouses with a term insurance on the life of the principal earner and a 10 to 15 year endowment policy on the life of the lower earning or non-earning spouse. The endowment policy provides a lump sum in the event of death but if the spouse is still alive at the end of the 10 or 15 year term, as hopefully he or she will, then the policy will pay out a useful lump sum which can be put towards the children's education.

But you must never lose sight of the main aim of life insurance. The objective must be to provide financial cover in the event of premature death. While that can be combined with saving for the future through endowment policies there are many other ways of saving. It is important to separate the twin objectives of protection for dependants and saving for the future. Be sure of what you need and what you are buying. These are just some general guidelines for deciding what type of policy you need. So how do you go about buying insurance and what about the fine print? Let us look first at the usual conditions that apply to life insurance.

A mortgage protection policy is normally taken out on joint lives ensuring that the mortgage is paid off if either spouse dies

How to buy assurance

It has become a lot easier for consumers to pick the best life insurance products for their needs. It still requires a bit of work but consumer protection laws mean that at least the consumer can get access to most of the information needed to make informed choices. Sellers are required to provide standardised information on the purpose of the product, all the costs involved and details of any penalties for early encashment. But the information is no good if you don't make use of it.

Before buying life insurance it is as important as ever to assess your needs and prioritise them. It is also important to take into account any cover you already have through a company pension scheme, for instance. And since it's a complicated area, some expert advice can be well worthwhile. Some advisers are paid through the commission they receive on the products they sell. Others charge a fee, often on a per hour basis, and give the client the benefit of any commission. Either way you need to assess the advice given.

Buying life assurance can be a far bigger financial decision than many people realise. It is a long-term contract which can cost a lot over the years and can involve considerable loss if cancelled too soon. So it is essential to make the right decisions at the start. Don't be afraid to shop around, ask questions, and take your time. Take advice from more than one person before committing yourself. You should first be clear on the type of policy you think you need and have the reasons clear in your mind.

What insurance cover do you need? Do you only need it for a fixed term until the children are older? What type of cover have you got already? Don't forget the cover you may have through a company pension scheme.

The disclosure requirements also apply, of course, to investment products

All too often in the past, life insurance was confused with saving. The two are still often combined but it's important when shopping around to be very aware of the distinction and of your own particular needs. Basic life insurance cover is somewhat like car insurance. It pays out if the insured person dies within a fixed term. If the person is still alive at the end of the agreed term then the policy lapses and nothing is paid out. The premiums have bought peace of mind.

Saving for the future may be linked to an insurance policy but it doesn't have to be. Consider your needs in both areas separately and satisfy yourself that there is some advantage in linking them – usually there isn't.

It can be well worthwhile getting independent advice. Financial intermediaries or brokers are regulated by the Financial Regulator within the Central Bank. There are two basic categories. There are authorised financial advisers who can provide advice on the full range of options and there are restricted advisers who can only advise on the products of those companies for which they hold agencies.

Even if a restricted adviser has a large number of agencies, they cannot cover the whole range of options since some insurance companies, such as Quinn Life, do not sell through the broker network. See the section on financial advisers on page 46. But then there is no guarantee that an authorised adviser will actually look at all the options.

Advisers have to be paid, of course. Some take their remuneration by way of commission on the products that they sell while others charge a fee for their services giving the client the benefit of any commission that might be payable. There is a wide range of regulations aimed at ensuring that advisers do the best job possible for their clients. Before offering advice at all they are required to spend some time doing what is known as a *fact find* designed to get information on the customer's requirements and personal circumstances.

Having obtained that information and having decided on a recommendation, the adviser is required to give the client a "statement of suitability" outlining why this particular product has been picked. The customer is also entitled to get a statement outlining details of the type of service provided by the adviser, the fees charged or commission collected, and an outline of the firm's complaints procedures. The statement also has to contain details of the compensation scheme that covers the transaction and be given a copy of the firm's Statement of Authorised Status as issued by the Financial Services Regulator.

Those requirements apply to the adviser. The insurance companies are also required to provide potential customers with a range of information on any life insurance products they intend to buy prior to the deal being concluded. The information includes:

- An outline of the main purpose of the product, is it primarily a savings or protection product and if there's insurance cover, is it for life or illness.

- Detailed information of all charges and of the commission that will be paid to brokers or salespeople.

- Examples of the expected return on savings and investment products together with details of any tax liability. A clear statement of any guarantees.

- Projected values if the product is surrendered early and details of the procedures for early encashment or cancellation.

An adviser must perform a fact find to access your financial position; any other assurance cover you have; your prospects for the future; the size of your family; and your plans for them

- Information on the insurance company and the broker or other intermediary with whom the customer is dealing.

- The premiums payable with details of whether they can be reviewed.

There are systems for dealing with complaints — for details see chapter 11.

The fine print

An important point to bear in mind with all insurance policies is the condition of 'utmost good faith' implied in all contracts. This simply means that you are required to tell the assurance company all the facts relevant to its assessment of the risk it is undertaking in assuring your life. If you withhold a relevant fact then the policy can be declared null and void and no payment will be made.

Recent court judgements have made the law less certain on this matter and the insurance companies are taking more care in asking the right questions and stressing the need for full disclosure of relevant details. It is important to give full details of past illnesses etc. but there is no need to get unduly worried if you forget to declare some minor illness.

Only surrender assurance policies as a last resort. There are other options worth considering if you can't afford the premiums or need to get some money

A further point is that you can only take out a life assurance policy on someone whose death will clearly involve you in financial loss. You must have an insurable interest in the person's life. A husband or wife is considered to have an infinite insurable interest in the life of his or her spouse and a child, of course, has an insurable interest in its parents. But the insurable interest of parents in their children is considered to be very small. This last point was written into law many years ago to prevent unscrupulous parents from taking out large assurance policies on their children and then being tempted to murder them.

With life assurance, the other sections of the policy are usually straightforward enough. They contain details of who is insured; conditions on the payment of premiums; how claims are to be made and paid. A point to bear in mind is that the name on the policy should coincide with the person's name on their birth certificate. Otherwise problems can sometimes arise. There will also be provisions on surrender values, conversion rights if applicable, and options available should you be unable to keep up your premium payments. Let's have a look at these in more detail as they can sometimes lead to difficulties and misunderstandings.

Surrender Values: On term assurance there is often no surrender value and certainly in the early years of a whole of life or endowment policy the surrender values are very small. So it is not something to be considered except as an absolute last resort.

Paid-Up Policy: If you find that you can no longer meet the premiums it may be possible to convert the policy into one that is 'fully-paid up'. Suppose you have a 20-year endowment policy on which you have paid premiums for 10 years and the life cover is €2,000. It is usually possible to stop paying premiums and continue to have a policy covering you for half (ten-twentieths) of the original sum assured.

Conversion Rights: If you have a policy carrying conversion rights — say a convertible term assurance — bear it in mind when you come to take out fresh assurance. You may have reached the stage where you can afford higher premiums so consider first whether it is better to convert an existing policy rather than take out a new one. If your health is failing, this option may be particularly valuable as you will not usually have to undergo a new medical test.

Selling a policy: If you have an endowment policy which you have to surrender it may be possible to sell it to an investor for rates up to 25% higher than the surrender value. It's better not to surrender a policy at all but if you have to, it can be well worthwhile shopping around and not simply surrendering it back to the insurance company. There are companies specialising in arranging this type of sale.

A policy with a surrender value is good security for a loan

Medical Insurance

While every Irish citizen is entitled to basic hospital care free of charge it is sometimes, but not always, possible to get speedier treatment if you are able to pay your own way. You also have a wider choice of consultants and the type of hospital accommodation you get. Private medical care can, however, be very expensive and is beyond the reach of most people who don't have insurance cover.

The VHI (Voluntary Health Insurance) had a near monopoly of the provision of medical insurance up until January 1997 when the law was changed allowing for competition subject to an overall condition that each company, while determining its own premium level, must provide cover at the same rate to all adults seeking it. This is known as "community rating".

Community rating still exists although it is currently being enforced by an artificial tax system that provides insurers with extra relief for older members. Unfortunately community rating has become less meaningful because of the wide range of different plans that are now available. There are over 30 basic medical insurance plans on offer from three providers and that's not counting add-ons and variations. All of the plans are designed to meet all or some of the cost of hospital treatment and accommodation and varying amounts of outpatient treatment. The amount of cover depends on the plan and the choice is wide and confusing.

The fact is that while there is obviously increased competition, consumers now have a near impossible job comparing products and choosing the one that provides the best value for their particular needs. A good starting point, however, is the guide "Selecting a private health insurance product" published by the Health Insurance Authority. It can be accessed on its website at www.hia.ie or requested by phone at (01) 4060080. It also publishes price comparisons between Aviva, Quinn Healthcare and VHI.

While community rating does still exist the varying rates charged for the many different plans on offer are undoubtedly contrary to its spirit. Companies are still not allowed to load premiums on the basis of age but there is nothing to prevent them from charging more for those products that are of particular interest to the elderly and that is what the insurers are doing. All of the companies also impose some restrictions in the form of waiting periods. At present, for instance, anyone joining VHI under 55 is not covered for pre-existing ailments for the first five years after joining and get no benefits for ailments arising in the first 26 weeks. Those aged between 55 and 59 on joining are not covered for existing ailments for seven years and get no benefits for ailments arising in the first 52 weeks. For those joining over the age of 60, there is no cover for pre-existing ailments for 10 years and no benefits for ailments arising in the first 52 weeks.

In a move that would further erode community rating there are proposals to allow insurers to charge higher premiums on those who join or upgrade their insurance cover after reaching age 35. It has been suggested that the loading could be as high as 80% for someone aged over 65 taking out medical insurance for the first time. Those aged between 55 and 64 on joining might incur a loading of 45% while a loading of 25% might apply to those aged between 45 and 54 and 10% on anyone aged between 35 and 44.

It is proposed that some credit be given for any previous period of cover. So someone taking out medical insurance at age 66, who had been insured for a period earlier in their lives, wouldn't incur the full 80% loading. While such loadings would be viewed by many as fair, there is no certainty that the proposals will make it into law.

All three companies allow a 10% reduction in premiums for those in group schemes. One way of getting this if you are not in a job-based scheme is to join a credit union. Many operate group schemes. Not only do you get a 10% saving on the premium but the credit union may also provide you with a cost-free facility for paying the premium in monthly instalments.

There are proposals to impose a loading based on the age of at which a person takes out their first medical insurance policy

5 Borrowing – it can often make sense

Sensible borrowing can play an important and beneficial role in managing the family finances. The operative word is sensible. There is a cost involved in borrowing. The benefits can, however, very often outweigh the costs particularly when interest rates are low but it all depends on what you use the borrowed money for. Just as a business loan makes sense if the borrowed money yields a return greater than the interest paid on it, a personal loan is justified if the returns, both tangible and intangible, outweigh the costs.

A loan can easily cost three times as much from one borrower than from another. Always shop around

Borrowing enables you to buy something now rather than having to wait until you have saved up the money. That's the main benefit. If delaying a purchase means that the price goes up, maybe simply because of inflation, then the savings you make, by buying now rather than later, help to offset some of the costs involved. So when considering interest rates it is important to also take account of inflation.

In some circumstances, tax relief can also reduce the cost of loans but, apart from business loans, tax relief is only allowed when the borrowed money is used to buy, maintain or improve your principal residence, certain other residences that you provide for specific people rent free, or to buy shares in your own company. Mortgage tax relief is detailed in Chapter 6 on page 129.

Apart from the interest charged on the loan there is another cost involved in borrowing. It's not a cost that can be accurately quantified but it is a cost nonetheless. It's the reduction in financial flexibility that results from having to meet the repayments on the loan. The lender, of course, takes the risk of not being repaid. But the borrower is also taking a risk. If he is unable to meet the repayments he could be forced to sell assets to meet the debt or even be declared bankrupt. At the very least, the borrower is taking on an extra burden and that involves risk.

Each individual will exercise a different degree of caution, but there is no need to be cautious to the point of not borrowing at all. Most reputable lenders will allow a degree of flexibility to help a borrower over an unexpected bad patch. If having considered all that, you still want to borrow, the next step is to shop around for the cheapest possible loan.

Shopping around

There is a wide range of options open to the would-be borrower: bank loans, finance houses, credit sales, budget accounts, HP, etc. And the cost can vary greatly. Except in the most general of advertising, all those providing credit, either by way of loans or by way of credit sales, are required to show the true rate of interest being charged on their loans in ads, sales literature, loan agreements etc. So it is possible to shop around by just keeping your eyes open and comparing rates.

The difference between the dearest and cheapest loan can be significant. Getting the cheapest available can save you a lot of money and remember the borrower is currently in a buyer's market. Lenders want to lend money: that is how they make a profit. If nobody borrowed, they would go out of business.

Where the loan is arranged by the seller of a product or service you should also carefully check the price you are being charged. It's no good saving on the loan and ending up paying over the odds for whatever you are buying.

Similar caution is necessary when buying goods or services on credit, perhaps paying by instalments. You may find that you are paying for so-called 'free' credit in the price of the goods and services you are buying. So shop around not only for the cheapest loan but also for the cheapest goods and services.

Borrowing is a normal business transaction, the lender is selling a commodity to the borrower. The commodity in this case is money. It might be more correct to say that the borrower is hiring the use of the money for a period and will be paying a rental — the interest — for the use of it. The lender has one thought in mind — will he get the money back? This is the risk factor, and the higher the risk he considers he is taking, the higher the interest he will charge. The longer the period of the loan, the greater is the risk he foresees: so normally the longer the term of the loan, the higher the interest rate. The major exceptions to this rule are mortgage loans on which rates are relatively low because of the security provided.

Most lenders, of course, have their interest rates fixed at any particular time and, as a result, have a set idea about the risk they are willing to take, or, in other words, the type of person they will lend to. Lenders want to lend the money — they just need convincing that you are a good risk.

Obviously, you want to pay the lowest interest rate possible, and as a rough guide the rates will go up as you move along the following list: mortgage lenders, the major banks, credit unions, finance houses, credit accounts, hire purchase, credit cards, money lenders. All lenders must declare the annual percentage rate (APR) charged on their loans. This can be defined as the true rate of interest and can be used to compare alternatives.

The APR shown on loan advertisements, shop notices and loan agreements has to be based on the global cost of the loan — interest and other charges. So it is ideal for comparing one source of finance with another — the lower the APR, the cheaper the loan.

For the sake of comparison, it does not really matter how the rates of interest are actually calculated so long as they are all calculated in the same way. That's the advantage of using

Monthly repayments on €1,000 loan

Interest rate	3 years	5 years	7 years	10 years
8%	€31.27	€20.21	€15.52	€12.06
9%	€31.72	€20.68	€16.00	€12.58
10%	€32.17	€21.14	€16.49	€13.10
11%	€32.62	€21.62	€16.99	€13.63
12%	€33.07	€22.09	€17.49	€14.18
13%	€33.52	€22.57	€18.00	€14.73

APRs. While they allow you to compare like with like, it is no harm having some understanding of what a true rate of interest is. Suppose you get €100 now and repay €110 this day next year — i.e., the initial €100 plus €10 interest — that is a true rate of interest of 10% — €10 on €100.

But suppose that instead of repaying in a lump sum, the repayments are spread over the full year and you still repay a total of €110, that is nearer a 20% rate of interest, since you did not have the use of the €100 for the full year. Indeed, you only had, on average, the use of €50 for the full year, since you had more than €50 for the first six months, but progressively less than €50 for the second six months.

As mentioned above, the borrower has a wide range of options open to him and the cost difference between the cheapest and dearest loans can be considerable. So it pays to shop around.

Overdrafts

To avail of an overdraft you need to have a current account i.e. an account that allows you ready access to your money by way of a chequebook, a Laser or ATM card. In effect you ask your bank manager if you can overdraw your account to a specified sum. If he agrees you can then spend that amount of money over and above the funds you have in your account. You only pay interest on the actual amount you have drawn and, as mentioned above, interest is calculated on a daily basis. If you don't make use of the overdraft permission you pay no interest.

Overdraft permissions, however, are only given to cover short-term borrowing requirements. There are no set repayments, but the account has to be back in credit at least within a year and the bank manager will want some assurance of that. So overdrafts generally have a limited use. They are particularly useful to cover the odd bad month when a number of large payments fall due. In other words it should be viewed like an advance, or a 'sub' on your salary or wages which will have to be paid off on the next pay day or at least over a few pay periods. Of course, it is a loan that you have to pay interest on and the interest rates are set substantially above the rates on personal loans and on the better credit cards. If you have a relatively low interest credit card charging less than 10%, it would usually be cheaper to use it to get over a short-term bad financial patch. If you need finance over the longer term, shop around for a personal loan with set repayments.

In some cases the flexibility offered by an overdraft can offset the higher interest rate and possible set-up costs. But you need to do the sums. Running up an overdraft, even for a short period, may lose you your right to free banking and result in you having to pay bank charges for a full three months. Those charges must be considered as additional to the interest in working out the true cost of an overdraft. You may also have to pay an arrangement fee of as much as €35 a year. Once an overdraft has been approved, it can be drawn on at any time without fresh recourse to the bank. Every cent put into the account immediately reduces the amount of the loan and, since interest is charged on the amount outstanding each day, there can be a significant saving.

Suppose, for instance, the borrower has his or her wages paid into the bank each month. Let's suppose that a net €3,000 is lodged. If that money is spent evenly over the month the customer has a net €1,500 on average in the account over the year — more than €1,500 early in the month and less than €1,500 later in the month but an average of €1,500. That's automatically reducing the size of the overdraft. At 10% a year the interest saving would be €150 to help offset the extra charges which might be incurred.

- **Budget Accounts:** Some banks and credit unions run budget type accounts where the customer sets out his spending requirements in advance. They are not unlike formalised overdrafts. The spending needs will not, of course, be spread evenly over the year but the bank allows for overdraft type loans to cover the lean periods while requiring fixed regular payments. It is simply a way of balancing out one's cash flow. But it is fixed and formalised — unlike the normal overdraft.

Term loans

Unlike overdrafts, term loans have fixed repayment commitments. Also, unlike an overdraft, the full amount of the loan is handed out to you or transferred into your current account and interest liability begins to accrue immediately. Interest rates can vary greatly depending on the lender, the borrower, the term of the loan, and even, in some cases, what the loan is for. It is up to the borrower to shop around and take care.

While lenders do have schedules of interest rates that apply in most cases, they can and do charge higher rates to some customers and for some purposes. It's important to check. In general the larger banks charge the same rate for normal term loans as they do for overdrafts but ignoring the impact of bank charges — as mentioned above — a term loan may prove more expensive for short term borrowing since you do not have the flexibility of drawing down only what you need. Repayments are normally set in monthly amounts extending over a fixed period.

Most term loans are given at variable rates of interest. The rate charged may change during the term of the loan in line with changes in wholesale interest rates. The rate may go up or down. If rates go up, some lenders will leave repayment levels unchanged and add some extra repayments at the end to cover the higher interest rate. Others may require an immediate increase in the repayments.

Save money by switching debt

☐ Financial decisions, once made, are all too seldom reviewed. This is particularly the case with personal borrowings. Built up over time for various different reasons, it is very easy to let each loan run its course. Yet personal circumstances change, interest rates vary, and the need for the debt may diminish as other assets become available.

So it's worth doing an occasional wealth check on your borrowings. It is possible to re-finance debt in order to alter repayment schedules or avail of lower interest rates. It may be worthwhile using savings to reduce or pay off a loan.

The biggest interest savings can be made by rolling up a number of loans into a mortgage top-up. The interest rates are the lowest available and the repayments can be spread over 20 or more years. It's an option which needs very careful consideration and it's not the only change which can produce savings.

Before you can make any decisions, of course, you need to take a little time to itemise your current loans and work out what they are costing you. Then you can start looking at the alternatives. But first list your loans. They are likely to fall into three categories.

<u>Mortgage:</u> You know how much you initially borrowed but how much do you owe now? How much equity do you have in your house? If it is worth significantly more than the outstanding loan you should be able to get a top up mortgage. What rate of interest are you paying? Is it fixed or variable? How does it compare with the competition? It can be worth switching mortgages and it's an option provided the outstanding loan is not more than about 80% of the current value of the property. But it is a big step and likely to require a heavy up-front cost. →

Fixed rate loans are also available but there are drawbacks. If variable rates are expected to rise, the fixed rate will be set higher than the initial variable rate. On average, fixed rate loans will be more expensive than variable rate ones. The borrower pays a premium for the security of knowing that the interest rate will not be increased during the term of the loan. If rates do go up it will have been worthwhile but if rates decline, a variable rate loan would have worked out

Don't, of course, switch out of a tracker mortgage. You are unlikely to be able to replace it with anything nearly as good or as cheap.

Bank Loans: We can include credit union and finance company loans in this category. You should check what rate of interest you are paying. There isn't a lot of variation at this time between one institution and the other but if you have a loan that's a few years old you may discover that you are still paying a fixed rate that's a little over the odds. If so, you need to find out if you can pay it off without penalty.

Also check your overdraft. An overdraft can be the cheapest form of bank borrowing since you only pay interest on the amount outstanding each day. So when your pay cheque is lodged to your account, your interest liability immediately goes down. A well-used overdraft can be cheaper than a term loan even though the interest rates are the same on both. But running up an occasional overdraft can be very expensive since it usually makes you immediately liable for bank charges during the relevant quarter and most banks impose a hefty arrangement fee.

Credit Cards: Credit cards should ideally only be used to secure free credit by paying the bill in full each month. Occasionally letting some of the bill run on for a month or two is not too costly but ongoing debt should definitely be avoided. The interest rates can be penal — over 20% on some cards.

It's easy to get into the habit of letting the credit card debt run on and on paying only the minimum requirement each month. The answer is to get a term loan to pay off the debt. If you then let the credit card debt run up again it may be time to bring out the scissors and cut the card in two.

cheaper. Remember you are doing the lender a favour by borrowing.

The major drawback with fixed rate loans is a lack of flexibility. There are usually penalties, sometimes quite heavy, for early repayment. Opting for a fixed-rate loan can make sense where the borrower needs assurance that the repayments won't increase. That can often be the case with a mortgage loan where the repayments represent a large proportion of the borrower's income. But it's less likely to apply in the case of a smaller term loan. The extra flexibility and potential lower cost of a variable rate loan usually makes it the best option.

Term loans are available from a wide range of lenders, banks, building societies, credit unions and finance houses. Building societies, better known for their mortgage finance, can and do provide unsecured personal loans. Credit unions have been increasing their range of services. They are covered in more detail below. Finance houses often provide loans through car dealers or shops. Sometimes they are at special low rates subsidised by the retail outlet. It is important to be sure, however, that you are not paying for the cheaper loan by paying over the odds for the goods or services being bought.

In other cases it is cheaper to go directly to the finance house itself rather than take out the loan through the retailer, service provider or agent. The intermediary often takes a commission — which you pay — and in any case you are in a stronger bargaining position when buying the goods if you arrange the loan yourself. As far as the seller is concerned, you are then a cash buyer.

Mortgages

Loans for house purchase are dealt with in Chapter 6, page 118 but there are other uses for loans secured with mortgages on the borrower's house or other property. Such loans are, of course, mainly used for house purchase but need not be. In the current climate it's not an option very readily available except, perhaps to those with very small mortgages relative to the value of their properties. Those with access to such loans can benefit from lower interest rates although they maybe partially offset by set-up costs.

Mortgage top ups are most suited for major spending needs such as home improvements or education and are best avoided by those who are easily tempted into running up debt — that obviously includes those who see it as a solution to an existing debt problem. It is, of course, possible to reduce monthly repayments by rolling up a number of debts into a single mortgage top-up and spreading the repayments over a longer period. But it is all too easy to let the debts mount up again and the second time around your home is being put at risk.

Topping up a mortgage sometimes involves taking out a new increased mortgage and paying off the existing one. But it is possible to top up an existing mortgage. A bank or building society with an existing mortgage on the property should be able to provide the top-up at the lowest cost but it is important to check interest rates. Because of the cost of setting up a new mortgage, you need to be borrowing upwards of perhaps €3,000 or even €5,000 to ensure that the saving in interest payments covers the set-up costs. And it is important to appreciate that the loan is secured on the property. The bank or building society has the right to sell the property to get its money back if the borrower defaults on payments.

Used sensibly, a top-up mortgage can save the borrower a lot of money. The interest rate on an unsecured personal loan can be about twice as high so the potential saving is significant, even allowing for some set up costs. But those who have any doubts over their financial discipline need to consider carefully why the interest rates on these top-up mortgages are low. It's because the loan is secured on the borrower's home. If you default on a personal bank loan the worst that can happen is that you're taken to court and ordered to pay what the judge decides you can afford. Default on a mortgage and your home could be sold to repay the debt. It doesn't happen too often but it does happen — unfortunately with increasing frequency.

Mortgage top-ups are most suited for major spending needs such as home improvements or education

Store budget accounts

Most of the larger stores have their own budget account facilities and a growing number of smaller stores have budget accounts run for them by finance houses. The interest rate is much the same as charged by the finance houses. The best advice is to avoid them. While a budget account is handy, it can be relatively expensive to run — it is cheaper to try to get a term loan from your bank or, cheaper still, your credit union. Budget accounts are flexible, however, allowing you to spend up to the maximum credit level at any time. The worst part, however, is that you have to use it in the one store, or group of stores, so there is a disincentive to shop around. Indeed, borrowing on your credit card is likely to be as cheap while still leaving you the freedom to shop where you like.

But in either case, of course, you may be tempted to spend more than you should, or really want to. The advice is to try to get a bank or credit union loan for major shopping sprees. If you want to have a store card to avail of special offers or promotions try to keep it on the basis of a monthly card. That should cost you nothing. If you actually do a lot of shopping in the one store there can be some advantage in having a card, even for credit purposes, since the card is generally free and the interest rate can be lower than that charged on a bank or building society card.

Credit unions

Credit unions are among the cheapest providers of loans but they are, of course, only available to members. Membership is open to those who are part of a 'common bond' i.e. live in the locality or work in the particular firm covered by the union. To qualify for a loan, it is usually necessary to be a member of some standing having shown an ability to save. But that can be well worth the effort. There are credit unions now based in most localities and in many organisations and large firms. The standard interest rate is 1% a month — an annual percentage rate of 12.6%. But many credit unions charge less than that and a few charge considerably less. They are non-profit making organisations. Any surplus made belongs to the members. Some credit unions use a portion of the surplus to give interest rate rebates to their borrowing members.

Limits may apply to the size of the loan and the cover is curtailed for the over 60s and not available for the over 70s. Another built-in insurance provides for the payment of a benefit to a member's estate in the event of death. In the case of a member aged under 55, the benefit is equal to the amount on deposit or in shares at the time of death. The benefit is lower for those over 55 and not applicable in the case of the over 70s.

Hire purchase

Hire purchase is generally an expensive way of buying on credit. Not only are interest rates high, but there are also high administrative charges built into the hire purchase price. Most people who buy on HP could borrow elsewhere. The best alternative for most people tempted to borrow on hire purchase is the local credit union.

Insurance

It is sometimes possible to borrow against the surrender value of with-profits endowment life assurance policies. Most insurance companies will provide such loans and the interest rates are usually relatively low. In some cases, there is no need to repay the loan, since the sum involved will be taken out of the final sum due on maturity of the policy. Indeed, the interest payments can also be rolled forward in this manner. But the policy does need to have a cash-in value higher than the size of the loan.

Credit cards

Credit cards are best seen as a means of getting short-term credit — they are a boon if used wisely in this way. They save you carrying cash; enable you to keep a record of your spending; and can provide you with a handy period of free credit. But used unwisely, they can be very expensive. If you exceed your permitted period of free credit you can end up paying a fairly high rate of interest on the outstanding amount — up to twice the rate you would pay on a bank or credit union loan. See the section on credit cards in chapter 2 on page 26.

Moneylenders

The best advice is not to borrow from moneylenders at all, whether legal or illegal. If there is no other alternative, pawnbrokers are not all that expensive provided you do not make a habit of using them.

Care is the watchword with equity release

Many of those currently in retirement didn't have the opportunity or fore-thought to fund pension entitlements although they may have a lot of money tied up in a house. Trading down to a smaller house is one way of releasing some of that wealth although seldom attractive for the over 65s particularly if it means moving to a new area. But there are other options available although during the economic downturn most have limited attractions.

An ideal way is to have the children borrow against their own houses and ad-vance the money to the parents in the expectation that the family home will be theirs in due course. But that doesn't suit every family situation. The alterna-tive is to opt for what is known as an equity release scheme. These fall into two broad categories. There is a basic loan scheme type similar to any other mort-gage secured on the house except that there are no regular repayments. The in-terest is rolled up and the loan is repaid when the borrower and his or her spouse eventually leave the house either on death or to move elsewhere.

The other type of equity release involves actually selling a share in the house for delivery when you and your spouse eventually move out of it. That's a more complicated option considered in more detail below. Neither option should be taken lightly. Long and careful thought should go into the decision making process. You should get independent advice.

Bank of Ireland was the first to offer a loan type product 'Lifeloan' but it is no longer actively marketed. The maximum loan depended on the age of the youngest applicant. It would lend 20% of the estimated value of the property to those aged 65 to 69 rising to 30% to those aged over 80. Other providers offer similar products but some set a lower age limit of 60.

Negotiating a value for the home is not of prime importance. The value does determine the maximum amount that can be borrowed but eventually the house will be sold on the open market. At that stage, the loan is repaid together with the accumulated interest and anything left goes to the borrower or his or her estate. In comparing loan products it is important to consider the interest rate which are usual fixed and can be very high with penalties for early repayment, for instance.

The other type of equity release scheme is more complicated. It involves actu-ally selling a share in the property. The decision making process is more →

involved. Valuing the property is, of course, crucial. It's easy if similar houses in the locality have been sold recently on the open market. But it is a lot more difficult with a unique house. Getting an independent valuation is important but that's only the first hurdle. Suppose you agree that the house is worth €400,000 and you want to sell half of it. That's currently worth €200,000 but because you and your spouse have the right to live in it for life you're not going to get €200,000.

The price you will get at this stage depends on age and gender. It should also, of course, depend on your health but it's unusual to take that into account although if you are in poor health it's well worth arguing for a higher pay out. In all cases you need to negotiate the best deal. Independent advice and careful consideration is essential.

Anyone considering equity release through the sale of a share in their home should steel themselves for hard and heavy negotiations. It's not like going into a shop or a bank and simply paying the asking price. Don't accept the first value put on your house. Be ready to bargain hard over the extent to which that price should then be reduced to take account of your lifetime right to live in it. If you are not up to hard negotiating, get someone to do it for you. The primary aim of the people offering these products is to make a profit for themselves. There's nothing wrong with that but be very conscious of it.

With a loan you know exactly what you are getting. You'll incur interest on the loan only until it is repaid. If you and your spouse were to die after a year then only a year's interest would have been paid. But if you sell a share in your home, the price you'll get is irrespective of how long you'll live. If you and your spouse were to live only a short while or the house was to rise significantly in value, you or the beneficiaries of your estate would have lost badly.

Another factor to consider in all cases is that the proceeds from loans or the sale of a share in your home could affect eligibility to means tested social welfare or health benefits. At present €190,460 of the proceeds from the sale of a house is ignored for social welfare means-test purposes where the recipient moves into more suitable alternative accommodation. But since you are not actually moving house this exemption doesn't apply.

☐ <u>Be very careful.</u>

Tackling debt problems

It is all too easy for debts to become a problem and when they do there is a strong temptation to bury your head in the sand and hope that the problem will go away. Of course, that just makes it worse. The only solution for those with debt problems — or heading that way — is to confront the difficulty head on. The quicker that is done, the quicker the problems can be solved.

There is no debtors' prison today and it is not possible to end up in prison simply for being in debt. But you can get locked up for failing to meet debt repayments decided on by a court and according to one estimate over 1,000 people have been imprisoned over the past decade for not complying with Court debt orders. Initially when a person is brought before a court for debt it will do no more than decide on equitable repayments in the context of the person's ability to pay and a court can always be asked to adjust a repayment order if circumstances change. It is only if those repayments are not met, that a person may face jail and then only for blatantly failing to pay.

Courts don't lock people up for debt but can if a debtor wilfully refuses to comply with a Court order

That was made clearer in new legislation passed in 2009 which requires a creditor to establish 'wilful refusal' or 'culpable neglect' on the part of the debtor. The law also provides that a debtor of insufficient means is entitled to apply for legal aid and, more importantly, must be informed of this right. Imprisonment is to be used only as a last resort when mediation or a variation of the original instalment order has failed, where the debtor has no assets/goods available for seizure and where the default is due to the debtors wilful refusal or culpable neglect.

But there should be no need for anyone to appear in court for debt. If creditors are kept informed of any financial difficulty, it is often possible to reschedule repayments and sometimes even have interest charges reduced. It is important to take action as early as possible.

Debt is not a bad thing, in itself. Borrowing, indeed, has an important role to play in most families' finances. But borrowing can get out of hand. Problems start to arise when a

Six point plan for tackling debt

☐ In brief, if you have a debt problem you need to face your problem, come clean with your creditors and make them an offer based on a full disclosure of what you can afford. Take it one step at a time.

ONE: The first step is to work out exactly what your income is. Get out a copy book or a few sheets of paper and detail your income — what actually comes into the house from all sources each week or month.

TWO: Next list your total spending needs. Do not leave anything out. There are the obvious things like rent/mortgage repayments, food, fuel etc. But do not forget to include the irregular spending items — clothes, TV licence and cable, the ESB or gas bill which only comes in every two months, insurance bills which may only come once a year etc. Bring it all down to a monthly or weekly figure.

THREE: Then compare your first list with your second. Check your figures again. Divide your spending into essentials and non essentials. Can you cut back? Is there anything you can sell to bring in money to reduce some debt — not goods that you have on HP, although if you do have goods on hire purchase and you have not paid a third of the price, the HP company may take them back.

FOUR: Examine possible ways of increasing your income. Are there any social welfare benefits you are entitled to — supplementary benefit or the family income supplement (see chapter 12). If you are on social welfare and have difficulty meeting your rent, you may be entitled to rent allowance under the supplementary benefit scheme administered by your local health board.

FIVE: List exactly how much you owe. Divide the loans into priority ones and others. The priorities would be rent/mortgage, ESB, other fuel bills. If you fall too far behind with these you could lose your house or have the electricity or gas turned off.

SIX: Lastly having gathered all that information, the final step is to talk with your creditors. Summarise the figures you have listed and let them see the details of your income and spending. That way they will realise how much or how little you can afford to pay. Make an offer.

person's — or a family's — spending needs start to outstrip their income. Initially it may seem possible to handle the problem. But it is usually only being compounded. The balance on the credit card runs up. The gas bill is missed so that something else can be paid. There is a hope that something will turn up. But it doesn't. Postponed debts do not go away. With interest added on they only get worse.

Swopping a number of small loans for one big one can be a big mistake too. You can, of course, reduce your monthly repayments by replacing some short-term expensive loans with a cheaper home mortgage loan spread over a longer period. But you may be only storing up problems for the future. If you do not meet the repayments on the mortgage you will be putting your home in jeopardy.

The quicker you face up to debt problems the quicker they can be solved

This is not the answer if you have major debt problems. If you see it as part of a solution you need to be absolutely sure that you will be able to meet the mortgage repayments and you also need to check that there are no heavy penalties involved in paying off your existing loans early. With many finance house loans there are such penalties. And there is no sense in replacing your loans with even more expensive ones. Overall there is no easy solution down this road.

Remember that you have to deal with the priority debts first. The top priority is usually the mortgage repayments or rent.

Dealing with mortgage arrears

Mortgage lenders are required by law to give borrowers every chance to meet their obligations. Even if it wasn't the law, it makes sense. Banks and building societies are likely to maximise their return that way and, above all, they want to be repaid. But there is no easy solution for either lenders or borrowers.

Short of filing for bankruptcy, that can currently leave a debtor under constraint for 12 years, there is no mechanism in Ireland for debt forgiveness. In the US most mortgages are what are known as 'non recourse'. The lender can't look for anything more than the return of the property against which the mortgage was given. So borrowers in difficulties can simply leave the keys at the bank and walk away.

But that is not the case in Ireland. A loan may be secured on a property but if the borrower gets into financial difficulty and its repossession and subsequent sale doesn't yield enough to pay off the mortgage, the outstanding amount continues to be owed.

The lender may decide that there is no point is pursuing the borrower immediately particularly if he or she has gone abroad or simply hasn't the money. But the debt is still due and may be pursued at a later date when the borrower has the means to pay.

But before it gets to that stage, lenders are required to consider every option short of repossession. They are subject to a statutory code that has been hardened up since it was first introduced. In addition, the main mortgage lenders, AIB, Bank of Ireland, EBS and Permanent TSB have signed up to the recommendations of a Government-sponsored expert group that the government promised to implement.

Lenders can not apply to the courts for a repossession order until at least 12 months after the mortgage went into arrears or after the borrower has failed to keep to a revised repayment agreement.

The group ruled out debt forgiveness and lenders, although they have been known to write off loans in the past, will be very slow, in the current climate, to allow mortgage borrowers off the hook. But borrowers in financial difficulties, who engage with their lenders in respect of mortgages on their homes, have the right to be assisted in every way possible to meet their obligations.

The code of conduct on mortgages has the force of law but it only applies in full where borrowers engage with their lenders in trying to resolve a mortgage arrears problem.

The code, which applies to loans on principal private residences, require lenders to draw up formal frameworks for handling mortgage arrears and also to have standard financial statements to be used in assessing the financial circumstances of borrowers in difficulties or likely to get into difficulties.

Lenders are required to have dedicated support units within their organisation to handle arrears and to provide training for all staff dealing with borrowers experiencing difficulties.

The onus is on the lender to contact errant borrowers as soon as an account goes into arrears or is at risk of going into arrears. The aim is to explore possible solutions at as early a stage as possible, in the light of the borrower's personal circumstances. There should be no assumption that the framework for tackling arrears problems can be devised on the basis that one size fits all.

A distinction must be made between borrowers who can't pay and those who won't pay. All of those with genuine problems must be treated sympathetically and positively, with the lender taking account of the borrowers' financial situation, total indebtedness and their ability to pay.

All options must be explored including temporarily deferring payments, extending the term of the loan, changing the type of mortgage or capitalising the arrears into the loan. The major lenders have agreed to consider, in appropriate cases, deferring the payment of up to a third of the interest on a loan for a maximum of five years or until the amount deferred exceeds 18 months interest. In this latter case, the deferred interest is not added to the loan and is not itself subject to an interest charge.

There is no requirement in the code for the lender to reduce the amount owning or to forego interest. Interest not paid is simply deferred for payment later.

In all cases the lender is required to keep the borrower fully informed

Lenders can apply to the courts for a repossession order 12 months after the mortgage went into arrears or after the borrower has failed to keep to an advised repayment agreement. Periods during which the borrower was complying with an agree alternative repayment arrangement or making a formal appeal or complaint are excluded from the twelve month calculation. At all times the lender must try to engage with the borrower seeking alternatives.

Lenders are required to leave repossessed borrowers in their homes long enough to allow the local authority to find appropriate alternative accommodation.

The Government is also committed to introduce new bankruptcy legislation and a legal but non-judicial debt settlement scheme that would allow people to reach agreement with creditors for a full discharge of their debt liabilities for the payment of so much in the euro. Schemes would have to be approved by creditors representing at least 60% of the outstanding debt with repayments extending over a number of years depending on the total size of the debt. It's likely that preferential creditors would have to accept the same deal as everyone else.

Such a facility has existed in Britain for some time but it's likely to be some time before the necessary legislation is signed into law here, although the urgent need for it is well recognised. It's not seen as a way of forgiving people their debts but rather of enabling them to repay as much as they can over a period of years and then get on with their lives.

The code isn't a panacea but it is obviously better to fall under its scope than not to. The worst possible option for borrowers in difficulty is not to engage with the lender. The solution arrives at by discussing the problem is certain to be no worse, and could be a lot better, than the solution imposed in the absence of such discussion.

The Department of Social Welfare supports a money advice and budgeting advice service (MABS) throughout most of the country. It's a free service of course. Ask about it at your local Social Welfare Office or public library. It has its own website www.mabs.ie which provides useful advice and the locations of its offices nationwide. Another scheme administered with help from the St. Vincent de Paul Society and credit unions, provides advice on budgeting and will negotiate with creditors on behalf of borrowers. It is not there to pay off loans but rather to help people budget their way out of difficulties. Arrangements may be made to pay off expensive loans and replace them with cheaper credit union loans.

The MABS service is free and can provide valuable assistance to all with debt problems

The European Consumer Centre, 13A Upper O'Connell Street, Dublin, phone (01) 809 0600 can help you prepare for a district court appearance over debts of up to €6,300. The legal adviser will provide advice but will not actually represent you in court.

> *A house may be large or small; as long as the neighbouring houses are likewise small, it satisfies all social requirements for a residence. But let there arise next to the little house a palace, and the little house shrinks to a hut — Karl Marx*

6 Putting a roof over your head

The sharp decline in house prices is beginning to put house purchase back within reach of those young people who viewed home ownership as a vain aspiration during the boom days of upward spiralling prices. The financial crisis is, at least, having the beneficial effect of bringing house prices back down to more reasonable levels and the decision to extend mortgage tax relief at the full rate to those buying in 2012 provides an added incentive. But there is an understandable reluctance to buy until it is clear that the market is at, or close to, the bottom, particularly since the rental market has become much more competitive.

Even with the drop in prices, the purchase of a house is likely to require many times the average person's annual salary and represents the single largest financial commitment of a lifetime. And if the money is borrowed, the repayments will take up a considerable part of the family budget.

Assuming that you do not pay an inflated price for the house, there is little doubt that it generally makes more sense to borrow and buy, rather than rent. But in the uncertain climate of late 2011 this conventional wisdom may not apply. With house prices falling, and rental properties readily available, there must be a temptation to delay a purchase until there is some sign of a market upturn and that could still be some time off. There are, of course, exceptions. Few people can hope to get in at the absolute bottom of the market and fewer still can hope to get their ideal home at a rock bottom price. So it may not be a good idea to wait until that once-in-a-lifetime dream home happens to come onto the market. Even if you don't manage to buy at the lowest possible price, you can be fairly sure of gains over the longer term.

Apart from the pleasure of living in a home that you like, you can be fairly sure that in the longer term, property values will rise faster than the rate of inflation unless the economy collapses completely. You need some money for the deposit and expenses and you also need to convince a lender that you will be able to meet the repayment on a loan. But there are plenty of lenders in the market. They may be a little more cautious than they were in the boom years but they still want to lend money. That's the business that they are in. It's important to remember, however, that there are traps along the way and a lot of critical decisions to be made. Unfortunately, many of those decisions have to be taken on the basis of assumptions about the future rather than hard facts. So what are the options?

Buying a house does not simply add to household expenses. It is a major investment decision as well, and the return on the investment can be sizeable.

What are the options?

The main constraint on what you can buy is the availability of finance. For most people this simply means the amount they are able to borrow. The range of borrowing options open to the house buyer has widened significantly in recent years with most lenders actively seeking mortgage business. The banks and building societies want to lend money so there is plenty of scope for the borrower to shop around. The choice is wide and you can never be sure of making the right decision. It's impossible to predict what is going to happen over the next 30 years. What appears to be the cheapest and best option now may prove to be otherwise over the course of time. A little care can help to reduce the risks. There are a number of factors to consider:

Interest rates: It is easy enough to compare interest rates so it is not too difficult to pick the cheapest loan on the basis of current rates. That's where you have to start. Have a look at the stated interest rate first and then at the monthly repayments. The repayments may be as good a guide as any. While all lenders have to show annual percentage rates of interest that take into account all the costs involved in paying off the loan they may not be strictly comparable. But look at both. Remember that it is the interest rate over the full term of the loan that matters, so do not be taken in by short-term catch-all promotions. If the rate is variable, it may change within months and what was cheapest when you borrowed may prove dearest in the long run. Some lenders offer a special low rate for the first year or so and that may look attractive. But the gains in the first year can very quickly be offset if the interest rate in subsequent years is higher than the competition.

At least in the long term it usually makes good financial sense to borrow to buy a house

It may, of course, be possible to switch lenders later but that can be costly enough – anything from €750 to €1,500. But even if there is a cost involved, switching shouldn't necessarily be ruled out because of it. Remember if you can save half a percentage point on a €200,000 mortgage, the annual saving is €1,000 gross or €800 after allowing for tax relief. So the cost of switching can be recouped over a few years. And most mortgages run for 25 or more years.

Fixed or Variable: It is impossible to know which is best in advance. As a rule of thumb, a fixed rate mortgage will tend to be more expensive in the long run. The lender will fix a rate on the basis of how interest rates are expected to move and then add a margin on to cover his risk.

So the borrower pays a little extra for the assurance that whatever happens to rates, his interest rate remains unchanged. But just as a bookie sometimes loses, so can a bank or building society. It is impossible to accurately foretell the future and if rates go higher than expected, a fixed rate mortgage will prove to be the cheapest. The only certainty is that one type of mortgage will definitely prove cheaper in the long run than the other but it's impossible to know in advance. So a choice has to be made on the basis of limited information and many borrowers will find that their repayments would have been lower had they chosen otherwise. But that doesn't necessarily mean that they made the wrong choice.

The borrower should not be trying to second-guess developments on the money market. At the time the mortgage is taken out, the money market believes that the fixed rate mortgage will prove more expensive than the variable rate one.

The fixed rate provides the borrower with a guarantee that repayments will not go up. He or she has to pay a premium for that insurance. The lender has to raise the money from depositors who expect to do better by fixing their rates. In other words, the market expects variable interest rates to be lower over that period than the fixed rates. The market may be wrong, of course, but the borrower does well to heed its view unless (s)he believes (s)he knows better than the money market moguls or else simply wants to gamble against the market.

The choice between a fixed rate and variable rate mortgage should not be made in the hope of picking the cheapest option. If that is the sole objective then the variable rate will most often prove the cheapest. That has to be true even if the market is only right half of the time since there is an insurance premium built into the fixed rate. That said, fixed rates are still the best option for many borrowers — those for whom a hike in interest rates would prove traumatic because of the impact higher repayments would have on their lives. The security of having fixed repayments can be well worthwhile if variable rates do rise. Buying that insurance is the only good reason for picking a fixed rate loan and it's as relevant now as it was in the past.

The choice between a fixed and variable rate mortgage has to be made without adequate information

In general, for those on a tight budget, a fixed rate mortgage is a good option for borrowers who could suffer severe difficulties if interest rates rise. Even if it doesn't prove cheapest in the long run they will have benefited from fewer sleepless nights. A variable rate mortgage is likely to be best for borrowers who can well handle a rise in interest rates and who are not of a worrying nature.

Lender: Different lenders may be prepared to lend different amounts. The traditional norm favoured by the Central Bank was to limit mortgage loans to $2^1/_2$ times the sum of a principal income and half of a secondary income. Lenders now apply more sophisticated stress testing taking into account both income and the potential impact of a sharp rise in interest rates. In some cases first time buyers may be able to get mortgages of 90% of the house value. Mortgage providers do want to lend money but it's now a lot harder to convince them that they are not taking too much of a risk.

Type of mortgage: Most borrowers choose the traditional annuity type where each repayment goes partly to pay the interest on the loan and partly to reduce the principal amount borrowed. Over the years the amount owed declines. The decline is relatively small in the early years and even 10 years into a 20 year loan three-quarters of each monthly repayment is still interest. The panel on page 123 outlines the advantages and disadvantages of other types of mortgage loan that may be on offer.

Speeding up your mortgage repayments doesn't always make good financial sense, see page 48

Local authority loans

Local authorities — county councils and corporations — have for many years provided house purchase loans for those on relatively low incomes and can also pay mortgage subsidies to tenants and tenant-purchasers of local authority houses who give up their houses to buy a private home. 'Home Choice Loan' is a Government-sponsored scheme that provides loans to first-time buyers who are unable to borrow sufficient finance from a bank or building society. 'Home Choice Loans' are administered by four local authorities, Cork and Dublin City Councils and Galway and Kilkenny County Councils. The finance is provided by the Housing Finance Agency and applications are made through a network of mortgage brokers throughout the country. Loans up to 92% of the market value of the property, subject to a maximum of €285,000 are available to first-time buyers of new homes or self-builders. At the end of 2011 the interest rate was 4.28%. Loans are repayable over a maximum of 30 years.

To qualify, buyers must earn at least €35,000 a year and have been in permanent employment for at least a year or, if self-employed be able to provide two year's certified accounts. Where the loan is being taken out by a couple their joint income must be at least €45,000. You can get a list of

Mortgage types

☐ **Annuity**: This is the most popular type of mortgage where each repayment covers the interest and also pays something off the loan. The amount owing goes down each year, slowly at first and then progressively quicker. But you are 15 years into a 20 year mortgage before you have paid off half the loan.

☐ **Endowment:** With the basic endowment mortgage the loan is not repaid until the end of the term. The borrower pays interest each year on the full amount and also pays money into an investment fund which should, at the end of the term, mature yielding at least enough to pay off the loan. Their attractiveness depends on how the investment fund performs and for most people the risk involved is not worth taking.

☐ **Current account:** Combines a normal current account with the mortgage account. Any money in the current account is automatically offset against the mortgage debt thereby reducing interest charges. Personal loans when agreed are at the mortgage rate of interest. Also sometimes known as an offset mortgage they may be linked to both savings and current accounts.

☐ **Tracker:** The interest rate rises or falls in line with a standard rate usually the European Central Bank rate. Other variable rate mortgages allow the lending institution to vary rates at its discretion. These are no longer available to new borrowers in Ireland.

☐ **Pension linked:** This is an endowment type mortgage linked to a pension scheme rather than an insurance policy. For a self-employed person it provides better tax relief since all of the contributions to a pension fund can be allowable for tax relief. The loan is repaid from the accumulated pension fund on retirement. This option is unlikely to be available to those in standard company schemes.

participating brokers at www.homechoiceloan.ie or by phone at 1890 252 842.

The older local authority loan scheme still exists but may be difficult to access. To be eligible, the applicant's income has to be below €50,000 in the case of a single purchaser or €75,000 in the case of joint purchasers. The maximum loan is €220,000. Home improvement loans of up to €38,000 may be given to eligible applicants. The maximum loan is

Under the Home Choice Scheme loans of up to €285,000 are available

€50,000 for those living on offshore islands and €15,000 for unsecured loans. In all cases the applicant must have been refused a loan by both a bank and a building society.

Costs of buying

Obviously, first of all, you need the cash for the deposit. In the new economic climate, post credit-crunch, you may find it hard to get more than 80% on an old house and even on a new house if you are not in a very secure job. If it is an old house which you are going to renovate, it may be possible to increase the mortgage later as alterations and additions are made. Check this with your lender. But there are also other costs. Auctioneers' fees are paid by the seller, so there is no need to worry about those, but there will be fees to the building society or other lender, legal fees and stamp duty that applies to all purchases of residential property. There will also be costs involved in satisfying yourself that the house has no structural flaws. Let us look at these in turn.

- **Fees to the lending agency:** These are not likely to break you, but it is as well to bear them in mind since they can stretch a slim budget. They include mortgage fees, survey fees, and search fees. The rates vary but the following provides a rough guide:

  - **Mortgage Law Costs:** 0.5 to 0.65% of the loan – some lenders charge a fixed fee of up to €300, others allow you to use your own solicitor.

  - **Application Fee:** From nothing to 0.2c per €1,000 of the mortgage to a fixed €60 fee depending on the lender.

  - **Survey Fees:** About €1.50 per €1,000 although some times a fixed fee is charged. There may also be travelling expenses for the surveyor.

  - **Search Fees:** These should not amount to much more than about €150.

- **Stamp duties:** Stamp duty on transfers of residential property is applied to slices of the property value. Since

December 8, 2010 the rate is 1% on up to €1 million and 2% on any amount above €1 million.

- **Legal Fees:** There are too many possible pitfalls in buying a house for you to dispense with the services of a solicitor. Ask him in advance what his fees will be – most solicitors will tell you as a matter of course. There is no fixed rate of charges, but about 1% of the house price plus VAT at 23% is not uncommon. The VAT only applies to the fees — not to the stamp duty which the solicitor may also collect. It pays to shop around and negotiate.

- **Indemnity bond:** If you borrow more than 80% of the house value the lender may require you to take out an indemnity bond. It can cost about 3% of the additional amount borrowed over and above 80% of the property value. That can be costly but some lenders don't require them.

Checking the house

There are, of course, other — mainly non-financial — matters to be borne in mind. These are the fairly obvious considerations of the location, house size, age, etc. In other words, is the house good value for money? Is it suitable for your particular requirements and are there any flaws which might make it bad value for money? Your solicitor is only concerned that the contract of sale does not put you at a disadvantage. Make sure that a check is also made for planning applications or approvals that might affect the value of the house.

The importance of location and size are matters for your own judgement, but you should never buy a house without having someone give it a professional once-over, unless it is a new house and the purchase contract provides for the making good of any structural defect appearing in the first two years. The lending agency will always send out its own surveyor to examine a house before agreeing to grant a mortgage. This provides some protection, since a mortgage will not be forthcoming unless the house is reasonably sound. But remember the lending agency is only concerned that the value of the house covers 80% of the price which it

Cost of buying a home

☐ The following example assumes the purchase of a €400,000 house with a mortgage of €250,000. This is only an illustration of the possible costs. There is plenty of scope for shopping around in the matter of legal fees but it's impossible to avoid Stamp Duty which is chargeable at the rates shown below. The 50% reduction that applies to transfers between certain relatives is to be ended from January 1, 2015.

Legal fees*	€3,000
Survey fees	€400
Land registry fees	€625
Search fees	€120
Stamp duty	€4,000
Total	**€8,145**

* There is no set scale of fees. They are negotiable. Check in advance and don't be afraid to shop around.

Stamp duty on home purchases

☐ Since December 8, 2010 stamp duty is levied on all residential property transactions with no distinction between first-time buyers and others. There are only two rates and they are charged on slices of the property value. So on a property sold for €1.5 million, the 1% rate applies to the first €1 million and the 2% rate to €500,000.

Total price	Tax rate
Less than €1,000,000	1%
Excess over €1,000,000	2%

is lending to you. So with a second-hand house it is a good idea to engage your own surveyor to carry out a more detailed examination. With a new house, ask your solicitor to ensure that the purchase contract contains a guarantee that any structural defects becoming evident in the first two years will be put right at the builder's expense. For preference deal with a builder who is in the National House Building Guarantee Scheme. If not, have a survey done.

Having satisfied yourself that the house is sound — or at least that you know of any major defects — the next thing to check is the possibility of any new building which might affect its value in the future. That is as important with second-hand as it is with new houses. It could be that the person selling knows of some development planned for an adjoining site that will impact on the value of what you are buying. So you need to check the planning applications and approvals for the area. This can be done at the offices of your local planning authority. There you can examine maps of your area showing the zonings — whether agricultural, commercial or residential — and see details of any planning approvals granted or applications pending. Such a visit is well worth making.

Rent-to-buy schemes

Rent-to-buy schemes which provide potential home buyers the chance to rent a property with an option to buy at a later stage are occasionally promoted by builders and developers faced with a depressed market. Such schemes have some attractions but there are potential pitfalls. At their simplest, such schemes give potential buyers the right to buy a house or apartment at a fixed price at any time over a set time frame. It may be two, three or more years. Sometimes the rent payable is higher than the current market rate but usually some, or all, of the rent is put towards a deposit on the property is and when a decision to buy is made.

Within that general concept, there is plenty of room for variation. There's the price at which the option to buy is set. There's the rent to be paid, whether it's below or above the market rate. And there's the amount of the rent, if any, that will be put towards the purchase price. You need to ask yourself a number of questions.

■ **Just how valuable is the right to buy at a fixed price in the future?**

It could be worth a lot if prices rise but, if they don't, you'll be left with either leaving a house that you may have settled into or buying at an unduely high price.

■ **Is the rent reasonable?**

Would you be paying more or less if this wasn't a rent-to-buy scheme? Even if you are going to get all or part of the rent back when you eventually buy the property, it's important to be aware of the real costs and benefits involved. You might be better paying a lower rent and saving in a regular saver account some of which are paying more than 4% on up to €1,000 saved each month.

■ **Do I have to pay a deposit up front?**

If you do, be very careful. Some schemes let you into the house under a caretaker's rather than a rental agreement. That means that you are effectively living in the house rent-free. In this case, the Revenue consider that you are getting a benefit-in-kind which is taxable. You will be liable for tax on the market rent you would have paid. In the absence of evidence to the contrary, the Revenue will take that to be 8% of the market value of the home. So on a €200,000 apartment you could be paying tax on €16,000 a year.

■ **What happens if I can't get a mortgage, or can't afford one, when the time comes to buy?**

The right to buy is likely to lapse and although you may be allowed to continue renting, you'll have gained nothing and may have lost out through paying over-the-odds in rent.

Mortgage tax relief

Mortgage tax relief will end for all owner occupiers by the end of 2017 although for some it will end before then. Unless there is a change in the law, mortgages taken out on or after January 1, 2013 will not qualify for any relief. For the tax years 2012 to 2017 inclusive, individuals who bought their first principal private residence between January 1, 2004 and December 31, 2008 will get tax relief at 30%. Owners of investment residential properties can claim tax relief on 75% of their interest payments. Such interest is viewed as a business expense to be set against rental income. There is no definite proposal to abolish it and any reduction would be a severe blow to many people who bought investment properties at or near the top of the boom.

The tax relief is allowed in respect of the interest on loans taken out to buy, maintain, or improve the taxpayer's principal residence, the residence of a former or separated spouse, or the residence of a dependant relative (other than a child) who is living in the house rent free. There is an upper limit on eligible interest for first-time buyers during the first seven years of €10,000 for single taxpayers; and €20,000 for married couples, widows and widowers.

Since January 2009 first-time buyers get tax relief at 25% of eligible interest paid during the first and second years and at the rate of 22.5% during the third, fourth and fifth years. Tax relief in the sixth and seventh year is given at the standard rate of 20%. From the eighth year onwards home buyers, who at that stage are defined as non-first-time buyers, are allowed tax relief at the reduced rate of 15% and only on a maximum of €6,000 a year (married and widowed) and €3,000 (single).

The tax relief is given at source but only if the Revenue know of your entitlement. It's up to you to ensure that you get it

Those who took out qualifying loans after January 1, 2004 will continue to get the relief until the end of 2017. But those who first claimed the relief during 2003 or earlier only got the relief for a maximum of seven years. It's the number of tax years that matters. Someone who took out their mortgage in October 2003 and claimed tax relief in that year

How much is mortgage relief worth?

☐ Mortgage interest relief is given on certain mortgages. To qualify, the borrowed money must have been used to buy, maintain, or improve the taxpayer's principal residence, the residence of a former or separated spouse, or the residence of a dependant relative (other than a child) who is living in the house rent free. First-time buyers get extra relief during the first seven years of their mortgage. Relief on other qualifying mortgages is allowed at lower rates for seven years from the date it was taken out or until the end of 2017.

Mortgages taken out after December 31, 2012 will not qualify for relief.

Maximum relief

	Allowable interest
First-time buyers	
Single	€10,000
Married, widowed	€20,000
Non-first-time buyers	
Single	€3,000
Married, widowed	€6,000

Rates of relief [1]

First-time buyers who bought between January 1, 2004 and December 31, 2008

In the tax years 2012 to 2017	30%

Other first-time buyers

Years 1 and 2	25%
Years 3, 4 and 5	22.5%
Years 6 and 7	20%
Non-first-time buyers	15%

☐ A first-time buyer is defined as someone who has bought their first home in the past seven years. Non-first time buyers can qualify for relief for seven years from the time a qualifying loan was taken out.

☐ **In saved tax, the maximum relief at 25% is worth:**

	............First time buyers........................			Other owner occupiers
	Years 1 and 2	Years 3 and 4	Years 6 and 7	
Couple	€5,000	€4,500	€4,000	€900
Single	€2,500	€2,250	€2,000	€600

---

ceased to be eligible for relief at the end of 2009 having got the relief during seven tax years.

It's not possible to re-qualify by simply switching lenders. But it is possible to start again on a top-up mortgage provided the money is spent on qualifying work such as structural improvements or extensions to your home.

Switching lender or the type of mortgage you have in order to achieve a better interest rate is not the same as taking out a new loan. However, a new mortgage, where you move home and take out a mortgage with a new or existing lender, is eligible for relief up until the end of 2017 provided it is taken out before the end of 2013.

You are considered a first-time buyer for seven years from the time you first claim the relief. In effect you get tax relief as a first-time buyer for a maximum of seven tax years. If you first claimed in 2005 you are still considered a first time buyer in 2012.

You are considered a first-time buyer for seven years from the time you first claim the relief

This will remain the case for those taking out mortgages this year. Under the current rules their seven years as first-time buyers will extend up to and including 2017 and they will get tax relief at those rates outlined above. But there will be no tax relief for anyone from 2018 onwards.

The tax relief is normally granted at source i.e. by way of a reduction in the repayments to the mortgage lender so it is important to ensure that the lender has been authorised by the Revenue to provide the relief. It is also important to ensure that your tax office has the full details of your mortgage account. If it hasn't been allowed at source, of course, you can claim it.

Where a taxpayer moves house and there is a delay in selling the original house, both houses can be considered to be the sole or main residence for up to one year. And during that year the interest on any loan taken out to buy the new house is allowed for tax relief in addition to the tax relief on the old loan - the limit is doubled.

Owners of investment residential properties can still claim tax relief on 75% of their interest payments. Such interest is viewed as a business expense to be set against rental income.

Maximum claim for rent tax relief

Tax year	Single under 55	Single over 55	Married under 55	Married over 55
2010	€2,000	€4,000	€4,000	€8,000
2011	€1,600	€3,200	€3,200	€6,400
2012	€1,200	€2,400	€2,400	€4,800
2013	€1,000	€2,000	€2,000	€4,000
2014	€800	€1,600	€1,600	€3,200
2015	€600	€1,200	€1,200	€2,400
2016	€400	€800	€800	€1,600
2017	€200	€400	€400	€800
2018	0	0	0	0

There are some other reliefs apart from the basic relief on investment properties mentioned above, some of which apply to owner occupiers. Their continuation must be in doubt although in the current climate they are possibly not costing the Exchequer much in lost revenue. There are capital allowances available to investors who own residential property in certain designated areas and there is additional tax relief for owner-occupiers of homes built or refurbished in certain designated areas.

These areas include the Upper Shannon Region Rural Renewal Scheme which covers all of Co Leitrim and Co Longford and parts of Co Cavan, Co Roscommon and Co Sligo. Also covered are 100 designated small towns. To qualify the property must be the sole or main residence of the individual claiming the relief. If it is a converted premises, there must be a certificate of reasonable cost obtainable from the Department of the Environment. Properties must be of a minimum size.

In these cases, tax relief is allowed each year for 10 years on 5% of the construction cost in the case of a new premises and 10% in the case of a refurbished premises. For example the construction costs of a new apartment selling for €280,000 might be about €180,000. The buyer is entitled to claim tax relief on 5% of that for 10 years. So relief is allowed on €9,000 a year. That relief is in addition to any mortgage tax relief calculated on the basis outlined above.

Rent relief

The tax relief on rent paid for private sector accommodation is being phased out. It is not available for rent paid on local authority houses or flats. The table on page 132 shows the maximum relief that can be claimed in each year up until 2017. It's a tax relief that is often missed because it has to be claimed. It is, of course, possible to backdate a claim — see chapter 13 — and in 2012 it can still be claimed four years back to, and including, 2008. The maximum amount that can be claimed for 2008, 2009 and 2010 by someone over 55 is €4,000 single, €8,000 widowed or married. The relief is restricted to the standard rate. The maximum allowance for those under 55 is €2,000 if single and €4,000 if married or widowed. .

Rent a room

Rental income up to €10,000 (€7,620 for 2007) may be received tax-free by owner-occupiers who rent out a room or rooms in their own principal residence. That relates to the total payment received. The person who is paying the rent may also be entitled to claim tax relief on it. The relief is not allowed if the person paying the rent is a 'connected' person, for instance a child.

> *Live as if you were to die tomorrow. Learn as if you were to live forever*
> *— Mahatma Gandhi*

7 Wills, probate and inheritances

The failure to draw up a will can cause many problems for dependants. It has also resulted in many bitter family feuds. Unless there is a properly drawn up will in existence, your property will be divided up, after your death, according to the dictates of the 1965 Succession Act. Such a division may not be in keeping with your wishes and could cause major problems for your spouse. Advance planning can prevent such difficulties arising and can also reduce the amount your dependants may have to pay in inheritance tax, particularly if some of the beneficiaries are distant relatives or friends.

The first concern is to ensure that your wishes are known. If there is no will, the law lays down how the estate is divided among your family. By making a will you ensure that your property passes to the people you choose — not to the people dictated in court according to the strict rule of law. There is the added advantage that you can appoint your own executor and the administration of the estate will be much easier.

A valid will can be made by anyone over 18 years of age — or younger if he or she is married. It must be in writing. While a simple will can be drawn up at home, it is well

What may happen when there is no will

Surviving Relatives	Distribution of estate where there is no will
Spouse and children	Two-thirds to spouse, one third to children in equal shares with children of a deceased child getting their parent's share.
Spouse, no children	Whole estate to spouse.
Children, no spouse	Whole estate to children in equal shares with children of a deceased child getting their parent's share.
Father, mother, brothers and/or sisters	One-half to each parent.
Parent, brothers and/or sisters	Whole estate to parent.
Brothers and sisters	All get equal shares with children of deceased brothers and sisters getting their parent's share.
Nephews and nieces	All get equal shares.
Other relatives	Nearest equal relatives get equal shares.
No relatives	The State.

worthwhile getting a solicitor to oversee the task. The few euro it costs can save a lot of trouble in the long run.

If you do decide to draw up your own will, remember to word it simply and clearly. Date it, sign it, and get your signature witnessed by two people. This means that you should sign it in their presence. They do not have to read the will. Neither of the witnesses should be a beneficiary under the will. It is normal to appoint an executor, or executors, to carry out the instructions outlined in the will although it is

There is usually no need to name a solicitor as executor

not essential. The executor can be a beneficiary under the will although he, or she, need not be.

For a simple will, where the main beneficiaries are members of the immediate family, it is common to name the principal beneficiary as executor. In most cases, this is the husband or wife. If either is reaching old age and might find the task difficult, it is useful to name a co-executor — perhaps an elder child or trusted family friend. It is not necessary to name a solicitor, accountant, or bank as executor. Usually a member of the family — or a friend whom you trust — is the best choice. He or she can hire a solicitor if needed at the time.

The will should, of course, be lodged in a safe place, and be sure that the executor, and some other people know where it is lodged. This is particularly important for people whose families are widely spread. There are many wills lying in solicitors' offices throughout the country forgotten and, for all practical purposes, lost. Once made, the will remains in force until a new will is made or the person who made it gets married. On marriage, an existing will becomes void and a new one should be drawn up. Remember also to review your will from time to time particularly if your life situation changes. Even if you do not want to change the provisions you may want to change the executor and it can be useful to reconsider the inheritance tax implications.

Power of attorney

A power of attorney is simply a legal authorisation to act on behalf of someone else. So a person who is physically incapacitated — perhaps not mobile enough to fully look after his or her business — may grant a power of attorney to a relative, friend, or adviser to carry out a range of transactions. This is known as a general power of attorney although it can be limited to certain transactions. A person may be given a power of attorney, for instance to handle a specific transaction like arranging the sale of a house. The person granting the power of attorney must have the mental capacity to withdraw the power of attorney should he or she wish

---

All married people should have a will drawn up. It costs little to have the job done correctly by a solicitor. Once made, the will should be reviewed from time to time

and, indeed, should he or she lose that capacity the power of attorney lapses. In such a situation it may be necessary to apply to have the person made a ward of court with someone appointed to look after his or her affairs.

So besides drawing up a will, it may also be worthwhile considering the possibility of losing the ability to take care of one's affairs as a result of an accident, disability or illness. These eventualities can be planned for by arranging to grant an *enduring* power of attorney to someone you can trust to act in your best interests and with your views in mind. Such an enduring power of attorney comes into force if, and when, the person who has signed it becomes mentally incapable of acting on his or her own behalf. It involves planning, of course, although many people in the early stages of Alzheimer's disease will be able to legitimately draw up a power of attorney. Before it comes into force, an enduring power of attorney has to be registered following an application to the High Court. Such an application is made when the person who drew up the power of attorney has become or is becoming mentally incapable. Legal advice is always advisable.

Both spouses should make wills

It is now usual for both spouses to share ownership in the family home. But there are still families where the bulk of the assets — perhaps home and/or farm — are held in the husband's name. It may be thought unnecessary, in such cases for the wife to make a will but nothing is further from the truth. In not making a will, the assumption is that she will always have time to do so, if necessary, after her husband's death. Yet this can lead to problems in an unfortunate situation where both die together — in a car accident, for instance.

It could happen in such a case that the husband dies first leaving his entire estate to his wife but that she then dies without having time to make a will. The estate would then be equally divided among the children — if there are any. That may be in accordance with their parent's wishes. But it might not, if one child, for instance, was still living at home and hoped to be left the house.

There is only one important restriction on the maker of a will. A spouse cannot be cut out of the estate unless he or she agrees to be, for instance as part of a separation agreement. Irrespective of what the will says, the spouse is legally entitled to one-third of the estate where there are surviving children, and one-half of the estate where there are no children. Apart from that restriction a person may dispose of his or her property as he or she thinks fit, although the courts can overturn the provisions of a will if, for instance, a child claims that he or she has not been adequately provided for.

Living wills

While a will outlines how property is to be divided up following death the objective of what has become known as a 'living will' is to influence events before your death. The idea is to let people know what you would like to happen should you become incapable of making or communicating decisions as a result of an accident or illness. Very often, a living will deals solely with views regarding healthcare but it can, of course, be more wide ranging. A living will has no legal standing so the wishes outlined in it do not have to be complied with, but at least they ensure that relatives and doctors know your views and those views will undoubtedly be considered.

Rights to the family home

In many cases family homes are jointly owned by both spouses but even where one spouse has formal ownership the other spouse, very often a non-wage earning wife, has certain rights in the family home under existing legislation. They are not rights of ownership although in the case of a judicial separation or divorce, a court may order a transfer of property from one spouse to another. Rights in this area are provided under the Family Home Protection Act; the Married Women's Status Act; and judicial separation and divorce legislation.

The Family Home Protection Act provides that both spouses must agree to the sale or mortgaging of the family home. But where the house is in just one name, the other spouse has no right to any proceeds from a sale unless he or she made some financial contribution to the purchase of the house.

There are also provisions protecting the rights of a spouse against whom a barring order is being sought. The first step in getting a barring order is to get a protection order. Where that has been obtained, neither spouse can remove or dispose of any household contents until a decision has been made on the barring order. A spouse must also be given the opportunity to take over the mortgage repayments on the family home where his or her partner has defaulted on the payments. And the courts can make orders for the protection of a home where a spouse is indulging in some actions which could lead to its loss.

Under the Married Women's Status Act, the courts can be asked to rule on the ownership of property, including a family home. But the courts will only grant ownership rights to a spouse who can show that he or she made financial contributions to the purchase of the house or to other household costs. Work done in the home or time spent rearing children is not taken into account.

The courts have much wider powers of discretion under the judicial separation and divorce legislation. Where a couple has been granted either a judicial separation or a divorce the court can make orders requiring the transfer of property from one spouse to another. In this case it does not matter whether or not a spouse has made a financial contribution. The courts may also make maintenance orders. Such orders can be reviewed from time to time, but orders made about property are permanent and a court will only review them if it can be shown that it was deliberately misled when the original order was made.

Both spouses have important rights to the family home even if they are not formally joint owners

Wills and tax planning

Tax is another thing to consider when making a will. Inheritance tax is not a problem for most people, particularly those inheriting from parents where the tax thresholds are still high despite the reductions of recent years. But the tax liability can be significant in some circumstances, for instance where an inheritance comes from a distant relative or friend. There are special concessions for farms and family businesses but there are conditions to be met. There is a section on tax planning for inheritances on page 274.

The duties of executors

The person making a will — the testator — should always seek the consent of a person named in the will to act as executor. It is, of course, quite in order to name more than one person, but there is no obligation on the persons so named to act. A person who does not wish to accept an executorship may renounce it by signing a form of renunciation before a witness. This can obviously create problems so it is essential to ensure that the executor named in the will is willing to act. An executor may benefit under a will but he is not entitled to any payment for his services unless it is specifically stated in the will that such a payment should be made. The executor can, however, claim for expenses actually incurred in administering the will.

You don't need to hire a solicitor to take out probate on a will. You can do it yourself

If it is decided to accept the executorship, the first move is normally to obtain a Grant of Probate from the courts. This will formally authorise the executor to collect the deceased's assets and carry out the provisions of the will. But the will itself is sufficient authorisation and even without a grant of probate, the executor can immediately take charge of the deceased's assets and start to carry out the provisions of the will.

A listing of all the deceased's assets should be made and valuations obtained where necessary. It is also necessary to obtain details of any outstanding debts. Usually these are easily ascertained but, if they are not, the executor can protect himself against further claims by putting a notice in the daily newspaper asking all creditors to supply details of their claims by a certain date.

If a creditor has not made a claim by that date, he loses the right to pursue his claim against the executor although he can still proceed against the beneficiaries under the will. If the executor does not put the statutory notice in the newspaper, he may protect himself by getting the beneficiaries to give an agreement in writing to indemnify him against any claims which emerge after the distribution has taken place.

Taking out probate

The Probate Office at 15/24 Phoenix Street, Smithfield, Dublin, 7, telephone (01 8886174) has a special application section for those who wish to take out probate themselves. Application for probate can be made there or to one of 14 District Probate Registries. It takes no great skill to take out probate on the average estate and for many bereaved it can be therapeutic. Doing the job yourself beats waiting around for progress reports from a solicitor.

There is no need to get a solicitor to do the job, particularly if it is a simple will, although the Court Service now operates a duel schedule of fees, one for solicitors and another for the rest of us. The solicitors pay half price. For instance, a solicitor taking out a grant of probate on an estate valued at €750,000 pays €375 in fees. A non-solicitor taking out the same grant of probate is charged €750. It's unfair and discriminatory but that's the way it is.

However, even with the extra probate office fees, there is money to be saved by taking out probate yourself. When solicitors were allowed to have an agreed scale of charges for probate work they charged 2% on the value of the estate, plus VAT and expenses. Some solicitors may still be using that formula when calculating their charges. Some may even charge more, but even a 2% fee represents a significant charge on even relatively modest estates – €10,000 on an estate of €500,000 that may comprise little more than a house.

Despite the fact that non-solicitors have to pay higher probate fees, substantial savings can be made by taking out probate yourself

With the standard scale gone, there is some competition in the market and some solicitors will quote a flat rate. It pays to shop around but with a restriction on advertising and with few solicitors willing to quote over the phone it can be hard to do. But even at their cheapest the solicitor's fees for taking out probate are sure to dwarf the relatively minor saving in probate office fees.

So there are significant savings to be made dispensing with the services of a solicitor and paying the higher probate office fees. But that still doesn't excuse the Court Service's discriminating fees structure.

It can, of course, claim that there is more work involved in providing a grant of probate to a non-professional. Undoubtedly there is in some cases but not in others. Solicitors may be as demanding on the time and expertise of the Court Service as any member of the public. Many solicitors will get their clerks to do the job and they may have had no formal training or experience. The Law Society does not have a great regard for their clerks. They won't accept them as trainee solicitors until they have worked a full 10 years in a clerking role.

The suspicion must be that the Court Service was responding to pressure from the Law Society lobby in adopting this dual fee structure. It was introduced very quietly without any fanfare and is totally against the spirit of the recommendations in the 2007 Competition Authority's report which were aimed at diminishing the monopoly power of the legal profession.

It you do need the services of a solicitor make sure to shop around and agree fees in advance

Solicitors have an effective monopoly, for instance, in the provision of conveyancing services. It is illegal for anyone other than a solicitor to provide and charge for such services. That's not the case in many other countries. In Britain there is a para-legal profession of conveyancer. Costs dropped significantly when they were introduced.

It makes sense but it requires a change in the law and the Government has been effectively dragging its feet on the issue. Building societies were to be given the right to provide conveyancing services under a 1989 Act. All that's needed is a ministerial order but that order has never been made and now the issue has been long-fingered again by simply putting it on a list of items to be considered by the proposed Legal Services Regulatory Authority.

So competition remains limited and solicitors will fight hard to keep it that way. Before the property boom, conveyancing accounted for almost a third of their fee income and even in the current climate, it remains a lucrative business.

On request the probate office will send out an application form which should be completed as fully as possible and returned. The probate office will immediately acknowledge receipt of the form and will ask the applicant to call in for a preliminary meeting. At that stage the applicant should present full details of the estate, a death certificate and the original will, if there is one. Statements of deposit accounts held by the deceased should be produced, as well as details of assurance policies and all assets owned by the deceased. A second meeting will be arranged to finalise any outstanding matters and the applicant will then be required to sign the completed documents, swear to the truth and accuracy of their contents, and pay a fee.

In some cases, it may take more than two meetings to finalise the matter but once probate has been granted, the executor will find it easier to transfer funds from bank accounts into his or her own name. It is best for the executor to open a separate bank account for this purpose. The executor has further duties in making returns to the taxman and settling any tax claims outstanding or arising as a result of the will. This includes making income and inheritance tax returns. Because of the tax implications it may be necessary to get tax clearance before withdrawing money from bank or other saving accounts.

Tax clearance is not always needed to withdraw money from a deceased person's account

Tax clearance

In the case of a joint husband/wife account, a surviving spouse is not required to present a tax clearance no matter how large the estate but the financial institution may require sight of the death certificate and/or will depending on the type of account i.e. whether or not two signatures were needed for withdrawals.

Tax clearance is needed to access an account in the deceased's sole name or in the joint names of the deceased and someone other than a spouse where the account has more than €50,000 in it, but such a clearance is granted quickly by the Capital Taxes Branch, Revenue Commissioners, Stamping Building, Dublin Castle, phone (01)6475000 or Locall 1890 201105. The financial institution may also have its own rules about having sight of the will, death certificate or grant of probate. For more details on joint accounts see chapter 2, page 21.

8 Enforcing rights as worker and citizen

The rights of employees have been greatly enhanced in recent years, mostly in line with EU directives, with the introduction of legislation providing minimum rights and protection in matters like hours of work, minimum notice of dismissal or redundancy, redundancy payments, holidays, discrimination, unfair dismissal, etc. The laws apply to both full-time and part-time workers. The definition of part-time includes those working under a contract of employment or apprenticeship and those employed through an employment agency. That even includes the right to overtime pay if they work extra hours provided equivalent full-time workers get extra pay for working overtime.

Some employers have been known to try to reduce their exposure to the employment protection laws by either contracting out work to self-employed workers, or by hiring employees under contracts which effectively prevent them acquiring their full range of rights.

To qualify for some employment rights, employees have to have a minimum amount of service. But under the Protection of Employees (Fixed-term work) Act that came into force in July 2003, workers on fixed term contracts may not be treated less favourably than other employees unless justified on objective grounds other than the fact that the worker is on contract. Under the Act, an employer proposing to renew a fixed-term contract of employment must explain to the employee in writing the reason for retaining the job as a contract rather than a staff job.

The Act also places a limit on the amount of time an employee may be required to work on fixed-term contracts. Any renewal contract offered to workers on fixed-term contracts should not extend their total period on contract to more than four years. Any contract, thereafter, is considered by law to be a permanent contract unless the employer can show reasons why it should be otherwise. The employer would have to show that a non-permanent contract was necessary in pursuit of a legitimate objective and that there was no other way of achieving it.

What constitutes a legitimate objective has yet to be fully determined. Disputes can be referred to a Rights Commission of the Labour Relations Commission. The Rights Commission's decision can be appealed to the Labour Court for a legally binding determination. See page 162 for details of addresses and phone numbers.

Even before the 2003 Act, there were limits to what employers could do with contracts. In general the contract must be seen to have a purpose other than simply to allow the employer avoid unfair dismissal legislation. A 1993 Act specifically provided that employers cannot avoid the Act by using fixed-term contracts and that a break of less than three months between two consecutive contracts does not constitute a break in service.

This may be true even for work of a seasonal nature. It may not be possible for employers to prevent workers building up entitlements under the Unfair Dismissals and Redundancy Acts.

The Employment Appeals Tribunal has upheld claims for continuity of service by seasonal workers who showed a pattern of such work over a number of years. A contract worker is not normally covered under the unfair dismissals legislation unless he or she did work other than that specified in the contract of employment.

You can't totally rely on others, inspectors, employers or even trade unions to defend your rights. You must be aware of your entitlements and ensure you get them

While workers in large firms with union representation can be fairly certain that their entitlements are not allowed to go by default, non-union workers, particularly in smaller firms, may find that their employers, either by accident or design, fail to give them their full entitlements.

Explanatory leaflets may be obtained from the Department of Enterprise, Trade and Employment, Conditions of Employment Section, Dublin 4

The following gives a brief guide to the more important legislative provisions. Explanatory leaflets may be obtained from the Department of Enterprise, Trade and Employment, Conditions of Employment Section, Dublin 4 which also gives further assistance and advice. In the case of disputes, you can seek redress through a Rights Commissioner who can be contacted through the Department. The rights of part-time workers under these labour laws should not be confused with social welfare entitlements. Part-time workers earning more than €38 a week have some cover under the PRSI system.

Redundancy entitlements

The economic downturn has brought with it an increase in the numbers losing their jobs through redundancy. It can be a traumatic experience even for those who can convince themselves, as they should, that it is the job that's redundant, not they themselves. The law provides some protection but that doesn't make the experience any easier. Under the Redundancy Payment Scheme and the Protection of Employment Act, an employer is required to give at least 30 days notice to the relevant minister of any intention to make collective redundancies.

Workers are entitled to minimum notice and to minimum lump sum payments based on the number of years service with the firm.

Who is covered? The scheme covers employees who are in employment which is insurable for all benefits under the Social Welfare Acts or who were in such employment in the four years prior to redundancy; are over the age of 16 and who are normally expected to work for at least eight hours a week for the same employer. Domestic servants and agricultural workers — who are not relatives and who do not reside with their employers — are also covered. The upper age limit of 66 was abolished some years ago.

An employee becomes eligible for redundancy pay if he has been employed by the same employer for at least two years after attaining 16 years of age and is dismissed as redundant, laid off, or kept on short-time at less than 50% of normal time for four consecutive weeks or a total of six weeks in a period of 13 weeks.

The lump sum: The statutory lump sum is based on two week's pay for every year of service over the age of 16 but no more than €600 a week is taken into account. In addition to the payment, based on service, there is an additional top-up of one week's pay. The number of years service is calculated backwards from the date of dismissal with any period of service less than a full year taken into account on a pro-rata daily basis.

Where a company is not going into liquidation but is simply rationalising its operations or just cutting back on staff it has become usual for the affected workers to demand and for the employer to pay, redundancy lump sums well in excess of the statutory requirements — in some cases up to seven weeks pay for every year of service. The employer can claim 15% of the statutory lump sum from the Department of Enterprise, Trade and Employment provided two weeks notice has been given. It was 60% up until January 1, 2012.

Tax and the lump sum: The taxation on redundancy lump sums can be quite high. As mentioned above, the statutory redundancy payment is not liable for tax. In addition at least €10,160 of any other extra redundancy payment is also tax free. That €10,160 is increased by €765 for each full year of service. That's the minimum entitlement. Another €10,000 may also be taken tax free provided that no other claim in respect of a lump sum has been made in the previous ten years. But that €10,000 is reduced by the amount of any tax-free lump sum taken from a pension scheme. That's the lump sum received or that will eventually be received when the redundant worker retires. Any refund of pension contributions is taxed at a flat 20%.

The calculation of the actual exemption starts off at €20,160, plus €765 for each full year of service. The €20,160 figure is reduced by the amount of any other tax-

Lump sums well in excess of the statutory minimum are often paid free payments received or credited. That does not include refunds of pension contributions but it does include tax-free lump sums from pension schemes. And it also includes a valuation put on any deferred payment from a pension scheme such as an entitlement to a future lump sum. In no case is the €20,160 reduced below €10,160.

To see how these calculations might work, let us first take the case of a man who is made redundant and leaves his pension contributions in the scheme as he is required to do. He has a right to a tax-free lump sum and a pension when he reaches retirement age.

A valuation is put on that lump sum taking account of the amount that will be paid out and the number of years to go before it is paid. Let's suppose that such a lump sum is valued at €4,500. The basic tax exemption on the redundancy lump sum of €20,160 would be reduced by that €4,500 to €15,660. If the value of the pension lump sum was €15,000, the exemption would only be reduced to €10,160 since in no case is it reduced below that level.

There is an alternative method of calculation which can give a higher tax-free figure for workers with long service. It is up to the worker. He or she has the option of calculating the tax-free lump sum on the following basis known as the Standard Capital Superannuation Benefit. The average annual salary over the last three years is multiplied by the number of years service divided by 15 and from that is deducted any tax-free lump sum from a pension scheme.

Whichever method produces the smallest taxable lump sum can be used. Initially, any remaining taxable lump sum, after deducting the tax-free element, is treated as income in the year in which it is received and taxed as such but the taxpayer can opt to have tax levied instead at the average rate paid over the three tax years prior to the year in which the lump sum is paid. The tax paid over the three years preceding the year in which the lump sum is paid is divided by taxable income over that period to give an average tax rate. Taxable income is defined as before tax credits and other reliefs that are given as a reductions of tax.

Someone who has opted for joint assessment with a spouse may, in making this calculation, use either the joint incomes and tax payable by both spouses or, alternatively, only the total income and tax payable by the spouse in receipt of the redundancy payment. A claim to have this average tax rate applied must be made to your tax office and if a refund is payable you normally have to wait until the end of the tax year. No part of a redundancy lump sum is normally liable for PRSI but the taxable portion is liable to the new Universal Social Charge.

It may be possible to shelter part, or all, of a redundancy lump sum by using it to make an additional voluntary contribution to a pension scheme. Employees can claim tax relief on at least 15% of income each year invested in an approved pension fund. The limit goes up to 30% for those over 50, 35% for those over 55 and 40% for anyone over 60. If the contribution is above those limits it may be possible to claim relief against income in the previous year or to carry it forward and claim the relief against future income.

It may be possible to save tax by putting part of a redundancy lump sum into a pension fund

The drawback of making extra contributions into a pension fund is that the money cannot be accessed before retirement. There is more about additional voluntary contributions to pension funds on page 183.

In some cases, a person leaving a job after less than two years service may be entitled to a refund of pension contributions. But usually only his own, not any made by the employer. It depends on the rules of the scheme. Such repayments, if taken, are taxed at 20%. As an alternative to a refund, a person may actually take a pension on leaving the job and as part of that pension get a tax-free lump sum of up to 1½ times final salary.

To qualify for a pension on retirement, a person must normally be of retirement age — at least 60 in most cases. In some occupations, retirement is allowed at an earlier age and the age limit is lifted in the case of retirement due to disability. To qualify for a tax free lump sum of 1½ times salary from a pension scheme requires 20 years service.

Holiday entitlement

The right to paid annual leave was first introduced into Irish law in 1939, three years after a similar law was introduced in Britain. It gave most workers the right to seven consecutive days off each year. That included Sundays. Matters have improved since then and many are entitled to more than the much-improved minimum rights thanks to locally negotiated agreements. But laws can be broken and in the current climate there is a danger that even statutory rights will come under pressure from some employers. But paid holiday entitlements have the backing of law and can't legally be withheld. Holiday entitlements above the minimum laid down by law are, of course, open to negotiation. They are a matter for agreement between employer and employee.

The minimum legal entitlements have remained unchanged since 1997. They are covered by the Organisation of Working Time Act which replaced an earlier 1973 Act. It covers all those working under a contract of employment or apprenticeship, employed through an employment agency, and most State employees other than the gardaí and defence forces. There is no qualifying period of service.

A 'leave year' normally means a year beginning on January 1 but any 12 month period may be used provided it is used consistently. Minimum paid holiday entitlements can be calculated in one of the following ways:

- Four working weeks where the employee has worked at least 1,365 hours in the year – this method is not used where a worker changes jobs during the leave year.

- One-third of a working week for each calendar month in which the employee has worked at least 117 hours.

- Alternatively the calculation can be based on eight per cent of the hours an employee works in a leave year subject to a maximum of four working weeks. In other words eight hours leave for every 100 hours or pro rata.

For the purposes of these calculations, hours worked include overtime, time spent on maternity or parental leave as well as holidays and public holidays taken during the calculation period. Holiday pay should be paid in advance at the normal weekly rate.

The final decision on when holidays are taken rests with the employer but under the Act he or she is required to take account of a worker's need to reconcile work and family responsibilities and his or her opportunities for rest and recreation. That sounds good but it may mean very little in reality since the decision can clearly be based on a range of subjective criteria. Where disputes arise they can be referred to the Rights Commissioner Service of the Labour Relations Commission. They can be contacted at www.lrc.ie or by phone at (01) 6609662. This is true of any disputes over holiday entitlements.

Most of the rights conferred by law are specific. For instance, the employer is specifically required to give at least one month's notice to the employee or his trade union of when holidays are to be taken and the leave must be given either during the leave year or within six months after it ends.

These are, of course, minimum entitlements which allow employers a lot of freedom in deciding when holidays are to be taken. But in most cases, leave rosters are worked out by agreement, taking account of the needs of the employer but also seniority and personal needs of the employees.

If an employee on leave sends in a medical certificate stating that he or she is ill, the time covered by the certificate is not considered as leave. Only that period during which the worker was medically fit for work is considered to be part of the paid holiday entitlement. The time covered by the doctor's cert is treated as sick leave.

After eight months work an employee is entitled to an unbroken period of two weeks holidays

Live-in workers are entitled to extra holiday pay as compensation for the loss of board and/or lodgings during the holiday period. This only applies, of course, where such board and/or lodgings is part of a worker's remuneration.

After eight months work, an employee is entitled to an unbroken period of two weeks holidays which may include public holidays. This entitlement may be ceded by mutual agreement. But it is illegal for an employer to make a payment instead of the minimum statutory holiday entitlement unless the worker is actually leaving employment. So a worker who is continuing in employment must at the very least be given his or her minimum holiday entitlements.

There is nothing illegal, however, in asking a worker to accept a payment for giving up additional holiday entitlements over and above the statutory minimum, just as there is nothing illegal about asking a worker to accept a pay cut so long as it wouldn't bring the pay level below the minimum wage.

In addition to the annual holiday entitlement, all full-time employees are entitled to extra pay or leave in respect of public holidays. Part-time and casual workers must have worked at least 40 hours in the five weeks ending on the day before the public holiday. The entitlement is to one of the following: a paid day off on the day, a paid day off within a month of the day, an additional day of annual leave or an additional day's pay.

The employee can have a say in which of those options is applied but if agreement cannot be reached, the final decision is up to the employer. The level of compensation may also be increased, of course, by negotiation.

If an employee asks an employer within 21 days of a public holiday to nominate which of the above options he or she wants to apply and gets no response the worker is automatically entitled to take a paid day off on the public holiday. There are nine public holidays: New Year's Day, St. Patrick's Day, Easter Monday, First Monday in May, First Monday in June, First Monday in August, Last Monday in October, Christmas Day, and St. Stephen's Day.

Working hours

The maximum working week has been progressively reduced since 1998 under the provisions of the Organisation of Working Time Act. Subject to a wide range of exceptions it is now set at 48 hours. That has applied since March 1, 2000. The Act doesn't apply to members of the defence forces, the Garda Síochána, junior hospital doctors, transport employees, those working at sea, workers who control their own working hours, or family members working on a farm or in a private house. The maximum working week may be averaged over 12 months, if workers enter into a Labour Court approved collective agreement. In the case of seasonal workers, it can be averaged over six months. Otherwise it can be averaged over four months.

Every worker is entitled to:

- An 11 hour rest period in every 24 hours.

- One period of 24 hours rest per week preceded by a daily rest period i.e. A total of 35 hours.

- Rest breaks of 15 minutes where up to four and a half hours have been worked or 30 minutes where up to six hours have been worked.

Night workers are defined as those who normally work at least three hours between midnight and 7am and who, during the year, work at least half of their hours during the night period. For night workers whose jobs involve special hazards or heavy physical or mental strain an absolute limit of eight hours in a 24 hour period applies.

Minimum wage

Most workers, over the age of 18, are entitled to be paid at least the national minimum wage which was increased to €8.65 in July 2011 having been earlier reduced. Those taking up new employment are only entitled to 80% of the minimum wage during their first year and 90% during their second year of employment.

Reduced rates also apply to those under 18 who are entitled to 70% of the basic minimum wage until they reach 18 rising to 80% on their 18th birthday and 90% a year later. Reduced entitlements also apply to workers who are still in training and attending prescribed courses. They are entitled to be paid for their work hours at a rate of at least 75% of the minimum wage during the first year of training rising to 80% in the second year and 90% in the third year.

The progression up the scale is faster where the training course takes less than three years, for instance if a course only takes one year there is an entitlement to 80% after four months — a third of the total duration — rising to 90% after eight months. Tips, gratuities, and extra payments for overtime, Sunday, holiday working or unsociable hours can not be considered as part of the minimum wage entitlement.

A portion of the minimum wage may be paid in kind in the form of board (food) and lodging. The maxima that can be taken into account are:

- €54.13 for full board and lodgings per week, or €7.73 per day

- €32.14 for full board only per week, or €4.60 per day

- €21.85 for lodgings only per week, or €3.14 per day

Workers in some sectors of the economy are entitled to minimum rates of pay in excess of the minimum wage as a result of registered collective agreements covering the drapery, footwear and allied trades in Dublin and Dun Laoghaire, the construction industry, electrical contracting and the printing sector in Dublin. The system under which such agreements are reached and implemented is to be changed under proposed new legislation. New provisions are also proposed for Employment Regulation Orders which, until July 2011, laid down minimum pay for workers in a range of sectors including the aerated waters and wholesale bottling sector, agricultural workers, catering, contract cleaning, hairdressing in Dublin and Cork, hotels outside of Dublin and Cork, law clerks, provender milling, retail, grocery and allied trades, the security industry, shirt making, tailoring, women's clothing and millinery. Those orders cease to have any statutory basis following a High Court decision.

The new legislation will remove the right to a Sunday premium payment from Joint Labour Committee agreements but employers will have to provide for Sunday working on the basis of a Sunday premium payments, a higher hourly rate throughout the working week or time off in lieu. Businesses will also be given the right to opt out of payment on the basis of inability to pay and require Joint Labour Committees, to set no more than one basic adult rate per agreement together with just supplementary minimum rates reflecting varying levels of service. It is proposed that all other rates of pay, including rates for those with long service or with particular skills, would be agreed at firm level.

Further details on minimum pay can be obtained from The National Employment Rights Authority, O'Brien Road, Carlow, telephone Lo-call 1890 80 80 90. Its website www.employmentrights.ie provides information in a range of different languages.

Sunday work

Workers who don't already get special compensation for Sunday work are entitled to a Sunday premium equivalent to that applying to similar workers elsewhere. The premium payable should be based on the closest applicable collective agreement that applies in similar employment.

Zero hours on-call

Where a worker is requested to be available for work he or she is entitled to be paid for at least a quarter of the on-call hours, even if not called upon to work, subject to a payment for a maximum of 15 hours. So if a worker is required to be available for 48 hours a week, he or she is entitled to a minimum payment for 12 hours (a quarter of 48) even if not required to work at all.

Unfair dismissal

The Unfair Dismissals Acts are aimed at protecting workers from being unfairly sacked by laying down criteria of what is unfair dismissal and providing an adjudication system for redressing such action. The Act applies to most workers who have at least a year's continuous service with the same employer. It does not cover those who have passed retiring age or those excluded from the redundancy payments scheme because they are under 16 or over 66.

Neither does it cover people working for a close relative and living in the same house or on the same farm, members of the defence forces, gardaí, FÁS/SOLAS trainees, apprentices, or most State and local authority employees.

Normally it is up to the employer to prove that a dismissal is fair and justified on the basis of the capability, competence, or qualifications of the worker, conduct, redundancy, or that a continuation of employment would breach another statutory rule.

Dismissals are deemed to be definitely unfair if it is shown that they result from the worker's trade union membership or activities outside working hours or within working hours if normally permitted by the employer; race; religion; politics; pregnancy or related matters such as breastfeeding; membership of the Traveller community; the exercise or proposed exercise of rights to maternity, adoptive or parental leave; age or unfair selection for redundancy. The normal requirement of having a year's service does not apply in cases involving trade union membership or activities, pregnancy, and maternity or adoptive leave.

An action against unfair dismissal should be taken within six months. This may be done by contacting a Rights Commissioner, through the Department of Labour, phone (01) 6765861, or by writing to the Employment Appeals Tribunal, Davitt House, Dublin 4. The time limit can be extended to 12 months in exceptional circumstances.

Where the dismissal is unfair, the Commissioner or Tribunal can order any of the following: reinstatement in the old job, re-engagement in the old job, or in a suitable alternative, or financial compensation up to a maximum of two years pay. Cases taken on the grounds of gender discrimination can be taken directly to the Circuit Court with no limit on the compensation that can be awarded.

Minimum notice

Any worker who has completed at least 13 weeks continuous employment with the one employer is entitled to receive minimum notice of dismissal. The notice depends on the length of service as outlined in the table below. An employee who has worked for over 13 weeks is required to give at least one week's notice of leaving the job to his employer.

13 weeks to 2 years	1 week
2 to 5 years	2 weeks
5 to 10 years	4 weeks
10 to 15 years	6 weeks
Over 15 years	8 weeks

Under the Employment Equality Act it is illegal for employers to discriminate against workers or potential workers in matters of pay, conditions of employment, recruitment, training and/or promotion on the grounds of sex, marital status, family status, sexual orientation, religious belief, age, disability, race, or membership of the Traveller community. Discrimination in the provision of services, etc. is prohibited under the Equal Status Act. Discrimination by individual employers is outlawed, as is discrimination in collective agreements, in advertisements, by employment agencies, in vocational training or by bodies such as trade unions and professional or trade organisations.

Harassment in the workplace is outlawed by the Act. That includes sexual harassment and harassment related to any of the other grounds for discrimination. Harassment is defined as any act or conduct that is unwelcomed and offensive, humiliating or intimidating including spoken words, gestures, or the production, display or circulation of written material or pictures. The obligation is on employers to take all 'reasonable' steps to ensure that harassment doesn't take place.

There are some exceptions allowed for in the Act. Sexual discrimination is allowed where the sex of the employee is an essential part of the job in areas such as acting or modelling for an artist. It is also allowed in the case of some foreign postings to areas where women, for instance, might not be accepted locally in certain jobs.

Discrimination in the provision of childbirth facilities or in the employment of care workers is also allowed, as is positive discrimination to maintain a desirable gender balance in the garda and prison services. Discrimination on the grounds of age is outlawed for all those between 18 and 65 years of age. Age-related pay scales are no longer allowed. An employer may discriminate against an elderly worker in relation to training, if it can be shown that the cost of the training would not be recouped before the worker retires.

There is a critical exception in the case of disability. An employer may discriminate against a disabled person if the cost

The obligation is on employers to take all 'reasonable' steps to ensure that harassment doesn't take place

of ensuring equal treatment is anything other than nominal. The original Bill, enacted in 1997, was found to be unconstitutional because it required employers to bear greater than nominal cost in providing facilities for the disabled. Another exception allows for discrimination on religious grounds in education and medical institutions where the discrimination is required to maintain a religious ethos. For public service jobs it is also permissible to require proficiency in the Irish language, residency in Ireland and/or Irish citizenship.

The Act also allows employers to discriminate in a positive fashion. It allows for actions specifically geared towards employing people over 50 years of age, people with disabilities, and members of the Traveller community. Employers may discriminate against men in measures or actions aimed at promoting equal opportunities for women in terms of recruitment and promotion including the provision of special training for women. Having laws that outlaw discrimination doesn't, of course, ensure that discrimination will be abolished. Equal pay for women wasn't achieved overnight following the enactment of the equal pay laws in 1974. Indeed some would claim that it hasn't yet been achieved.

To qualify for equal pay under the 1974 Act, it was necessary to show that someone doing equal work was being paid more by the same or associate employer 'in the same locality' but that is no longer required. The Equality Authority, which oversees the law, doesn't itself rule on equality issues but its job is to work towards the elimination of discrimination and the promotion of equality of opportunity in employment on all of the nine discriminatory grounds covered by the Act.

The Equality Authority provides advice on pursuing equality rights. It can be contacted at 1890 245545

So the first port of call for people with a grievance should be the Equality Authority. It can be contacted at 1890 245545. It can help individuals and groups to make their case and get redress. A person who believes that he or she has been discriminated against has the right to seek and get information necessary in drawing up a case from the supposed discriminator. Most cases go to the Employment Tribunal which can award pay arrears for up to three years in equal pay cases and compensation of up to two years pay. The maximum compensation is €12,700 in other cases. To comply with a judgement of the European Court of Justice, cases involving discrimination on the grounds of gender can go straight to the Circuit Court with no limit on the compensation that can be awarded.

Emergency time off

Employees are entitled under the 1998 Parental Leave Act, to limited time off for family emergencies resulting from an accident or illness. The entitlement is to paid leave. Emergency leave can consist of one or more working days subject to a maximum of three days in each 12 months or five days in 36 months. The employee must show that because of an injury to or illness of a family member, his or her presence is indispensably required.

Also entitled are non-parents, including same-sex couples, who are in a relationship of domestic dependency.

Maternity and parental leave

There is a basic entitlement to 26 weeks maternity leave during which time Maternity Benefit is payable, if PRSI contribution requirements are met. This benefit is tax-free. There is no obligation on the employer to continue to pay the worker although many do top up the social welfare benefit to the equivalent of full pay. At least two of the 26 weeks must be taken before the birth although that can be increased at the discretion of the worker provided at least four weeks are taken after the birth.

There is a further entitlement to a maximum of 16 weeks leave during which no Maternity Benefit is paid. Full maternity leave entitlement is also available to women who suffer a still birth or miscarriage any time after the 24th week of pregnancy.

Employers are entitled to adequate notice. Four weeks notice must be given of the intention to take maternity leave and four weeks notice must be given of the intention to return to work. The worker continues to earn holiday entitlements including bank holiday entitlements, during the full period of maternity leave.

Leave entitlements can only be transferred to a father in the tragic situation where a mother dies within 24 weeks of giving birth. But, in all cases, a father is entitled to some unpaid parental leave.

That's in addition to maternity leave and applies to all parents or those acting in *locus parentis*. The entitlement is to a maximum of 14 weeks parental leave, unpaid and without any social welfare entitlement. It is normally taken in blocks of at least six continuous weeks before each child is eight years old. That is extended to 16 if the child is disabled.

In the case of an adopted child, who is aged between three and eight at the time of adoption, the leave must normally be taken within two years of the adoption order. As with maternity leave the worker retains employment rights and is entitled to return to the same job under the same contract of employment unless the employer can show that it is not "reasonably practical". In such a case the worker is entitled to suitable alternative employment.

Existing social welfare rights are also protected by the granting of credited PRSI contributions during the period of leave. The employee, who must normally have at least one year's service must give six weeks notice of taking paternal leave and the employer has the right to postpone it where it would have an adverse impact on the business. In some cases those with only three months service may be entitled to pro-rata paternal leave.

An expectant mother is entitled to take time off without loss of pay for ante- and post-natal medical examination and tests and both she and the expectant father are entitled to limited time off, again without any loss of pay, to attend ante-natal classes. She may attend one set of ante-natal classes under this provision with the exception of the last three classes in the set when she would normally be on leave.

Fathers have a once-off right to attend the two pre-natal classes immediately prior to the birth. Employers are entitled to be given two weeks notice in writing of appointment dates.

Adoptive leave is granted on much the same basis as maternity leave. The entitlement is to 24 weeks on social welfare and a further 16 weeks without social welfare payments. The adopting parent is usually a woman but a man can qualify, in certain circumstances, where his partner has died or where the child is being placed solely in his care. The conditions as to notice etc. are similar to those that apply to maternity leave. Adoptive parents are also entitled to time off without loss of pay to attend pre-adoption classes or meetings. Attendance must be a requirement of the adoption and notice must be given.

Breastfeeding mothers who have given birth within the previous six months are entitled, without loss of pay, to either a single one hour break or two half-hour breaks during each standard working day. Alternatively an employer who can't provide breastfeeding facilities must facilitate an adjustment of the mother's working hours. There is provision for both maternity and adoptive leave to be postponed in the event of the child being hospitalised or the mother falling ill.

Where a child is hospitalised an employer can be asked to postpone some of the maternity leave but the request can be refused. If it is granted, the mother returns to work and takes the remainder of the leave starting not later than seven days after the child is discharged from hospital.

Adoptive leave is granted on much the same terms as maternity leave

If the mother falls ill during the extended period of maternity leave i.e. the period during which no Maternity Benefit is payable, she may request the employer to end the maternity leave period. If granted that allows her to claim Illness Benefit but there is no entitlement to reclaim the maternity leave foregone.

Apart from the entitlement to maternity and adoptive leave, all employees are also entitled under the 1998 Parental Leave Act to limited time off for family emergencies resulting from an accident or illness. The entitlement is to paid leave. These two entitlements are completely separate although provided for under the same Act. See page 159.

Terms of employment

All employees are entitled to get a written statement of the terms and conditions of employment within two months of starting a job. Those who were in jobs before the Act came into effect, on May 16, 1994, are entitled to a statement within two weeks of requesting it. The statement should include a job description, expected duration if temporary, starting date, hours of work, details of pay, overtime, bonus and holiday entitlements, and details of sick pay and pension arrangements.

Getting redress

Trade union members can refer disputes over any of their employment rights to their union representation but those who are not in trade unions have to seek redress themselves. Further information on entitlements can be got from

- **The Department of Jobs,**
     Enterprise and Innovation,
     Employment Rights section
     Davitt House, 65 Adelaide Road,
     Dublin, 2.
     Telephone (01) 6313131 or 1890 201615

Other disputes can be referred to the Rights Commissioner Service of the Labour Relations Commission at

- **Rights Commissioner Service**
     Labour Relations Commission,
     Tom Johnson House, Haddington Road,
     Dublin, 4.
     Telephone (01) 6609662

For assistance on matters of discrimination contact

- **Equality Authority**
     Clonmel Street
     Dublin, 2.
     Telephone (1890) 245545

Most equality claims are decided by

- **The Equality Tribunal**
     Clonmel Street
     Dublin, 2.
     Telephone (1890) 344424

> *To get the best insurance quote you have to shop around.*
> *Now, there's a very quotable quote — Anon*

9 Insuring home and possessions

The single largest asset owned by most people is a house or apartment. Fire, burglary, accident, flood and storm damage can, and does, result in substantial losses every day of the week. It is up to the individual to decide whether he wants to bear the full risk of such losses himself or spread it around by taking out insurance. For this is what insurance does — spreads the risk. A large number of people pay a small premium so that the few who actually suffer loss can be reimbursed. And you could be one of the few.

Now that a bit of competition is coming back into the house and car insurance markets, it's more important than ever to shop around. There are significant savings to be made. Don't rely solely on a broker to do the shopping around for you. There are very good deals to be got by phoning around or by seeking online quotes.

Don't assume that the first quote you get is the best available. Discounts can make a big difference where they apply and not all companies are the same. Most, but not all, give discounts for smoke detectors and burglar alarms. Senior citizens can also claim discounts from some insurers. 'Senior' can mean over 50 in some cases and over 55 in others. A couple of insurers also give discounts to people who also insure their cars with them.

The cheapest policy is not always the best, of course. Cover can vary significantly and it is often difficult to compare policies before you buy since you don't get the full documentation until you have paid the premium. But there are a few questions you can ask.

- Does the policy cover accidental damage to household items? Are you covered, for instance, for damage to the TV if you simply let it fall moving it from one room to another? Not all policies cover accidental damage.

- If one item of a suite of furniture is damaged does the policy cover replacing the whole suite or just that item even if a good match cannot be obtained?

- What limitations are placed on the cover for high value items including cash?

- What portion of any claim will you have to meet yourself? This is known as the excess. You may be able to choose a figure yourself. The higher it is, the lower the premium should be.

- Are there any discounts for having an alarm or because of my age? – over 50s sometimes qualify.

You may even get a lower quote from your existing insurance company if it thinks that you are a new customer or if you approach it in a different way, on the internet, for instance

These are just some of the questions to consider when choosing a policy. Once you get the policy document make sure to read it carefully. Make sure you know what is and isn't covered. The cover may be more extensive than you realise. For instance it may cover the replacement of locks if you lose your keys or cover for items lost from your car.

You may have more cover than you realise in some areas. But every policy also imposes a range of restrictions on your cover in other areas. It's as well to be aware of them too. Take the case of John who brought a complaint to the Insurance Ombudsman. His house was burgled while he was attending a street party and he made a claim for about €2,000 to cover the items stolen.

The insurance company refused to pay on three grounds. An inspector had difficulties gaining access to the house after the burglary. Some of the goods taken belonged to a woman with whom the claimant had been living. The policy only covered goods belonging to members of the claimant's

Valuing your house for insurance

☐ The Society of Chartered Surveyors, 5 Wilton Place, Dublin 2 issues annual guidelines for valuing houses for insurance purposes. Copies are free on request but please enclose a stamped addressed envelope. The following is a summary of their 2011 figures in euro per square foot. Based on March 2011 costs, they are designed to cover rebuilding costs including site clearance.

House type		Dublin	Cork	Galway	Waterford	Limerick
Terraced —	2 bedroom 750 sq. ft.	€169	€130	€128	€128	€130
	3 bedroom 1,023 sq. ft.	€162	€123	€120	€121	€122
Semi —	3 bedroom 1,023 sq. ft.	€163	€124	€122	€122	€123
	4 bedroom 1,270 sq. ft.	€161	€122	€121	€120	€119
Detached — 4 bedroom 1,270 sq. ft.		€164	€124	€121	€124	€124
Bungalow — 4 bedrooms 1,572 sq. ft.		€159	€122	€119	€116	€125

Garage: Single attached garage €13,527, double detached garage €24,282

family. And the alarm was not turned on. That was a breach of a policy condition. The Ombudsman found in favour of the company on all but the first ground. It transpired that the claimant's wife had moved back into the house after the burglary and she had refused the inspector entry. That wasn't enough to refuse the claim, the Ombudsman decided.

But not turning on the alarm was a sufficient reason for not paying up since the claimant had got a 10% discount on his premium on the understanding that the alarm would always be turned on when the house was not occupied, even for a short period. And the policy clearly stated that only property belonging to the claimant and his family was covered.

So paying the insurance premium isn't enough. You need to read the fine print to see what is and isn't covered and you also must abide by any conditions such as turning on alarms. You also need to answer the questions on the proposal form truthfully and fully. In another case, the Ombudsman found in favour of an insurance company that had refused to pay out on a claim for damage resulting from a chimney fire. The claimant had not disclosed that she had previously claimed for similar damage from another company.

Greater losses can result from a failure to fully value the contents of your house or to underestimate the costs of reinstating the house after a fire. Overestimating will push up your premiums but underestimating can result in any claim being scaled down as a result of the 'average clause' included in most policies.

The average clause causes many misunderstandings and problems, so it is as well to understand what it is about. It can best be explained by a simple example. Suppose your house is worth €300,000, but you only have it insured for €150,000. If your house is completely destroyed, you would only expect to get €150,000 from the insurance company since you are only half insured. But suppose your house is only damaged. If the damage is estimated at, say, €40,000 then the insurance company will still consider that you are only half insured and pay out €20,000 – half of the €40,000 damage.

A house owner who complained to the Financial Ombudsman when his insurance company applied the average clause lost his case. His claim for €145,000 was reduced to €132,000 because, according to the company, his property was underinsured. He had relied on indexing the amount of cover but the Ombudsman found that this was not sufficient. In coming to his decision he took account of the guidelines issued by the Society of Chartered Surveyors.

Because of the average clause, it is important to reassess your insurance needs each year as you renew your policies. You don't have to be absolutely precise but you do need to be fairly close to the correct valuations. In the case of building insurance, of course, you need to insure for the reinstate-

Don't assume that your building society insurance provides adequate cover

It is important to reassess your insurance needs every year taking account of replacement costs ment cost of the house. That may bear no relationship to the market value.

Similar houses in different areas may have very different market values but exactly the same reinstatement costs apply to both. The Society of Chartered Surveyors, 5 Wilton Place, Dublin, 2 issues annual guidelines for valuing houses for insurance purposes. Copies are free on request but please enclose a stamped addressed envelope.

In the case of older houses or those with unusual once-off designs it's as well to get some professional advice on reinstatement costs. Don't rely on the market value. It is seldom, if ever, a good guide to valuation for insurance purposes.

It pays to shop around or get a broker to do it for you. Don't forget, of course, that there are some companies that don't deal through brokers. You need to check them out yourself. Make sure your home is adequately insured, but don't be scared into over-insuring it.

There are four general areas of risk which the average householder should consider covering by insurance. These are: damage or loss of the house itself; damage or loss of contents — furniture, etc; liability for damage to third parties arising out of defects in the building; and all risks insurance for specific items, i.e. jewellery, etc. Very often all four types of risk can be covered by the one general policy, although individual policies covering any one type can be taken out.

Read the proposal form and the policy carefully to discover just what's covered and what's not

The house itself

For the sake of the relatively small premium involved it is not worth taking the risk of not insuring your house. If the house is rented, check if you are liable for insuring it. With a short lease you possibly are not. With a long lease you may be. If you are buying a house with a mortgage, the bank or building society will require you to insure it and in some cases will have done it for you.

Most policies cover damage to the basic structure of the house itself, the garage and certain outbuildings, together with walls, gates and fences. Also covered is damage to fixtures and fittings such as washbasins, toilets, pipes etc.

Public liability cover, up to a fixed sum, is usually included as standard to cover your liability for injury or loss suffered by another person as a result of an accident which occurred on your property. It is also usual to have some cover for the cost of alternative accommodation if the house is left uninhabitable. It may be necessary to specifically request and pay extra to get cover for damage to underground water pipes running between your house and the boundary of your land, damage to radio and television aerials and breakage of glass, etc. The basic policy usually covers:

Fire, explosion, lightning, thunderbolt, falling aircraft or other aerial devices: Damage resulting from terrorist attack may be excluded.

Flood damage: Flood damage may not be covered in some areas. Storm damage to fences and gates or damage to television aerials may be excluded.

Burglary, housebreaking or any attempt there at: The buildings policy simply covers damage to the house itself — not the contents. The cover does not apply if the house is left unfurnished, or even if it is furnished, is left uninhabited for more than a set period. If you are leaving your house vacant it is best to check with the insurance company to ensure that you are covered. If you are leaving it unfurnished you will have to take out a special policy.

Bursting or overflowing of water tanks or pipes: Again it is usual to exclude some small part of any claim under this heading — the first €50 say — and the conditions on leaving the house vacant are the same as above.

Impact: Damage caused by impact with the buildings, walls, gates, fences of any road vehicle, horses or cattle not belonging to or under the control of yourself or your family.

Loss of rent: If the house is left uninhabitable you are usually covered in this regard up to a set percentage of the sum insured on the building — often 10%.

Liability to Public: If you are proved liable for damages caused to another person by an accident which occurred on your property, the normal building policy will provide cover up to about €65,000.

When you are taking out insurance you should read the proposal form carefully to see what risks are excluded and decide whether or not you want extra cover. It is a good idea to look at your insurance policies at least once a year, preferably long before the renewal date so as to give yourself ample time to shop around for a better deal.

House contents

Premiums for house contents insurance vary greatly depending on where the house is, the company providing the cover and the type of cover given. Many companies give discounts where the occupants are over a certain age, for being in a neighbourhood watch scheme, or for having an approved alarm system. You can also qualify for reduced premiums by accepting to pay a larger fixed amount of each potential claim yourself.

If the contents of your house are not insured, you may be running a serious risk of loss — tot up the value of the contents of your kitchen for instance. Could you afford to replace them yourself? If it would impose an undue burden, then you would do well to be insured. Do not assume that you are insured just because the bank or building society that holds your mortgage looks after your insurance. It is normally only interested in having the buildings insured. Insuring the contents is generally left up to yourself. The normal contents policy covers loss arising from the same causes as the building policy. Extras which may be included as standard in some policies include:

Tenant's liability to landlord: Useful if you are in a rented house, this clause provides cover for damage to fittings, etc., for which the tenant may have to reimburse the landlord.

Employer's liability: This covers claims by people employed to work in the house – anything from full-time domestic staff to tradesmen, who may be doing repairs about the house.

Liability to third parties: This provides cover for claims arising from accidents occurring in or about the house to visitors or their property. This could, for instance cover acci-

Phone and card insurance is often bad value

☐ There's a temptation to believe that taking out insurance somehow safeguards your property. That if you have insurance on your mobile phone, for instance, there is a reduced chance of it being stolen or lost. Of course there isn't. That's obvious when you think about it. And if you really think about it, taking out insurance on your mobile phone doesn't really make sense at all.

The real trauma involved in losing your mobile phone has a lot more to do with the inconvenience of losing the information in the phone's memory than it has to do with the cost of replacing the phone itself.

If you comply with all the conditions, an insurance policy may reimburse you for most of the cost of replacing the phone. But it won't compensate you for the trouble and strife involved in getting a replacement and programming it to your particular needs.

And having insurance doesn't, in any way, reduce the odds against your phone being damaged, lost or stolen – unless, of course, there is really something in that old belief that a slice of bread always falls buttered side down.

Is it really worth paying €5 a month to cover a potential loss of maybe only €100. You wouldn't dream of taking out insurance to cover the possibility of losing the €100 or so you may occasionally carry around in your pocket. So why take out cover on your mobile phone? You should be able to cover that sort of financial loss yourself without too much difficulty.

But many people do take out insurance on their mobile phones simply because they are not paying too much attention when filling out the application form and it's very often easier to say yes rather than no. The person selling the phone will usually have an incentive to sell the insurance. It's a lucrative business for the insurance companies and they pay generous commission.

While many people take out this form of insurance, few people bother to read the fine print. Very often the first €30 or so of any claim is disallowed. That's called the excess. Usually the owner of the phone is required to take good care of his or her phone.�

Companies will, for instance, refuse to pay out if the phone was left unattended, say in a car or in a jacket left on the back of a chair. This type of condition also applies to credit card insurance which is even less useful than insurance on a mobile phone.

Under the terms and conditions of most credit card agreements there is an upper limit on the cardholder's liability if the loss of a card is reported promptly. It's usually no more than about €60 and often only half that. In many cases the card companies don't even bother collecting that money.

Of course there is no limit on a cardholder's liability if he or she has been negligent or has acted in a fraudulent manner. Negligence might include simply leaving a card unattended but it certainly includes carrying a PIN number around with the card. The cardholder's potential liability can be very high if both card and PIN number fall into the wrong hands, particularly in some countries abroad where the upper limit on cash withdrawals is very high.

That's the type of liability against which it would be nice to have insurance. But it's not covered by the standard policy or indeed any policy that I know off. The standard policy costs about €16 a year. It isn't much. But it can't be good value when the most you are likely to ever claim is about €60.

Credit card companies also offer payment protection policies. They are similarly bad value. Yet it is all too easy to tick off the 'yes' box when filling out the application form for the credit card or when buying a mobile phone.

The typical charge is 60 cent a month for every €100 outstanding. At first glance that seems to be a small amount but it adds up to 7.2% a year on your debt. That's a lot, particularly for what you get. The typical policy provides a benefit if the cardholder is disabled or loses his or her job. But it only provides for the phased repayment of the debt, perhaps over 12 months. The debt isn't automatically cleared.

In all these cases, save yourself some money by thinking twice before saying yes to taking out insurance.

dental damage to property owned by someone other than yourself or a family member.

Most policies also include provision for replacing items on a new-for-old basis provided it is not more than (usually) five years old. Suppose, for instance, your cooker gets burnt it will be replaced with a new cooker of the same type. Some companies, however, only provide this as an extra, so check.

There can be some important exclusions which need to be borne in mind. There may only be limited cover for loss or damage to articles temporarily removed from the house. Usually if the value of any one article — a piece of jewellery for instance — is more than 5% of the total sum insured, a special policy will be required. Cash and bank notes are often only covered to a maximum of 5% of the total value insured. But there may be an even more onerous money limit, as low as €30. Usually the following items are not covered at all: deeds, bonds, bills of exchange, promissory notes, cheques, securities for money, stamps, documents of any kind, manuscripts, medals, coins, motor vehicles, accessories, and livestock.

Some insurers offer discounts for homes with alarms but be careful before applying for such a discount. There may be a condition attached that the alarm is always switched on when there is no-one is the house. If the policy does contain such a condition then you may not be insured at all if you forget to turn on the alarm. Most companies now have what is known as a 'best endeavour' clause rather than a complete exclusion clause so that you are covered as long as you did not blatantly refuse to turn on the alarm. But before looking for a discount or accepting one make sure that onerous conditions do not apply.

Personal liability

You, as a house owner or occupier may be held liable for damages caused by your negligence. A passer-by may be hit by a tile falling off your roof. A guest might trip over a carpet. Most household policies provide some cover for such claims. With some policies the cover extends to incidences unrelated to the house.

You can cause damage in many different ways. You could hit someone with a golf ball, close a door on someone's fingers, or cause an accident by walking out on the road in front of a cyclist. If you are found to be negligent in such cases, you could be liable to pay damages. Apart from the cover given by some household policies it is also possible to take out stand-alone personal liability insurance to provide you with cover against such claims up to a maximum sum. It's possible to get cover of up to €100,000 for an annual premium as low as €1.

All risks

As mentioned above, the normal policy on house contents does not provide cover for articles whose value represents more than 5% of the total sum insured. So if you have a valuable piece of jewellery, a camera or a painting, you may find that you are not covered for its loss. If you have such valuable items, an all-risks policy is worth having. Usually a valuation certificate is required for each article worth more than about €120. Rates vary considerably and range upwards of €1 a year for every €100 insured — a lot more for bicycles. Some insurance companies have a minimum all-risks premium so it may cost no more to put a few items on the policy than it does to simply cover one item.

10 Planning for your retirement

While it makes sense to save for retirement, the incentive to do so has been greatly eroded in recent years. Pension funds, in line with most investment funds, continue to yield dismal returns and there has been some curtailment of the available tax relief although the threat to restrict it to the standard rate of tax has been postponed, perhaps indefinitely. People are saving more but with a precautionary motive in mind they are tending to opt for shorter-term and safer investments. Managed pension funds did reasonably well in the early part of 2011 but lost most or all of those gains as the European financial crisis rumbled on.

With the average fund showing little or no growth over the past decade, doubt has been cast on the old conventional wisdom that such funds can be expected to yield real returns over the medium to long term despite short-term fluctuations. Tax relief has proved a saving grace up to this. The poor investment performances have, in many cases, been more than offset by the impact of tax relief on contributions. This is particularly so for those who can claim it at the top rate of 41%.

Even before the EU/IMF bail-out deal, the Government had decided to remove the anomaly whereby those paying tax at the top rate got tax relief at 41% on pension contributions while those paying tax only at the standard rate got relief at 20%. But the proposal on the policy document, National Pensions Framework, published in 2010 to standardise the relief at an effective 33%, was overtaken by a commitment in the EU/IMF bail-out agreement to move to standardising the relief at 20%.

Prior to the 2011 election, Fine Gael advocated a levy on pension funds as an alternative. That has been introduced and the rates of tax relief are to remain unchanged at least for the present although some change is still being considered according to the 2012 Budget statement.

As for the longer term investment outlook, it can be argued that the last 10 years have not been typical for investment performance and that funds can be expected to perform better as the world economy recovers from the deepest recession since the great depression of the 1930s. There is also scope for better management of pension funds and for a significant reduction in charges. And tax relief, even at 20%, effectively provides an up-front top-up of €1 for every €4 invested.

A person can expect to spend over one year in retirement for every three in the paid workforce. That average is based on someone working from 18 to 65 and then living another 16 years. That's about the average life expectancy at age 65. But people are living longer and more active lives, entering the labour force later and at least planning to retire earlier. It's no wonder we're told that it is never too early to plan for retirement.

Tax relief will still be available at 41% for the foreseeable future

Many people spend a lot of time planning their careers but there is frequently a reluctance to even think about the post-retirement years. Quality of life depends on a range of factors from health to wealth. The latter is the easiest to plan for. Planning is about anticipating change and preparing for it. Planning for retirement involves preparing for the changes that will take place in your income and expenditure patterns when you give up work. Your income is reduced but your spending needs are unlikely to decline to the same extent. A new income source will be needed.

So where is that income to come from?

Change in State pension entitlements

STATE PENSION AGE

The following changes were outlined in the 2010 Pensions Framework and seem certain to go ahead while other elements of the plan won't.

2014 Transition pension abolished raising the effective pension age to 66
— affecting those born on or after January 1, 1948
2021 State pension not payable until age 67
— affecting those born on or after January 1, 1955
2028 State pension not payable until age 68
— affecting those born on or after January 1, 1961

☐ **STATE PENSION qualifying rules**

2012 From April 6 a minimum of 520 paid contributions are required to qualify for the State pension.

There will be a scaled reduction in the pension payable to those qualifying after September 2012 with an annual average of between 20 and 47 PRSI contributions a year.

2020 Pension entitlements are to be based on total contributions rather than on a yearly average

---

The quality of life in retirement can be much improved by a bit of advance planning

The majority of workers retiring in the future will be entitled to a contributory old age pension when they retire. But even at the full rate that's far from enough to provide a comfortable living. The more you can put aside to supplement it the better. If you're self-employed, it's entirely up to yourself. If you're a PAYE worker you may be in a company pension scheme and be inclined to leave it at that.

But you can always top up your benefits if they are inadequate. All the options involve saving. Some people save by investing in their own businesses or directly in shares or property. But the most common way is through a pension scheme.

A recent study concluded that a man aged 20 would need to invest about 15% of his income each year to fund a civil service type pension at age 65. That's assuming he achieves a reasonable rate of return on the invested money. If he wanted to retire at 60 he'd need to invest 19% of his income or 23% if he wanted to start drawing his pension at 55. A woman would need to invest more since women tend to live longer than men. However slightly less than one in two workers is in a company or other occupational pension scheme in Ireland. While over 80% of public sector workers are covered, the figure is a much lower 38% in the private sector. It's as low as 19% in the distribution sector. The majority of self-employed workers don't make any pension provision for themselves either.

There are pluses and minuses to formally investing in a pension fund. Even with the ending of relief from PRSI and levies, those paying tax at the top rate of 41c in the euro can effectively get a top up of €41 for every €59 they put into a pension fund. That's a major plus. There are some set-up and management costs to take into account but you'd have to pay those anyway on most alternative investments. They can be substantial so don't just accept them. There is competition in the market and charges can be negotiated down.

Charges on pension funds can be significant. Don't just accept them as given. Check them out and shop around

There is, of course, one major drawback to investing in a pension fund. The money has to remain untouched until retirement. But that's not a drawback if your objective is really to save for your latter years. Restrictions on what can be done with the accumulated funds on retirement have, in recent years, been greatly eased in respect of personal pension funds and additional voluntary contributions to occupational schemes.

Saving is about accepting present pain for future gain and that future gain is almost certain to outweigh the current pain in foregone spending, particularly when saving for retirement. So should you be saving for retirement?

Should you be saving?

Only you can decide the level of income you would like to have in retirement. Obviously the more the better but securing an adequate pension requires a lot of saving. The standard civil service pension envisaged as a result of changes currently proposed can be used as a benchmark against which to judge your current entitlements or to set as an ideal to strive for.

- A pension of one-eightieth of pay for each year of service up to a maximum of 40/80ths i.e. half pay. Pay is to be defined on the basis of a career average and not final pay as is currently the case.

- A tax-free lump sum up to one and a half-year's salary is also payable on retirement.

- Post retirement increases at least in line with the Consumer Price Index.

- A continuing pension for a surviving spouse equal to half the original pension.

You may need to save 15% of income over your working life to secure a good pension on retirement

The best of private sector schemes promise similar benefits with the pension based on one-sixtieth of final pay up to a maximum of 40/60ths or two-thirds, reduced to take account of the tax-free lump sum.

But many such schemes have run into funding difficulties and the pension promise is only as good as the ability of the employer to meet the funding deficit and/or the willingness of the members to make additional contributions. Few of these schemes are open to new entrants.

Reviewing your pension options

There is a wide range of options from which to choose. The factors that you need to consider depend initially on whether you work for yourself or for someone else.

■ You work for someone else

If you are already in a company or occupational scheme you need to ask:

- How good is the scheme? If it's a defined benefit scheme (see page 181) is it adequately funded?

- What pension can I expect?

- Am I entitled to other benefits?

- Can I improve my entitlements by making additional contributions?

If you are not in a scheme you need to think about:

- Joining one if there is one to join,

- getting your employer to set up a scheme, or

- contributing to your own personal pension plan or PRSA.

■ You work for yourself

If you are self-employed, then your only option is to contribute to your own pension fund. There are a number of questions that you need to consider. For instance, if you work for your own company you may be better off setting up a company scheme and have it make the contributions. But either way ask yourself:

- How much should you be investing?

- Should you make regular contributions or invest occasional lump sums?

- Where do you invest your money? There are many companies and a range of funds to consider. There's even the option of administering your own fund. The following sections will help to provide answers to those questions.

Occupational pension schemes

Less than four out of every 10 private sector workers are in company pension schemes. That includes those who are in industry-wide occupational schemes. Even if you are one of the lucky ones, it doesn't mean that you can look forward to an adequate pension. Much depends on the type of scheme and its rules. They can vary greatly from one to the other. If you are not in a scheme and there isn't one for you to join, you can either get your employer to set one up or else contribute to a personal pension plan of your own in the same way as a self-employed person might.

Rights of pension scheme members

☐ **INFORMATION ENTITLEMENTS:** Members of pension schemes are entitled to the following information: basic information about the scheme's benefits, contributions etc; copies of the trust deed and rules of the scheme; an annual statement showing the individual's current entitlements; annual reports giving audited accounts; actuarial reports; and an investment report. Some of that information must be given automatically to members, prospective members and their trade unions. All of it must be available at least on request. Schemes with more than 100 members must produce a statement of investment policy, principles and objectives.

TRUSTEES: Members in schemes covering more than 50 people are entitled to elect at least two trustees if requested by 15% of members or a trade union.

PRESERVED PENSIONS: A pension fund member with over two years qualifying service is entitled to a preserved pension if he leaves the job. Alternatively pension entitlements may be transferred into a new pension scheme, a PRSA or into an approved pension bond. Refunds are not allowed.

CONTRIBUTION PAYMENTS: Contributions stopped by an employer from pay have to be lodged to the pension fund within 15 days of the end of the month in which the deductions were made.

INDEX LINKING: Pensions don't have to be index-linked to inflation or wage increases but the actuarial reports on pension schemes have to comment on the effects that indexing would have on the fund.

FUND SURPLUSES: In the event of a wind-up or transfer, employers and trustees have to consult with members on the treatment of any surplus that may be in the fund. But having consulted they can take any action allowed under the scheme rules.

WORKERS ON LOW PAY: The minimum pension payment must be at least equal to 120% of the member's personal contributions plus interest.

PENSIONS BOARD: The Pensions Board can be contacted at Verschoyle House, 28-30 Lower Mount Street, Dublin 2. Phone 1890 656565.

PENSIONS OMBUDSMAN: Complaints with regard to the mal-administration of schemes can be made to Paul Kenny at The Office of the Pensions Ombudsman, 36 Upper Mount Street, Dublin, 2. Phone (01) 6471650.

Employers have to at least collect contributions from pay for those workers who want to save for retirement through a PRSA although they do not have to make contributions themselves. (See the next section). If you are in a company or other occupational pension scheme how good is it? If it doesn't rate too highly there are ways to get a better pension.

There was a proposal in the National Pensions Framework to introduce auto-enrolment pension schemes for all workers who don't already have pension coverage. The target date was 2014 but it is unclear if the proposal will go ahead. Workers enrolled in these schemes would be required to contribute 2% of their pay which would be matched by 2% from the employer and, as originally proposed, by a 1% State top-up. That top-up would be equivalent to tax relief at the rate of 33% which was to be applied to all pension contributions. But that is at odds with the subsequent proposal to standardise tax relief at 20% which was also in doubt at the end of 2011.

■ How good is your scheme?

There are two basic types of pension scheme, defined benefit and defined contribution. In a defined benefit scheme, the pension payable is usually based on final salary and years of service. Worker contributions, if required, are usually fixed as a percentage of pay. The employer accepts an open-ended commitment to make whatever additional contributions are necessary to fund the guaranteed level of pension. Most older schemes are of this type but many have closed for new entrants while others have funding difficulties that are being addressed in a number of ways.

Some are hoping for an upturn in investment fortunes and are being allowed time to try to meet the funding standards laid down by the Pensions Board. Contribution levels have been raised in many cases.

In a defined contribution scheme, as the name implies, it is the level of contribution that's fixed. Usually both employer and employee contribute a set percentage of pay. The eventual pension depends both on the amount contributed over the years and the performance of the funds into which the money is put. The pension level is not guaranteed and the employer is not faced with an open-ended commitment as in the case of a defined benefit scheme. The best defined benefit schemes provide:

- An initial pension of 2/3rds final pay after 40 years service,

- A built-in widow/er's pension which can be as much as the full pension,

- Annual increases after retirement at least in line with inflation, and

- No reduction in the pension to take account of State pension entitlements.

A company pension scheme can provide a pension of two-thirds final salary plus social welfare although very few actually do.

That was the standard to aim for but for the foreseeable future it can only be a dream for those not already in such schemes and, for many of those who are, it must be viewed as a promise that may not be realised. But those pension entitlements are broadly in line with the maximum benefits allowed by the Revenue Commissioners. Contributions aimed at funding benefits over and above that level aren't eligible for tax relief. The Revenue rules are fairly liberal with regard to fine print conditions attaching to pension schemes. Some schemes are much more restrictive in the definition of final pay, for instance:

If your **defined benefit** scheme provides less than the maximum allowed by the Revenue rules, or if you won't have sufficient service to qualify for the maximum pension, then you should qualify for tax relief on additional voluntary contributions made to enhance your benefits. If you are in a **defined contribution** scheme you need to be constantly checking the build-up of your fund and the benefits you can expect. The annual statement, that you are entitled to, is required to show a reasonable forecast of what you can expect on the basis of expected contributions and investment returns.

■ Improving your entitlements

If you decide that your pension entitlements are inadequate and you don't have much hope of having your pension

Last minute voluntary pension contributions

☐ There is no time limit on the making of additional voluntary contributions to a pension scheme. They can be made any time during your working life. The earlier you start, of course, the better the return will be in terms of an enhanced pension. The sooner the money goes, in the longer it has to grow. But so long as you qualify for tax relief at a rate higher than you'll be paying in retirement it's possible to make a return on contributions made even in the last few weeks before retirement. The attraction is greatly diminished for those getting relief at only 20%, and on current plans, that will be everyone from 2014. But there is still some gains to be made.

Even if you are going to qualify for the maximum pension under your particular scheme, that may be less than the maximum allowed by the Revenue Commissioners. Your scheme, for instance, may only take basic pay into account while the Revenue allows you to fund for a pension based on a wider definition of pay including overtime, shift allowances and the value of benefits-in-kind. Your scheme may only provide for a pension of two-thirds final pay including your social welfare pension. Most defined benefit schemes do. But Revenue rules allow you to fund for a pension of two-thirds final pay plus social welfare and still qualify for tax relief. There may even be scope for claiming tax relief on additional contributions even if you are going to qualify for the maximum public sector pension. The Revenue recently conceded that with interest rates so low, this level of pension entitlement falls short of the maximum allowed for tax relief.

Those who make last-minute AVCs can backdate a claim for tax relief over two years on a maximum of 40% of pay in both the current and previous tax years. That 40% applies only if you are over 60 and includes any basic pension contributions that are being made. So if you are already putting 5% into the scheme, you can claim tax relief on a further 35% for each year. On retirement the money accumulated in the AVC may, in some cases, enhance the tax-free lump sum that can be taken immediately. If the maximum tax-free lump sum is already being taken, the AVC money can be transferred into an approved retirement fund (ARF or AMRF). Provided the pensioner has other income of at least €18,000 a year, the money in that fund can be drawn down at will. Otherwise it has to be left until he or she is 75. Money drawn out is subject to tax in the normal way but many pensioners are exempt from tax and few are subject to tax at the top rate. So in many cases the AVC money that qualified for tax relief when it was put into the fund can be drawn out tax free.

scheme improved, then your only option is to start saving to secure improved benefits for yourself by making additional voluntary contributions (AVCs). Most private sector schemes allow members to either contribute more money to the existing pension fund or, alternatively, to contribute to their own personal fund such as a Personal Retirement Savings Account (see page 187).

There are pros and cons for both options. Setting up a scheme of your own involves costs that may be avoided by contributing extra money into the company scheme. But a personal scheme is more flexible particularly in the choice of investments.

But whatever option you choose, there is no doubt that if your aim is to boost income in retirement there's a clear advantage in saving through a pension fund. That way you can get tax relief on every cent you save up to generous limits laid down by the Revenue Commissioners. Contributions up to the following percentages of pay are allowed in full for tax relief on condition that they won't provide you with benefits in excess of the very generous maximum levels set by the Revenue Commissioners. The maximum earnings taken into account in applying these percentages is €150,000 in 2010 and €115,000 in 2011. For a high earning 60 year old, the maximum contribution allowed for tax relief in 2012 and 2011 is €46,000 – 40% of €115,000.

Age	Limit	Age	Limit
up to 30	15%	30 but less than 40	20%
40 but less than 50	25%	50 but less than 55	30%
55 but less than 60	35%	60 or over	40%

There is an added advantage in that the fund built up through AVCs doesn't have to be used to buy a pension on retirement as was once the case. Up to a quarter of the fund can be withdrawn immediately on retirement tax free, subject to a maximum of one-and-a-half years salary. Salary is defined by Revenue to include overtime and other additional earnings that may not be taken into account in the benefits provided by the occupational scheme. Money accumulated through additional voluntary contributions does not have to be used to buy an additional pension for life. There are other options. For details see page 189.

Whether you are self-employed or working for someone else you can set up your own personal pension plan. If you work for yourself, it may be your only option but if you are an employee, you may see it as an alternative or addition to an occupational scheme. If you are self-employed and work for your own company, you can have it set up a company pension scheme even if you are going to be the only member. The alternative, which is also open to employees, is to contribute to your own pension scheme or open a PRSA. The following are points to consider in making the choice.

■ Company schemes

Where the self-employed person works for his or her own company, there are advantages in having the company set up the scheme. The net cost is likely to be lower and the restriction on the size of contributions that qualify for tax relief is less onerous. There can also be tax advantages in having your company pay all the contributions rather than paying them yourself into a personal plan. Also, where an employer is willing to make some contribution to an employee's pension, it can be more tax efficient to set up a formal scheme rather than paying the worker the extra money and letting him or her take out a personal pension plan.

Apart from the possible tax advantages within a company scheme there can be more flexibility in opting for early retirement. The balance of advantages depends on individual circumstances. Where a company scheme is deemed best it may even be worthwhile setting up a company simply to avail of that option but that has other implications. Professional advice is advisable.

■ Personal pension plans and PRSAs

If you are self-employed, or in a job with an inadequate pension scheme or no pension scheme, then you can contribute to your own personal pension plan or Personal Retirement Savings Account (PRSA). You pay all the contributions and you decide where the money is to be invested. If you want to save for your retirement then it's about the best option available.

- You get tax relief on the contributions.

- The tax relief also applies to contributions made to a life insurance policy that is part of the plan.

- You can withdraw 25% of the fund tax free on retirement.

- Subject to some conditions the remainder of the fund does not have to be used to fund a pension.

It's not difficult to set up a personal pension plan. The options have been widened greatly with the introduction of Personal Retirement Savings Accounts (PRSAs) which, although aimed mainly at employees without pension cover, are also an option for the self-employed.

Self-administered pension schemes

If you are putting sizeable sums into a pension fund it is possible to control your own investment strategy and even have the fund borrow to finance property or other investments. The costs of establishing and managing such a fund are significant and only worthwhile if the fund is fairly large so they are really only an option for relatively high earners. Self-administered pension schemes usually have fewer than 12 members, but Revenue approval for borrowing is only given to single member schemes. There are restrictions on the assets that can be held by such schemes. It is not permissible to buy, sell, lease or rent property to or from any beneficiary of the scheme. In other words you can't get the pension fund to invest in your house or in property used by your business. Neither can it invest in 'pride of possession' assets such as works of art, a holiday home, antiques, etc.

Picking the right plan

There is no single pension plan that is best for all people. There's even an element of luck involved in making the choice since there is no way of knowing in advance how various investments are going to perform in the future. But you are more likely to make a good choice by asking the right questions and getting good advice. The following are some of the basic choices that have to be made.

Personal Retirement Savings Accounts

☐ Personal Retirement Savings Accounts (PRSAs) offer a low cost, flexible way of saving for retirement. They can be used by the self-employed, employees who are not in occupational pension schemes and even by employees who are in pension schemes but who want to improve their pension entitlements by making additional voluntary contributions (AVCs). They may or may not be more attractive than existing AVC arrangements. It's important to look at the costs and how the money is being invested.

A PRSA is simply a personal investment account subject to the restriction that the funds cannot be accessed until retirement. They are issued by insurance companies, banks and other financial institutions and are open to everyone even those who are not employed subject to a minimum contribution of €300 a year. They are flexible in that there must be a facility to vary contributions from year to year. Tax relief can be claimed on contributions while the proportion of income on which the relief can be claimed varies with age.

Age	Proportion of pay	Age	Proportion of pay
Under 30	15%	50 to 54	30%
30 to 39	20%	55 to 59	35%
40 to 49	25%	Over 60	40%

☐ Irrespective of income, an individual contributing to a non-AVC PRSA can claim tax relief on up to €1,525 a year. An individual not liable for tax can carry that relief forward to set against a future tax liability. The maximum income taken into account is €150,000 in 2010 and €115,000 in 2011. The charges on standard PRSAs may not exceed 5% of each contribution plus an ongoing management charge of 1% of the accumulating fund. Those are maximum levels. Some companies charge less. There is no cap on the charges in respect of non-standard PRSAs and no reason to believe that they will on average perform any better than their standard counterparts.

☐ Employers who do not operate company pension schemes for all their employees or who do not offer an AVC arrangement are required to set up at least one standard PRSA for their workers. They must arrange to stop contributions from pay but they do not have to contribute themselves. They do, however, save employer's PRSI on the contributions made by their workers since they are not considered to be income for tax or PRSI purposes. On retirement, usually after age 60, a quarter of the value of the PRSA can be taken as a tax-free lump sum. The remainder can be used to buy a pension or be put into an Approved Retirement Fund (ARF) – see page 191.

■ Personal pension plan or PRSA

There are technical differences between the two but these are of less importance in making a choice than the actual specifics of the individual options. So the decision is best made on the basis of other criteria such as cost, flexibility, the investment options available.

■ Cost

The costs involved in building up a pension fund usually include a set-up cost applied to each contribution and an annual management charge applied to the ongoing value of the fund. The rates vary from company to company and may also vary from fund to fund. On standard PRSAs, the charge on contributions can be no more than 5% while the annual management fee can be no more than 1%. No other charges are allowed on standard PRSAs.

■ Regular premium or lump sum?

Most of the newer personal pension plans and all PRSAs allow you to alter contribution levels from year to year. That flexibility can be very important to someone whose income may fluctuate. An alternative is to make annual lump sum contributions into a pension fund. Each investment is a separate transaction. The lump sums may go into different funds or even different companies.

If you work for a company and make regular contributions through the payroll, you will automatically get the tax relief. If you make lump sum contributions on your own, you have to pay the gross amount up front and claim the tax relief.

The advantage of contributing occasional lump sums is flexibility. One disadvantage, apart from the delay in getting your tax relief, is that it is too easy to forget the initial good intentions and fail to make the investment each year. With regular contributions there is an element of compulsion.

■ Type of fund?

The final decision is where to invest your money. There are many companies and a wide range of funds to consider. Professional advice is well worthwhile. The investment performance of the fund can make a very significant difference to the size of pension you eventually enjoy. So too can the set-up and ongoing management charges. They differ from company to company and sometimes even from fund to fund. Equities are an ideal choice for investments made well before retirement.

Over the longer term, equities have yielded a far better return than bonds or bank deposits although over the shorter-term, and sometimes even over the medium terms, share values can be volatile as has been very evident in recent years. As a good rule of thumb it makes some sense to invest in equity funds for the best long-term returns before moving into safer investment options closer to retirement. The risk varies with the type of fund and you can always mix and match to build up your own portfolio. It is up to you to work out your own attitude to risk. Then take advice, and make your choice remembering that it is prudent to reduce your exposure to risk as you approach retirement age.

Collecting your pension

Members of occupational pension funds often face difficult choices when they reach retirement age. There's possibly little that can be done about the overall value of pension entitlements at this stage but there are usually decisions to be made about how the entitlements should be taken.

- Is it best to take the maximum possible lump sum?

- Is it best to accept a reduced initial pension to secure entitlement to a survivor's pension for your partner?

- If you have been making additional voluntary contributions, is it best to use the accumulated fund to buy an enhanced pension or to transfer it into an approved retirement fund?

Choices have to be made and there is no way of knowing in advance what decision is going to prove the most financially advantageous. But you stand a better chance of getting it right by carefully considering all of the options in the light of your best assumptions about those factors over which you have no control. Let's have a look at each of those issues in turn.

■ Tax free lump sum

The generous tax relief allowed on pension contributions is justified as an incentive to encourage people to save for retirement. The Revenue requires that the bulk of the money be used to provide a pension for life but the rules do allow a portion of it to be taken as a tax-free lump sum. Different rules apply to the self-employed and those with personal pension plans but here we are only considering workers in company pension schemes.

The size of this lump sum depends on the length of service up to a maximum of one-and-a-half times final pay after 20 years service subject to a cap of €200,000 from 2011.

Sums between €200,000 and €575,000 are taxed at 20% and sums above €575,000 are subject to tax at the person's marginal income tax rate.

There is a choice between taking the lump sum and getting a lower pension or not taking the lump sum and qualifying for a higher pension. The actual sums will vary from individual to individual. So which is best?

As a rule of thumb it is better to take the tax-free lump sum. With most pension schemes the actual pension is only guaranteed for five years. If you die within that period it continues to be paid until the end of the five years and then stops. If you die after five years it stops right away. Usually if you were to invest the lump sum in a deposit account it wouldn't yield enough to make up for the pension foregone. But you'll have the lump sum and have got it tax free while the pension would be taxable although that is only relevant if you are liable for tax. If you live a very long life it might work out that you would have been financially better off by not taking the lump sum. But you will have enjoyed extra flexibility by having the money under your control.

■ Widow/er's pension

Some pension schemes have a widow or widower's pension built in. There's no choice to be made. Very often the surviving spouse gets half of the original pension for life. But if there isn't an automatic survivor's pension built in, you may be given a choice between taking a smaller pension and the knowledge that the surviving spouse will continue to get half of it on your death or a larger pension that will die with you. For someone with inadequate pension entitlements to start with, it can be a very hard choice.

If your spouse dies before you, the choice will have been immaterial and you may have given up some of your pension for nothing. It's a very personal decision and can't be made solely on financial grounds although the extent of any other resources that would be available to a surviving spouse is obviously relevant. It's a decision that no-one should be asked to make particularly at a time when they are facing a traumatic change in their lives.

■ AVCs, PRSAs and personal pension fund

If you have built up your fund through a personal pension, a PRSA or with AVCs, or in a defined contribution scheme, you face a range of options on retirement. Those options also apply to someone in a company scheme who owns more than 5% of the company. In these cases, a quarter of the fund can be withdrawn as a tax-free lump sum.

The remainder can be used to buy a pension for life — an annuity, or invest in an approved retirement fund (ARF) or an Approved Minimum Retirement Fund (AMRF). The choice is up to you although the Revenue Commissioners do set some limitations. Any money that hasn't been taken as a tax-free lump sum or used to buy an annuity has to be invested in either an ARF or an AMRF. Unless the pensioner has an income of at least €18,000 (one-and-a-half times the maximum Contributory State Pension) some of the fund must be kept in an AMRF until the pensioner is 75. Any money not required to be kept in a fund as a result of this rule can be drawn down so it is possible to take a regular income. Canada Life has an ARF product which allows for a guaranteed income for life to be taken from the fund.

It is possible to take a regular income from an Approved Retirement Fund. One provider offers a guaranteed income

The disincentive against drawing down too much, too quickly, is that money taken out of the fund is subject to income tax in the normal way. In 2007 a notional 1% of the value of an ARF fund was deemed for tax purposes to have been withdrawn, whether it is taken out or not. That notional 1% was added to the taxable income of the ARF's owner. The notional withdrawal was raised to 3% in 2009, 5% in 2011 and 6% in 2012 on funds valued more than €2 million. The amount to be kept is a minimum of whatever is left after taking the maximum tax-free lump sum subject to a maximum of 10 times the maximum Contributory State Pension (about €120,000).

Up to, and including, 2010 the income requirement to avoid having to put money into an AMRF was €12,700 and the maximum that had to be kept in the fund was €63,500. Those with an existing AMRF can have it redesignated as an ARF, and thus get access to the money, if their income in 2011, 2012 and 2013 goes above €12,700. From 2014 the new level of one-and-half times the maximum annual Contributory State pension will apply.

An ARF or AMRF must be managed by an approved fund manager such as an insurance company, bank or an investment intermediary who are licensed to hold money on behalf of clients and there are some restrictions on how the money can be invested. It used to be possible to invest some of the money in personal use assets such as yachts or holiday homes. But that is no longer allowed. Any money left in the pension fund on death becomes part of the deceased person's estate. There is no tax on its transfer into a ARF in the name of a surviving spouse. In other cases, liability for income tax at 30%, inheritance tax or both can arise. The rules are complicated. If there is a lot of money involved get professional advice.

Marital breakdown

The rights of spouses to benefits from a pension scheme are not defined in any law. But the laws covering judicial separation and divorce allow the courts to make orders allocating such benefits between spouses in the event of separation or divorce. So part or all the pension rights of one spouse may be allocated to the other even though he or she had not made any financial contribution to it. The actual application of these powers depends on the courts and individual circumstances. All pension rights are covered from both defined contribution and defined benefit company schemes, personal pension plans and State schemes.

> *I asked God to increase my profits but I know that it doesn't work like that,*
> *so I ripped off the customers and asked God for forgiveness — Anon*

11 Using your rights as a consumer

Consumers enjoy a far greater degree of protection from mis-selling, fraud and incompetence than they did even a short few years ago and rights were further enhanced by the enactment of the Consumer Protection Act 2007. Since then there has been new codes of conduct introduced for providers and financial services and protections for those with mortgage arrears. The National Consumer Agency has taken over the educational and information role in the area of financial services that was formally the remit of the Financial Regulator and there is a proposal to merge it with the Competition Authority. There are also major changes proposed in the legal services area.

While many of the provisions of the 2007 Act were simply a consolidation of previous legislation, it also transposed into Irish law the EU Directive on Unfair Commercial Practices, the provisions of which greatly extend consumer rights. It makes it unlawful for businesses to exploit consumers by the use of unfair commercial practices. A practice is considered unfair if the trader is not acting in good faith or without the standard of care and skill that would be reasonably expected by an 'average consumer'. The European Court of Justice defined an 'average consumer' as one reasonably well informed and reasonably observant and circumspect. That's a general provision and the Act includes some examples:

- The provision of false and misleading information with regard to anything from the prior usage of a second-hand item to the country of origin.

- Trying to pass off products as something they are not by use of misleading or counterfeited trade names.

- Withholding or concealing material information of a product or service or of its full price.

- Measures aimed at pressurising, intimidating or taking advantage of vulnerable consumers.

- Persistent sales techniques.

There are bound to be grey areas with regard to all of those and it may require test court cases to determine where the boundaries lie between unfair and acceptable. Some of those cases may be taken by consumers but the Agency may take some cases itself to test the waters and create precedences.

Some commercial practices are deemed unfair in all circumstances

There are some practices, however, that are deemed unfair in all circumstances and therefore prohibited. They include making false claims such as:

- Having the endorsement of a regulatory body.

- Being about to cease trading.

- Providing a cure for illnesses.

- Promising free goods or services when it costs money to claim them.

- Claiming that a product is in short supply to promote sales.

- Sending out false invoices.

- Demanding payment for unsolicited goods.

- Directing advertising at children.

Where to complain

FINANCIAL SERVICES	Financial Regulator Dame Street, Dublin 2. Tel. 1890 777 777
	Financial Services Ombudsman 3rd Floor, Lincoln House, Lincoln St, Dublin 2 Tel: 1890 88 20 90
Insurance companies	Irish Insurance Federation, Russell Court, St. Stephen's Green, Dublin 2.
GOODS AND SERVICES	National Consumer Agency 4 Harcourt Road, Dublin 2 Tel. 1890 432 432 www.Irishconsumer.ie
DATA PROTECTION	Data Protection Commissioner, Station Road, Portarlington, Co. Laois Tel. 1890 252 231
SOLICITORS	The Law Society, Blackhall Place, Dublin 7. Independent Adjudicator of the Law Society, 26/27 Upper Pembroke Street, Dublin 2.
PENSIONS	The Office of the Pensions Ombudsman, PO Box 9324, 36 Upper Mount Street, Dublin 2. Tel. (01) 6471650.
EUROPEAN UNION	The European Ombudsman, 1, avenue du President Robert Schuman, B.P. 403, F - 67001 Strasbourg Cedex.

Also prohibited under the Act is pyramid selling and 'gifting' schemes. While most of the Act only covers transaction that are of a business to consumer nature, these activities are banned even when they involve consumer to consumer transactions and they can attract severe penalties. Pyramid selling offences carry a fine of up to €150,000 and/or imprisonment for a term of up to five years. Those convicted of other breaches of the Act also face hefty penalties of up to €600,000 and 18 months in prison. The Agency has other options besides taking errant traders to Court. It can impose compliance notices or seek an undertaking that doubtful practices will be discontinued. Such undertakings may include an agreement to compensate affected consumers. So the Agency can directly help consumers and should be the first port of call for those with complaints.

Aggrieved consumers can alternatively seek redress through the courts and, under the Act, they can be awarded both damages for any loss suffered and also exemplary damages. The Agency can take cases on behalf of consumers but it is more likely to take test cases on practices that affect large numbers of consumers rather than just one individual.

It has considered taking such an action against airlines over their pricing and information practices particularly on their web sites but it seems to prefer getting agreement on change without the need for Court actions.

For instance, it managed to get compensation for Barbra Streisand fans who were less than impressed by the organisation of her Irish concert and it also lodged a formal and very detailed submission on proposed changes to Dublin's toll bridge charges.

But the Agency can and does tackle individual complaints and because of its powers to seek undertakings from traders including agreement on compensation payments, it is, in all cases, a good place to start if you have a complaint to make. Its website is a mine of information on consumer rights and it has also published a range of booklets and leaflets. It can be contacted through the website www.Irishconsumer.ie or on its phone helpline at 1890 432 432.

Financial services

The National Consumer Agency has a role in providing consumer information in this area but the Financial Regulator continues to oversee the activities of all financial intermediaries. That includes insurance intermediaries, financial advisers, brokers, etc. It doesn't deal with complaints, however. There is an ombudsman who adjudicates on disputes involving financial institutions and another dealing with the mal-administration of pension schemes.

The Financial Services Ombudsman can make awards of up to €250,000 to individuals which are binding on both parties subject to an appeal to the High Court. The scheme covers banks, building societies, insurance companies, credit unions, mortgage, insurance, credit intermediaries, stockbrokers, pawnbrokers, moneylenders, bureaux de change, hire purchase providers and health insurance companies.

He can consider complaints relating to events that occurred within the previous six years. Before going to the Ombudsman, you must first make a complaint to the company itself. All the banks and building societies have designated managers to deal with complaints. Obviously you should try to sort out any problem at local level first, then take it to the head office of the bank or building society. If you are still not satisfied, you can then take the matter to the Ombudsman.

He is unlikely to look at a complaint unless it has been through the complaints procedures of the institutions involved. He is open to complaints from individuals, organisations and sole traders and will also consider complaints from companies whose annual turnover is under €3 million. He can't consider matters of company policy. For instance, he will not adjudicate on a complaint about the general level of bank charges. But he can, of course, deal with a complaint about the application of those charges in an individual case.

If your claim is for less than €2,000, another option is to take a case to the Small Claims Court. It need cost no more than €15 and is no more complicated that making a complaint to the Ombudsman. While the Ombudsman normally operates in private, cases heard in the Small Claims Court are open to the public and the prospect of adverse publicity may help to speed up a settlement. See page 201 for details about how to go about it.

The Consumer Credit Act provides protection against unscrupulous lenders while a range of regulations make it com-

Consumers have plenty of legal safeguards but they are useless unless they are enforced

Where a claim involves less than €2,000 the Small Claims Court offers an alternative to the Financial Services Ombudsman pulsory for life insurance companies and intermediaries to give consumers more information on, among other things, the costs involved in buying their products. Through the Small Claims Courts consumers have a low cost means of processing claims of up to €2,000. Some of these protective measures have the backing of law while in other cases professional bodies operate their own regulatory codes.

Financial advisers

The operations of all financial advisers are regulated by the Financial Regulator. Only those authorised advisers who are also authorised cash holders can handle a client's money. With all other advisers, the money transaction takes place directly between the consumer and the investment company itself. The Regulator has drawn up very detailed codes of how intermediaries must operate including a requirement that they draw up a statement indicating why they believe that a suggested product is suitable for the particular client. For more details see page 46.

The law also requires companies to produce a wide range of information to customers on the true cost of a product, the amount of commission and other remuneration that will go to the intermediary, the exact purpose of the product and the penalties that may be incurred on early encashment. For further details see page 93.

Solicitors

Self-regulation of the legal professions is to be abolished under new legislation that was before the Dáil at the end of 2011. There is to be a new authority to regulate both solicitors and barristers. Only four of its 11 members will be nominated by the Law Society and Bar Council. The role of the taxing master in resolving disputes over fees is to be taken over by a new Legal Costs Adjudicator. There is a promise of more transparency. And an independent complaints' structure is to be established.

These are definite steps forward but many other changes recommended by the Competition Authority, and in various other reports since the 1980s, have been effectively long fingered. The new Legal Services Regulatory Authority will have wide ranging powers. But at this stage it is only being charged with reviewing and coming up with proposals on a multitude of reforms that have already been explored in detail over the years and on which the Competition Authority and others have made very specific recommendations.

It could take time and for the present the old procedures still apply. Solicitors are members of the Law Society of Ireland and it is to that body that complaints should first be directed after, of course, they have first been made to the individual concerned. The Law Society has its own complaints procedures. Complaints may be referred to the Disciplinary Tribunal of the High Court or, in the case of excessive fees, to the Taxing Master, at the Four Courts, Dublin 7.

Where a complainant is dissatisfied with the manner in which the Law Society has dealt with a complaint, he or she may refer it to the Independent Adjudicator of the Law Society whose role is to ensure that complaints are dealt with fairly and impartially by the Law Society.

The Adjudicator only considers the Society's handling of a complaint against the solicitor, not the actual complaint itself. The Adjudicator cannot award compensation and cannot consider any matters which have been dealt with by the Society's Compensation Fund Committee, the Disciplinary Tribunal of the High Court or the Taxing Master. Complaints have to be made in writing and should include a copy of the Society's decision and confirmation that the subject matter of the complaint has not already been considered by the Disciplinary Tribunal of the High Court.

In all cases the first complaint is made to the Law Society

Access to personal files

Some leading telecommunications companies were prosecuted during 2011 for breaches of the direct marketing provisions of the Data Protection Act. The cases, brought by the Data Protection Commissioner, related to both phone calls and text messages and were prompted by complaints received from consumers. In the dock were Eircom, O_2, UPC and Vodafone.

All four admitted breaches of the Act but may be considered to have got off lightly. UPC was fined €7,100 and Vodafone, €3,850. Eircom and O2 were let off having agreed to donate €2,000 each to designated charities. But while the punishment was relatively light, the Commissioner believes that taking the cases has sent a strong message to businesses that they need to comply with the law.

It's a message that clearly needs to be got across not only to business but also to consumers who can all too easily leave themselves open to junk mail and spam that they would prefer not to receive and who don't know how to stop it. Stopping the unwanted intrusions is not always easy. Much depends on the type of junk or spam that you are getting. The following is a brief guide.

■ ## Post

Businesses are required to comply with written results to cease sending marketing materials by post. One letter to the Irish Direct Marketing Association, 8 Upper Fitzwilliam Street, Dublin 2, will cover many of the largest direct marketing companies.

This only covers mail sent to you under your own name and not flyers and local newspapers etc that are simply dropped into the letter box.

■ ## Phone calls

For fixed lines you can contact the company to which you pay line rental informing it that you don't want to receive marketing calls. That preference is then recorded on the National Directory Database and has to be complied with except by businesses to which you have given specific permission to contact you.

To stop marketing calls to your mobile, you simply have to ask the caller not to call again. It's against the law to ignore such a request.

■ ## Electronic mail

The rules with regard to emails, text and voice messages etc, are a bit more complicated. The Data Protection Commis-

You have a right to see any information being held about you by individuals or businesses

Making use of the small claims court

☐ Have you ever bought faulty goods or paid for less than adequate service? Who hasn't? Complaints often go unheeded but you can take your case to the Small Claims Courts for only €15. The most you can claim is €2,000 and the dispute must normally relate to the purchase of goods or services from someone selling them in the course of business. Also covered are claims for damage to privately owned property. Precluded are claims for accidents, damages or for the recovery of payments under a loan or agreement. Landlord/tenant issues are dealt with by the Private Residential Tenancies Board.

The scheme is administered by the Small Claims Registrar at local District Court Offices throughout the country. You can look up the address and telephone number in the telephone directory or on the internet at www.courts.ie. The first approach is to the Registrar who will provide help in drawing up a statement of claim. A special form makes the job relatively easy. A non-refundable fee is payable at this stage. A copy of the claim is sent to the person against whom it is made. If no answer is received within 15 days, the claim is treated as undisputed and the District Court will make an order for the amount claimed to be paid within a stipulated time.

If the claim is disputed, the Registrar will try to reach an agreed settlement between the parties at an informal meeting. This is held in private. Both parties may be asked to outline the facts of the case and they may be asked questions by the Registrar. His aim is not to make a judgement but rather to reach an agreed settlement. Either side can bring forward witnesses or present expert reports. But the parties have to pay for these themselves. If the Registrar fails to get a settlement agreed, the matter is referred to the District Court and is heard before a judge. The hearing may not be in private and will, of course, be more formal. The parties may be asked to answer questions on oath. The Registrar attends the Court hearing to outline the facts.

There is provision for witnesses to be summoned to appear before either the Registrar or the Court. The Registrar will help in issuing the summons but it is up to the individual requesting the witness to pay any expenses involved. There is nothing to stop either party hiring a solicitor to represent them but the whole idea is to keep the cost down and there is no need for a solicitor. People who don't get their awards can go back to the Small Claims Registrar and have the matter passed to a sheriff or county registrar for collection. But even that is not a surefire way of getting the money. Not all the decrees passed to sheriffs for collection are enforced. Still most claimants win something.

sioners accepts that a business may consider to have some relationship with a consumer for twelve months after the last transaction.

At the time they obtain your personal data businesses are required to tell you why they need the information and who it may be disclosed to. They must also tell you how you can, without cost, withdraw your consent to having your personal data used for direct marketing purposes.

■ Electoral register

Local authorities maintain two versions of the electoral register. The information on what is know as the "edited version" can be used by direct marketeers. You can check whether or not your name is on the "edited" version at your local public library or garda station. You can also check at www.checktheregister.ie. Your local authority can arrange to have your name removed from the "edited" version.

The number of businesses holding personal data has increased dramatically. The Date Protection Commissioner keeps a register

Many companies, organisations and public bodies gather personal information on individuals and can hold it on file in any form of structured filing system. Subject to certain limitations they have a right to do so but the individual has a right to access that data, in so far as it relates to themselves, and to have it changed if it is factually incorrect. Those rights are given under the Data Protection Act and, in the case of public bodies, the Freedom of Information Act which also gives rights of access to a much wider range of information.

Under the Data Protection Act, individuals have a right of access to most personal files relating to themselves held on computer by companies and other organisations. Public sector organisations, financial institutions, providers of credit ratings, holders of direct mail lists, and those who keep sensitive information about such things as racial origin, political or other beliefs etc. are required to register with the Data Protection Commissioner. That register is open to the public and contains details of the type of information held.

The right of access covers not only the files of those companies and organisations required to register but anybody with personal information on file. In response to a written enquiry you have the right to be told what sort of information is kept on file and to see files relating to yourself. You are also entitled to be informed of the source of any data kept about you although the holder of the data can refuse to tell you if getting the information would involve "disproportionate effort" or affect trade secrets or copyright.

There is no legal right to have data removed from company files provided it's correct and has been properly collected for an explicitly stated purpose. But you have a right to access most personal files relating to yourself held by companies and other organisations either on computer or in paper based files held in a structured filing system. You can check that it's correct and is only being used for the stated purpose and no other.

To access the information, of course, you need to know that it exists and there is no sure-fire way of knowing who is keeping tabs on you. An ever increasing amount of personal data is being collected and retained in both private and State data bases. Lending institutions share information on your credit worthiness. Supermarkets use loyalty cards to collect information on your shopping preferences. Doctors and hospitals keep medical information about you. Even voluntary organisations, such as charities, very often maintain data bases of actual and potential contributors.

In response to a written enquiry you have the right to be told what sort of information an organisation or business keeps on file and see the files relating to yourself. Some data including police and prison files is exempt. Your first approach should be to the person or organisation you think is holding files on you. You should write to them along the following lines -

"Please send me a copy of any information you keep on file about me. I am making this request under the Data Protection Act."

You should give any information which might help the individual or organisation to identify you. You should get the information within 40 days and you may be asked to pay up to €6.35. If you experience any difficulty or if you want to see the register of data holders you can contact the Data Protection Commissioner at Canal House, Station Road, Portarlington, Co. Laois phone (057) 868 4800 or 1890 252 231.

There is no legal right to have data removed but you can have it corrected

If the information on file is wrong you have, of course, the right to have it corrected and you may have the right to have information completely erased. Corrections must be made to factually wrong data but you have no right to have opinions changed. If, for instance, a school is keeping assessments of its pupils the individual has a right of access to the data and could have actual markings changed if they were wrong. But there is no right to have teachers' opinions with regard to ability, etc. changed.

Where information is being unnecessarily kept, there is a right to have it erased. As mentioned above, the holder of data must have a stated reason for holding it. If the information held is not necessary for that purpose, then you can have it erased. For instance, information on a person's religious beliefs may be appropriate to files held by a hospital, but would be unnecessary to the files of a finance company.

There are many files out there that may be worth looking at and checking. Your employer may have some files, so too might your trade union. Most schools keep files on pupils. Then there are the banks and other financial institutions that maintain credit ratings. They are certainly worth checking if you have had any difficulty getting approval for a loan.

Holders of data have to exercise great care in how they gather and keep it. The data must be obtained fairly, it must be accurate, and it must be kept up to date. It must also only be used for a stated purpose. The purpose for holding the data has to be stated in advance and data said to be kept for one purpose cannot be used for another. The information kept must be adequate for the purpose; it must be relevant and not excessive. It must be erased when it is no longer needed for its stated purpose. Employers are not allowed to use the Act to force employees or job applicants to reveal personal data about themselves. They cannot, for instance force job applicants to produce their detailed personnel files from previous employers.

Freedom of Information Act

The Freedom of Information Act came into force in 1998 and provides wide ranging rights to access information held by public bodies. It doesn't apply to private companies or organisations. Rights under the Act play a role in consumer protection in so far as all citizens are consumers of many State services. In this regard an individual has a right to access his or her own personal files and to have them amended if they are incorrect or misleading. There is also a right to access official files dating back to April 21, 1998 when the Act came into force subject to some limitations. To get access to the information you are looking for you should write to the head of the relevant government department or organisation saying that you are making the request under the Freedom of Information Act.

A fee of €15, or €10 for anyone with a medical card, must accompany the request unless the information sought relates to personal data relating to yourself. You may also be charged for the cost of gathering and photocopying the information. Decisions to refuse access to information can be appealed first to the body concerned and then, if necessary to Emily O'Reilly, Information Commissioner, 18 Lower Leeson Street, Dublin 2, phone (01) 6785222.

Credit ratings

The Irish Credit Bureau, of which most of the leading finance houses are members, provides members of the public with details of their personal credit rating as shown on the Bureau's books. It has been doing this since before the enactment of the Data Protection legislation. The information provided includes the name of the company which registered the information, the relevant account number and what is called the 'conduct grading' of the account — likely to be only one word 'satisfactory' or 'unsatisfactory'.

Most banks, finance companies, building societies and many credit unions are members of the Bureau. It can be contacted at Newstead House, Newstead, Clonskeagh, Dublin 14. Another agency is Experian Ireland, Park House, North Circular Road, Dublin 7. If you are finding difficulty in getting loan finance and you have no idea why, then you should contact the Bureau, Experian Ireland and your bank and ask for details of the information they have on you. Mistakes have been made. The Ombudsman for the Financial

Most financial institutions use credit reporting bureaux to maintain credit ratings on customers and potential customers

Institutions once granted an award for damages to a man who had been refused business loans as a result of a mistake in the information held on a bank's files. The fact that he had paid off a loan early was mistakenly entered as something else on his file and he was effectively blacklisted. So it can happen.

Office of the Ombudsman

The Ombudsman, Emily O'Reilly who is also the Information Commissioner, investigates complaints from individuals about government departments, local authorities, the HSE and the postal services. The office is independent of government and has powers to inspect files, require officials to give information, and make recommendations for redress including compensation. While she has no power to force acceptance of her recommendations, if they are not accepted and acted upon, she can report the fact to the Dáil and Seanad. Complaints, in writing, can be sent to her office at 18 Lower Leeson Street, Dublin 2, phone (01) 6785222, within a year of the action, or lack of action, that is the subject of the complaint.

Consumer Credit

There is a common misconception that banks don't like lending money and are somehow doing customers a favour when they advance them a loan. Nothing is further from the truth, of course. Banks, building societies, finance houses, moneylenders, and pawnbrokers all make their profits by lending money. It's important, of course, that the money is repaid. So lenders do need to be convinced that the borrower won't renege on the repayments. But the borrower is the customer and the lender wants the custom and there is enough competition in the market now for borrowers to use their power as consumers.

That means shopping around for the best possible deal. That's not too difficult to do. But there are other protections. The following are imposed on lenders by either the Consumer Credit Act, the EU Directive or the binding code of conduct.

Creditworthiness: Lenders are required to carry out credit-worthiness checks before loans are granted or rescheduled.

Information: All loan agreements have to be written in plain language and contain a minimum amount of information on interest rates, charges, repayments, what happens if there is a default, etc. If there are two possible meanings to any clause, the Courts have to favour the one most beneficial to the borrower. That provision applies to all consumer agreements under a general consumer protection legislation which ensures that the Courts will not uphold 'unfair conditions'.

A condition is considered to be 'unfair' if, contrary to the requirement of good faith, it causes a significant imbalance in the parties' rights and obligations under the contract to the detriment of the consumer. The borrower must also be given time to read and understand the agreement.

A legal provision, which doesn't apply to bank or building society loans, allows the borrower to apply to the Circuit Court claiming that the terms of an agreement are 'excessive'. The Court will take all the circumstances into account including "the age, business competence and level of literacy and numeracy of the consumer". The Court can effectively rewrite the agreement reducing or eliminating further repayments.

Refused a loan: A person who is refused a loan has the right to request and get information including the name and address of 'any single person' from whom the lender sought information on the financial standing of the would-be borrower. The request has to be made within 28 days and the lender has 14 days to comply.

Interest Rates: The only interest rates that can be quoted in advertisements and agreements are annual percentage rates (APRs) worked out under a fixed formula so that the consumer can compare rates on a like-with-like basis. All costs involved in getting a loan must be included in the calculation including, for instance, the annual Stamp Duty charged on credit cards and fees or commission paid to intermediaries.

Cooling-off Period: Under the EU Directive all loan agreements for between €200 and €75,000, except for mortgages must allow for a 14-day cooling-off period during which the consumer can withdraw from it. Under the Consumer Credit Act, which is still in existence but superseded in this case, consumers were entitled to a 10 day cooling-off period but could waive that right and sometimes did when they were very anxious to get a loan. But consumers are no longer allowed to waive their rights in this regard.

Early Repayment: Lenders are not allowed to charge early repayment penalties on payments of less than €10,000 in any one year. Where penalties are applied to early repayment on fixed rate loans, they cannot exceed 1% of the payment where more than 1 year of the fixed term remains or 0.5% where less than a year remains.

Mortgage lenders are subject to strict legally binding rules on their interactions with borrowers in arrears.
See page 114

Enforcement: There are some limitations imposed on lenders' rights to contact customers. They are barred from contacting consumers at their place of work except in some cases where the borrower has a live-in job. Any contact at home, by phone or personally, has to be between 9 am and 9 pm. The lender has to give 10 days notice in writing of any action he wants to take under the agreement. He also has to detail the action and the date on, or after which, it is intended to take that action.

Where the action has been prompted by a breach of the agreement on the part of the borrower no action can be taken for 21 days. If the borrower gets back on track within that time the lender must not include any reference to it in the customer's credit record.

Lender's Liability: Lenders may be liable to make good any defect in the goods or services bought with a loan. In certain circumstances where the loan is arranged through the supplier and the money is paid directly to the supplier of the goods or services the lender can become liable. Customers must first pursue their rights against the supplier but where that fails the claim can then be pursued against the lender.

Buying house insurance

Mortgage lenders often suggest that borrowers take out house insurance with a particular company or even from one of a group of companies but they cannot force a borrower to do so. However they can require that insurance be taken out and they may impose a charge if the insurance is taken out with a company other than one of those recommended. Taking out house insurance through a building society or bank need not, of course, be a bad thing. Some lenders offer very attractive house insurance packages which are cheaper in many cases than the alternatives.

European Union

There is a European Ombudsman who investigates complaints about mal-administration by institutions and bodies of the European Community. These include the Commission, the European Parliament, the Committee of Regions, the European Investment Bank, and the European Investment Fund. You don't have to be personally affected by the mal-administration, but you must first contact the institution or body concerned to inform it of your complaint. A letter of complaint is sufficient. Complaints should be made in writing. There is a standard form which may be used if you like. You can get a copy from the Ombudsman's office — see page 195 for the address. The Ombudsman tries to find a mutually acceptable solution to the complaint. He can recommend how it might be solved. If the recommendation is not accepted, the Ombudsman can make a special report about the case to the European Parliament.

Goods and services

If the retailer, shopkeeper, or what have you, refuses to rectify a claim, the final judgement on who is right has to be made in court. The Small Claims Court offers a low cost route where the amount involved is less than €2,000. If you have a complaint, your claim is against the retailer or service provider. If you fail to get redress you could try the Small Claims Courts.

The National Consumer Agency can investigate various practices and take direct action against traders who do not comply with the general provisions of the Act and it can help a consumer to get redress but in the absence of an agreed settlement the final recourse has to be to the Courts.

In matters concerning the supply of goods and services consumer protection legislation relates mainly to dealings between a trader and an end-consumer. Most of the protections do not apply to deals between two traders — a retailer and wholesaler, for instance so a consumer may not be covered by the full Act if he does a deal at a "trade price".

When something goes wrong it is almost always the retailer who is, in law, responsible for putting things right. It is he who sold the goods and it is between him and the consumer that the contract was made — a contract for sale, remember, need not be in writing. Even if the manufacturer provides a guarantee against defect in the product it is still the retailer who is responsible to see that things are put right. The law gives the consumer five areas of protection.

- **The goods sold must be made of 'merchantable quality'.** The goods must be capable of being used for the purpose for which they are normally sold. It does not matter if the retailer did not know about the fault. He has a responsibility to the consumer but if there are defects he may cover himself by pointing them out. Goods marked 'seconds' or 'slightly defective', for instance, would not be expected to be of top quality. The buyer also has responsibilities — he or she is expected to have examined the goods and have no complaint if the defects could reasonably have been noticed before purchase.

- **The goods must be fit for their intended purpose.** In some cases the purpose is obvious but in other cases the consumer may be relying on the retailer for advice and he is expected to have some skill in this matter. If he says the product or service will do the job, or serve the purpose, then you have a claim against him if it turns out otherwise.

- **The goods must be as described.** Goods can be described in advertisements, pictures, or orally by the salesman and if these descriptions are not in keeping with the truth, the purchaser has a claim for redress. The trader may also be liable for criminal prosecution under the 1978 Consumer Information Act.

- **The goods must conform with the sample.** This provision applies when the consumer buys on the basis of seeing a sample of the goods.

- **The trader can be assumed to be able to pass ownership.** This is a difficult area of law but, in general, the trader is assumed to be able to pass ownership of the goods to the purchaser. If, for instance, there is an unpaid hire purchase debt on the goods and the hire purchase company comes looking for them, the buyer may have a claim against the seller.

These rights are enshrined in law and in general, the trader cannot limit them. If a consumer has a valid complaint, then in general, he has a right to get his money back. He may, in some cases, be entitled to compensation and may have a claim against the manufacturer if the goods are so defective that they caused damage. But that is another area of law. Retailers cannot rely on such notices as 'no exchange', 'no money refunded', 'returned goods only exchanged for credit notes', or 'no liability accepted for faulty goods'. Indeed such notices are illegal.

Unfair consumer contracts

If a contract is unfair, it is unenforceable even if read, freely entered into and graced with the consumer's signature. The law no longer assumes that the consumer is a completely free agent. That was made very evident in regulations introduced by the government at the beginning of 1995 to comply with an EU Directive. The regulations apply to contracts entered into by personal consumers with suppliers of goods or services and they greatly enhance the rights of consumers. A consumer cannot be assumed to have signed his or her rights away just because of a signature on a practically unintelligible contract written in legalese and produced in small fine print. That doesn't mean that contracts can be signed with impunity and repudiated afterwards. The old adage of *caveat emptor* (let the buyer beware) still applies.

The regulations don't apply to core provisions of a contract such as the price or other terms that were individually negotiated with the consumer. They are aimed more at the type of standard clause often written into contracts to protect the seller or supplier without providing any benefit to the consumer — the type of clause included in the fine print and imposed on the consumer in a take-it or leave-it fashion. Such clauses are not automatically unfair and unenforceable. Only a court can decide that but the regulations lay down guidelines.

They require all consumer contracts to be written in plain and intelligible language. Consumers must be given a reasonable opportunity to read the contract and fully understand what's involved. Any term that allows the supplier to hold onto a deposit if the consumer pulls out of the deal must be matched by a similar clause providing equal compensation for the consumer if the supplier fails to deliver. An individual consumer may go to court to have a clause in a contract declared unfair. This may arise where a consumer is looking for compensation and the supplier is relying on the fine print of a contract to avoid payment. Alternatively it may be used by a consumer as a defence against a seller or supplier who is looking for extra payment.

So how does a Court decide if a clause in a consumer contract is unfair? It has to take a range of factors into account including the balance between supplier and consumer in terms of rights and obligations and the strength of the consumer's bargaining position. A contract that imposes severe sanctions on a consumer for late payment, for instance, without imposing similar penalties on the supplier for late delivery might well be considered unfair, for instance.

In each case the final decision is up to the courts so it can be expensive finding out. But as outlined on page 201 the Small Claims Courts provide access to legal redress for claims up to €2,000 for a flat fee of €15. So if you are being held to a clause in a consumer contract that you believe to be unfair and you are willing to cap your claim at no more than €2,000 then the Small Claims Courts are worth a try. There's little to lose.

Using your rights

It is one thing having rights as a consumer, but it is another thing altogether using them. The consumer may have a claim against the trader but how does he get redress, and what form will this redress take. The National Consumer Agency has suggested the following guidelines:

- If the goods are incapable of doing what they are supposed to do from the very beginning, it is likely that the consumer is entitled to a full refund, and may refuse all offers of repair, replacement, or adjustment.

- If goods are not as described, the consumer is not bound to accept them. This is an important provision since it can be difficult for a retailer to claim that even a minor instance of false description was not important.

- The consumer's right to reject goods could be lost if he does not act promptly on discovering the cause of complaint. It could also be affected if he altered the goods or if he does anything which implies that he has accepted them.

- If the goods have been used for some time before the fault is detected, a repair may be all that the consumer can expect but the repair should be a permanent one which restores the goods to the quality that they should have been when sold allowing, of course, for wear and tear.

- If the consumer is entitled to his money back, a credit note is never good enough.

12 Social welfare — some basics

The social welfare system is every bit as complicated as the tax system and there are few people with a full knowledge of its working. Tax advisers can find paying clients but social welfare claimants can seldom afford to pay for advice. The system is wide-ranging and complication. This chapter provides no more than an overview of some of the schemes. But there are many sources to draw on for more detailed information and advice. Booklets and leaflets on various aspects of the system are available from Information Service, Department of Social Protection, Áras Mhic Dhiarmada, Dublin 1, from local social welfare offices and Citizens Information Centres throughout the country. You'll get a list of your local information centres under Citizens Information Centres in your phonebook.

Details of most schemes are also available on the Citizens Information Boards's web-site www.citizensinformation.ie. More detailed information on policy, guidelines and the procedures for determining entitlement to the various payments can be accessed on the Department's internet website at www.welfare.ie. Everyone has a right to this information under the Freedom of Information Act.

If you haven't got access to the internet, you can request the information at any social welfare office.

Main 2012 Budget changes

- Child benefit remains unchanged for the first and second child but is reduced by €19 a month to €148 for the third child and by €17 a month to €160 for the fourth and subsequent children.

- The €20 weekly fuel allowance will be paid for 26 weeks a year rather than 32. Payments will stop three weeks earlier in April 2012 and start three weeks later in October.

- New claimants for the One Parent Family Payment Benefits will cease to be eligible when their youngest child is 12. The age limit is being reduced to seven on a phased basis. The income disregard is reduced from €146.50 to €130 from January 2012.

- From July 2012, Job Seeker's Benefit will be based on a five-day week for those working part of the week. So someone working three days will get two fifths of the weekly benefit rather than three-sixths.

- From September 2012, new claimants for the Transitionary or State pension who have average annual contributions of between 20 and 47 will have their benefit calculated on a sliding scale. At present they qualify for a pension only €4.50 less than the full pension.

- From April 2012, late claim payments will be limited to six months.

- From July 2013, a total of 520 paid PRSI contributions will be required to qualify for a Widow(er)'s or a Surviving Civil Partner's Contributory Pension.

- From January 2012, new participants on Community Employment Schemes will not be able to claim another social welfare payment at the same time but will receive the standard payment of €20 per week.

- Back to School Allowances will no longer be paid in respect of children aged under four. The benefit is cut from €200 to €150 for children aged four to 11 and from €305 to €250 for children aged 12 or over.

- In assessing eligibility for Farm Assist from January 2012, actual income from self-employment will be reduced by 15% rather than 30% and deductions for children are being halved to €127 for the first two children and €190.50 for each subsequent child.

- Tenants in receipt of Rent Supplement will, from January 2012, have to contribute a minimum of €30 a week if single and €35 if married.

There are two basic types of social welfare payment — benefits and social assistance or allowances. Entitlement to benefits is based on meeting certain PRSI contribution requirements and also meeting some other conditions such as being unemployed, over 65 or widowed etc. Most workers earning €38 or more a week are covered by social insurance. Entitlement to social assistance is based solely on need, usually assessed by applying a means test.

Most public servants who entered the service after 1995 pay full rate PRSI. The self-employed have been paying PRSI since 1988. For details of the changes that apply from January 1, 2012 see page 247.

With a few limited exceptions entitlement to any social welfare *benefit* is not affected by the claimant's means. Entitlement to social *assistance*, however, is dependent on satisfying a means test. An example of the difference between the two is that the State Pension (Contributory) is a benefit — there is no means test — while the State Pension (Non-contributory) is a form of social assistance subject to a means test.

Part-time workers

Part-time workers who earn €38 a week or more are covered for all social welfare benefits including jobseeker's benefit, illness benefit and invalidity pensions. As with full-time workers, there is no PRSI on the first €127 earned each week and the exemption outlined above also apply.

To be eligible for benefits, part-time workers need to have worked for 39 weeks in insurable employment and also have 39 contributions paid or credited in the relevant contribution year. For those claiming in 2012 the relevant tax year is 2010. The same 39 contributions may satisfy both conditions. Having satisfied these contribution conditions, part-time workers are entitled to the same PRSI benefits as full time workers but unemployment and disability benefits may be paid at reduced rates. Those benefits are paid on a pro-rata basis depending on the part-timer's weekly earnings during a specified tax year.

In order to qualify for the State Pension (Contributory) it is necessary to have a minimum annual average of contributions either paid or credited over a specified number of years. The number of years can, however, differ with the individual — a fact which can result in some anomalies. A man who paid contributions for only five years could get a full old age pension while someone who paid for over 10 years can find himself on a reduced pension or even ineligible for any pension. Those reaching retirement age before April 6, 2012 can qualify if you have at least 260 paid PRSI contributions. Those reaching retirement age on or after April 6, 2012 need 520 contributions to qualify. The entitlements of those reaching retirement age after 2020 are to be based on total contributions during their working lives rather than on the basis of an annual average.

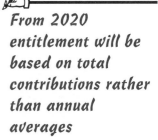

From 2020 entitlement will be based on total contributions rather than annual averages

The retirement age will have been raised to 66 in 2014 and would be raised to 67 until 2021, so if you were born after 1 January 1954 and reach retirement age in 2020, under these proposals, you will need a total of 30 years contributions, either paid or credited, to get the maximum State Pension. The minimum pension, based on five years paid contributions, will be one third of the maximum rate with 1/30th of the full pension added for each additional year of contributions.

No more than 520 credited contributions will be taken into account in calculating entitlements but it will be possible to gain additional entitlements by continuing to pay full-rate contributions after reaching pension age. It will also be possible to qualify for an increased pension by opting to defer the claim.

That's for the future: a future that will apply to most of those currently in the work-force. But those reaching retirement age before 2020 will have their entitlements calculated on the basis of annual average contributions.

A claimant must have an average of at least 10 contributions either paid or credited for each year between the date he or she first entered insurable employment and the end of the

Child Benefit and pre-school payment

☐ Child Benefit is payable in respect of all children under the age of 16 or 18 if the child is in full time education or disabled. The rates of payment from January 2012 are as follows:

First and second child	€140
Third child	€148
Fourth and subsequent child	€160

The pre-school Early Childhood and Education Scheme (ECCE) applies to children aged between 3 years 3 months and 4 years 6 months. Children born between 2 February 2008 and 30 June 2009 are eligible to enter the scheme for the year starting September 2012.

contribution year prior to reaching age 66. Pre-1953 contributions are taken into account in some circumstances. An average of 48 contributions a year is normally required to qualify for a full pension while an average of 10 will be enough for a 'reduced' pension. Those with an average of 20 to 47 contributions a year qualify for a pension of 98% of the maximum rate while those with between 15 and 19 contributions qualify for a pension of 75%. Those with between 10 and 14 contributions get about 50%. Contributions credited during periods of unemployment or illness can be used to meet the contribution requirements.

In assessing a claim, the Department first looks at the insurance record back to 1979 and if the claimant qualifies for a full pension on that basis they do not look back any further. If the claimant does not qualify for a full pension on the basis of his or her contributions from 1979, then the rules outlined earlier are applied.

Where entitlement can be based solely on self-employed contributions, prior employee contributions are not taken into account. This is an important concession since, if earlier contributions were taken into account, the claimant's working life might have to be spread over a larger number of years thereby reducing the average contributions per year.

Full rate PRSI became compulsory for most private sector workers from April 1974. Before that, non-manual workers earning above fixed income levels did not have to pay social insurance. If they did not make voluntary contributions they ended up with a gap in their contribution record. Those who came back into the PRSI net from April 1, 1974 get reduced rate pensions provided they had a minimum yearly average of at least five contributions. A similar scheme exists for people who stopped paying full rate PRSI on joining the public service. The rules are complicated. Full details are available from the sources mentioned above. A good starting point on the web is the Department itself at www.welfare.ie/EN/Schemes/Pension/Pages/spc.aspx

The Contributory State Pension is payable from age 66. Subject to the same contribution conditions the Transitional State Pension is payable at age 65 provided the claimant has ceased working. He or she can have an income of no more than €38 a week or, in the case of the self-employed, €3,174 a year and still be eligible. The proposed increased in the retirement age to 66 is to be achieved from January 1, 2014 by ending entitlement to the Transitional Pension to new claimants from that date.

Under the Homemakers Scheme, up to 20 years spent caring for a family can be disregarded in determining entitlement to a State Pension Contributory. A year is defined as a full tax year outside the work-force. It was proposed that from 2012 claimants would be given credit for years spent caring for a child or for an ill or disabled person subject to a maximum of 20 rather than having them simply disregarded in the calculation. The changes were to apply to those born on or after January 1, 1946 who reach pension age in 2012 and beyond but the change has been deferred.

In assessing a claim for a contributory old age pension the Department initially looks at the records only as far back as 1979

The proposal to grant PRSI credits for periods spent in homemaking has been deferred

Family income supplement

This scheme provides a supplementary benefit for families on low incomes. To be eligible, it is necessary for one member of the family to be working for at least 19 hours a week and for the family income to fall below set levels depending on family size. If both partners are working, their

Family Income Supplement (FIS)

☐ To be eligible your net weekly income in 2012 must be less than the figure shown below. The thresholds remain unchanged from 2011 The payment is 60% of the difference between your net income and the income in the table.

Family size	Family income must be below	Family size	Family income must be below
One child	€506	Five children	€950
Two children	€602	Six children	€1,066
Three children	€703	Seven children	€1,202
Four children	€824	Eight children	€1,298

hours can be combined to make up the 19. It is also necessary for some member of the family to be entitled to the normal Child Benefit. The aim of the scheme is to help families on low wages who might otherwise be better off on social welfare. Claiming the benefit does not affect eligibility for a medical card and it is tax free.

The family income supplement payable is 60% of the difference between actual income and the prescribed income given in the table above. Actual income is defined as pay after tax, PRSI, health levy and any contributions to a pension scheme. The figures in the table are those which apply from January 2011. They remain unchanged for 2012.

Once the actual income level is established, the FIS payment remains unchanged for some time. It doesn't fluctuate up and down on a weekly basis according to the earned income in the previous week. To qualify it is necessary to show that the employment will last at least three months. Job-sharers can qualify.

The rate of payment is adjusted immediately on the birth of a child. Application forms are available from social welfare offices or from: Social Welfare Services Office, Ballinalee Road, Longford, phone (01) 7043481 or (043) 40000.

Medical cards

Eligibility for a medical card is usually based on the claimant's means. There are some exceptions. Subject to some conditions, the dependants of people working in other EU countries or drawing State pensions from EU countries are entitled to medical cards irrespective of means and until 2009 so too were all people aged 70 or over. The over-70s are now subject to a means test on the basis of income before tax and any other State deductions and the return they are getting from assets calculated either on a notional basis or on the basis of the actual real return. The income thresholds are higher for the over-70s and the notional basis for assessing the return on assets is different from that applied to other claimants.

The over-70s who already had a card prior to January 1, 2009 were asked to submit themselves for the test if they had any doubt about their eligibility. New applicants are automatically mean tested and subjected to means-test thresholds of €700 a week single (€36,500 a year) and €1,400 married (€73,000 a year). The full medical card provides access to general health services free of charge. There is also a GP-only card, available only to the under-70s, which only provides free access to GP services. Since October, 2010 medical card holders are required to pay a prescription charge of 50c subject to a maximum of €10. To qualify for a card the applicant's means must be lower than a set threshold level.

The threshold levels, detailed in the table above, vary depending on circumstances and age. For the under-70s, income is defined as net income after deductions for tax and PRSI. In assessing eligibility, the income limit is increased by 'reasonable' amounts in respect of rent or mortgage repayments, childcare and the cost of travelling to and from work. The HSE, which issues the cards, can also take factors other than means into account. These include "exceptional personal and financial burdens arising from medical or social circumstances".

The assessors are instructed to issue a card if, in the light of all relevant circumstances, they consider that the applicant

Medical card means test thresholds

☐ To qualify for a medical card the applicant's weekly income must be below the thresholds set out below. See the main text for details of how means are assessed. The method of assessment is different for those over 70 being based on actual income from assets rather than a notional income.

PERSONAL	Up to age 66		Age 66 to 69		70 and over
	Medical card	**GP visit card**	Medical card	**GP visit card**	Medical card
Single, living alone	€184.00	**€276.00**	€201.50	**€302.00**	€700
Single, living with family	€164.00	**€246.00**	€173.50	**€260.00**	€700
Married couple	€266.50	**€400.00**	€298.00	**€447.00**	€1,400
DEPENDANTS	Under 16		Over 16		
Allowance for first two children	€38.00	**€57.00**	€39.00	**€59.50**	
Allowance for third and subsequent child	€41.00	**€61.50**	€42.50	**€64.00**	
Other dependants in full time education not getting grants	€78.00	**€117.00**			

Additional allowances are given in respect of reasonable outgoings on rent or mortgage repayments, expenses in travelling to work and reasonable childcare costs — see text.

would suffer 'undue hardship' or if it would be 'unduly burdensome' if they had to pay for medical services.

Usually the full cost of housing and childcare is taken into account. The cost of travelling to and from work is based either on the cost of public transport or, for car owners, a rate of 30c a mile plus €50 a week to cover depreciation and running costs.

Savings and other assets are assessed as providing an income. In calculating the return from assets owned by the under-70s, the first €36,000 is ignored in the case of a single claimant and €72,000 in the case of a couple. The next €10,000 is taken to yield a weekly income of €1 per €1,000; the next €10,000 an income of €2 per €1,000 and the remainder i.e. anything over €40,000, is taken to yield an income of €4 per €1,000. In the case of a couple, the first €36,000 is ignored.

Where a claimant has savings such as Savings Certs which only yield a return at the end of a period longer than a year, he or she may request the return be only taken into account when the investment matures. The actual return used in the calculation is the return before DIRT.

The calculation for the over-70s is slightly different. As with the under-70s. The first €36,000 is ignored (€72,000 for a couple) and the remainder may either be assessed on the basis of the actual income produced or on a notional basis as yielding 3% a year. That's the rate applied by the HSE at the end of 2011. It can change from time to time in line with changes in bank deposit rates.

Alternatively the means can be assessed on the actual interest earned. So those getting less than 3% are not penalised. But they have to produce certificates of interest earned during the last full calendar year. As with the under-70s, claimants may also have the return on investments, such as Savings Bonds to be assessed, on an actual rather than the notional basis. The return is taken into account when it actually materialises. In the case of Saving Bonds it is at the end of the three years. So there is no income in the first three calendar years and all the return is taken into account in the fourth year when the Bond matures.

The assessment of savings is different for the over-70s

That could result in a claimant qualifying for a medical card in some years and not in others. That's not an ideal situation but those are the rules. An asset that produces no income is ignored, even though like land, for instance, it has the potential to provide an income.

Some people are entitled to medical cards irrespective of means. For instance, the dependants of people working in other EU countries are entitled to medical cards without any means test as are those drawing state pensions from other EU countries who are neither employed nor self-employed in this country. So someone whose spouse is working in Britain or in Germany is automatically entitled to a medical card – there is no means test. The same applies to someone who has retired here and is drawing a social welfare pension from an EU country provided they do not earn more than €3,175 a year in Ireland.

Drugs payment scheme

No individual or family is required to pay more than €132 a month for prescription drugs included on a list of 'essential medicines'. The threshold was €120 in 2011 and raised in the 2012 Budget. The scheme is based on a system of registration. The necessary forms can be obtained from GPs, pharmacies or health board offices. Immediate registration is possible when an individual or family unexpectedly incurs expenditure in excess of the monthly threshold. The aim is that all individuals will have plastic cards, similar to credit cards, to be presented at any pharmacy where the details of the transaction is automatically passed to the central computer.

Long-term illness scheme

People suffering from certain long-term illnesses, not including asthma, are entitled, without charge, to the drugs, medicines, medical and surgical appliances prescribed for that disease. This benefit is not means tested. The diseases covered include: mental handicap, mental illness in persons under 16, phenylketonuria, cystic fibrosis, spina bifida, hydrocephalus, diabetes mellitus, diabetes insipidus, haemophilia, cerebral palsy, epilepsy, multiple sclerosis, muscular dystrophies, parkinsonism and acute leukaemia. People suffering from any of those diseases get a long-term illness card from their local health boards.

Nursing home 'fair deal'

The long awaited "fair deal" nursing home subvention scheme was generally welcomed when introduced in late 2009. It brought an element of fairness to a previously chaotic and inconsistent range of State supports for the elderly in need of nursing home care. In particular, it protects family homes, requiring no more than 5% of their value each year to be contributed for a maximum of three years. But it's not all sweetness and light. That three-year time limit does not apply to other assets, a fact that has recently been causing fresh concern among some farm families.

The HSE is allowed to apply some discretion in its treatment of farm and other family business assets under the scheme. But making use of that potential concession requires a timely transfer of assets to successors and there is no clear indication, as yet, of how that discretion is being exercised or whether it is being applied consistently.

In general under the scheme nursing home residents have to contribute 80% of their income and up to 5% of the value of their assets each year towards their nursing home care. But the family home is only included in the calculation of assets for the first three years. So only a maximum of 15% of the value of the family home will have to be used to help pay for nursing home care. That three year rule is also applied to farm and family business assets but only in what seems to be limited circumstances where the person requiring long-term nursing home care has suffered a sudden illness or disability and where he or she, or a partner, was engaged in the daily management of the business up to the time of the sudden illness or disability.

Farm and family business assets can get favourable treatment under 'fair deal' scheme

There is also a requirement that a family successor continues on the management of the farm or business.

The emphasis is on 'sudden' where a person did not have an opportunity to put appropriate succession arrangements in place. But it may well result in the claimant enjoying the same three year cap on assessment that applies to the family home on their farm and business assets as well. It depends on how the rule is applied.

While this three-year rule provides some certainty and protection for the family home, it is not a great concession. The vast majority of residents are in nursing homes for less than three years and in many cases the 5% of assets will cover the full cost of care.

So how exactly does it work?

To qualify, a person first has to be assessed as in need of nursing home care. The assessment is made by health care professionals employed by the HSE. Residential care is likely to be seen as a last resort. The policy is to improve community care facilities with a view to reducing the number of people needing nursing home care. Those who were already in nursing homes before the "fair deal" scheme was introduced are not reassessed even if they choose to move over to the new scheme. They also have the choice of staying on whatever subvention scheme that they are currently on.

Those assessed as in need of long-term residential care automatically qualify for the scheme if they want to take it up. There is no age limit and, once assessed as eligible, a person can pick any available nursing home either private or public. The scheme operates exactly the same for both.

The 5% assessable on the claimant's home is only payable for a maximum of five years

Those who opt for this scheme are required to make a contribution towards the cost of the care up to 80% of his or her disposable income and 5% of the value of any assets owned in excess of €36,000 in the case of a single person or €72,000 for a couple. The assets taken into account initially include the individual's home.

But the 5% assessable on the home, and in some cases on farm and business assets, as outlined above, is only payable for a maximum of three years and will not be collected until the individual dies, or later still if a spouse or a dependant is still living in the home. In effect, the State provides a loan of that money and will take a mortgage charge on the home or other assets.

Let's take an example.

Mary has a pension of €230 a week. She has €86,000 in savings and owns a house worth €500,000. The first €36,000 of her savings is disregarded so Mary's total assets are deemed to be worth €550,000. Her contribution to the nursing home cost will consist of 80% of her pension which works out at €184 and 5% of her assets which works out at €27,500 a year or €528 a week. That's a total of €712.

The €25,000 assessed on the value of her home (5% of €500,000) will not be collected until after her death and that

5% will only be assessed for three years. There is no time limit on the 5% collected on other assets such as her savings. So in the fourth year if she still has savings of €86,000, the first €36,000 would be disregarded and she would be liable to contribute 5% of the remaining €50,000 or €2,500.

If Mary's house was worth say €800,000 she'd possibly be contributing almost enough to pay the full cost of the nursing home. But she'll never have to pay more than the full cost.

Assets disposed of within five years of applying for assistance during the scheme can be taken into account in the means assessment. Unfortunately that may encourage some elderly people to dispose of assets well in advance of needing nursing home care or they may be encouraged by others to do so. But that can leave an elderly person very vulnerable. Married and other couples, including same-sex couples, who are cohabiting as life partners, for at least three years, are assessed on half their income and assets.

Free travel

Free travel is available to the following: All those aged 66 years or over residing permanently in the State; those receiving Invalidity Pensions from the State, those receiving a Disability Allowance, Blind Person's Pension, Carer's Allowance and people aged 18 or over who are registered with the National Council for the Blind. Also entitled are people who have been getting an invalidity pension or a benefit continuously for at least a year from another EU country or a country with which Ireland has a bilateral social security agreement.

If you are married or cohabiting and entitled to a free travel pass your spouse or partner is entitled to travel with you free. This facility is included on the pass provided you have specifically applied for it. All wheelchair users, blind people and those on an Invalidity Pension, who are entitled to free travel, are also entitled to a free travel companion pass as are those who are being cared for by someone in receipt of a carer's allowance.

If you are married or cohabiting and entitled to free travel your spouse or partner is entitled to travel with you free

Anyone aged 75 or over, who is medically assessed as unfit to travel alone, is eligible for a free travel pass for a companion. The pass enables the holder to have any person aged 16 or over accompanying him or her free of charge on public transport. People who transfer from Invalidity Pension, Disability Allowance or Blind Person's Pension to another social welfare pension such as a widow's pension are entitled to keep their entitlement to the free schemes.

There is also an entitlement under the scheme to free travel on all bus and rail services in Northern Ireland. Spouses, partners and companions, entitled to travel with you free, are covered for cross-border journeys but not for travel on public transport within Northern Ireland. You need a special Senior SmartPass card to avail of services within Northern Ireland. You can get an application form from your local social welfare office or by ringing 1890 20 23 25.

The application form has to be returned in person to your local social welfare office. You'll need your current Free Travel Pass, evidence of your address, (an electricity or phone bill) and evidence of your identity, (a driver's licence, passport or other photo identification). It can take up to six weeks to process an application.

Household benefits package

Everyone over 70 years of age is entitled to the Household Benefits Package which includes free units of electricity or gas. With some exceptions, applicants under 70 must be living alone or with a dependent spouse or partner; an invalid; dependent children under 18, or under 22 if still in full time education; or, if the applicant is an invalid or infirm, one other person who provides care and attention for him/her. Widows and widowers, aged 60 to 65, whose late spouses had entitlement to free schemes retain that entitlement. If they meet the 'living alone' condition, those over 66 may qualify if they are:

■ receiving pensions from the Department of Social, Community and Family Affairs; social security pensions from other EU countries or from countries with which Ireland has a bilateral social security agreement;

any other social welfare payment; or an ordinary garda widow's pension.

- pensioners who do not have social welfare pensions but whose total weekly income is not more than €38 above the contributory old age pension rates plus any appropriate allowances e.g. living alone allowance. People under 66 years of age can qualify if they are in receipt of an Invalidity Pension; Blind Person's Pension; Unemployability Supplement or Worker's Compensation Supplement; Disability Allowance; Disability Pension/Benefit (or equivalent) for at least 12 months from another EU country, or another country with which Ireland has a bilateral social security agreement, people getting Carer's Allowance or caring for people getting Constant Attendance or Prescribed Relative Allowance.

The allowance covers 300 units per two-monthly billing period, winter and summer. The annual maximum is 1,800 units. As an alternative, the claimant can have a natural gas allowance of €48.20 per two monthly period from June to November and €107.20 per bill from December to May. Another alternative, but only open to those who have not got gas or electricity, is an allowance towards the cost of bottled gas.

Application forms can be obtained from any Post Office or Social Welfare Office. The package also includes an entitlement to €18.36 a month towards telephone expenses. The account doesn't have to be with Eircom. Also included is an entitlement to a free TV licence. Lifetime TV licences are issued that don't have to be renewed each year.

13 Guide to the tax system

While the main income tax credits and bands remain unchanged in 2012, there were a number of significant tax changes unveiled in the 2012 budget. The most wide ranging in terms of impact is the lifting of the exemption threshold for the Universal Service Charge from €4,004 to €10,036. It has no impact on those earning less than €10,036 but an estimated 330,000 low earners are expected to benefit. Other changes include increases in the tax rates applied to deposit interest, capital acquisitions and capital gains. There was also a new household charge, increases in the carbon tax and in the motor tax.

Some expected changes such as a further reduction in the age exemption limits did not emerge while Mortgage Tax Relief was extended to those buying in 2012. There was also a major extra concession in the form of extra Mortgage Tax Relief for first-time buyers who bought during the boom years 2004 to 2008.

Reducing your tax bill

Most people believe that they are paying too much tax, on the basis that any tax is too much. There are certainly many people paying more tax than they need to – simply

Budget 2012 — the main tax changes

□ **INCOME TAX**
— First-time home buyers who bought between January 1, 2004 and December 31, 2008 allowed tax relief on up to €10,000 in interest paid per individual for the tax years 2012 to 2017.
— Interest paid on qualifying home loans taken out during 2012 to qualify for tax relief up until the end of 2017.
— Tax exemption limits for over 65s remain unchanged.
— DIRT and investment exit tax rates raised by 3 percentage points.
— Exemption on first 36 days of Sickness Benefit removed.
— Surcharge of 5% on income sheltered by property tax reliefs earned by those with earnings over €100,000.

□ **PRSI**
— Employers to pay full PRSI on employee contributions to pension schemes.

□ **UNIVERSAL SOCIAL CHARGE**
— Low income exemption raised to €10,036.

□ **CAPITAL ACQUISITIONS TAX**
— Tax rate raised to 30% from December 6, 2011 and Group A threshold lowered to €250,000 from the same date. Other thresholds remain unchanged.

□ **STAMP DUTY ON NON-RESIDENTIAL PROPERTY**
— From December 6, 2011 a single rate of 2% applies.

□ **CAPITAL GAINS TAX**
— Rate increased to 30% on disposals made after December 6, 2011.

□ **HOUSEHOLD CHARGE**
— Fixed charge of €100 per home paid by owner. Those claiming Mortgage Interest Supplement or living in defined ghost estates are exempt.

□ **CARBON TAX**
— From December 6, 2011 the Carbon Tax on motor fuels was increased from €15 to €20 per tonne. The increase applies to heating oils and LPG from May 1, 2012. It does not apply to solid fuels.

□ **MOTOR TAX**
— All motor tax rates increase from January 1, 2012.

because they do not claim all the allowances they are entitled to, or because they are not making use of every tax avoidance measure possible. Tax avoidance is no crime. It is simply using the tax system to the best advantage. It is tax evasion which is illegal.

The following are some ideas worth considering. Further details on each option are given later, in this chapter, or in chapter 14 on page 279.

■ Make sure that you are claiming all the tax credits and reliefs to which you are entitled. PAYE taxpayers are likely to lose rather than gain by not making an annual return. That is not always true but it generally is. Do you claim for medical expenses? Are you eligible for the home carer's tax credit which has wider application than many think? Have you a claim in respect of rent? You can go back four years so during 2012 you can still make a claim for 2008. A careful read of the following pages could be worthwhile.

■ If you are self-employed, consider employing your children on a part-time basis. As a family, you can save some tax that way. If your spouse does some work in the business it may be worthwhile formally employing her so as to gain the extra standard rate band enjoyed by two-income couples. But a tax saving of up to €4,998 is possible for 2012. **See page 280.**

■ The cap on the tax relief, available on pension contributions introduced in 2009, only affects those on incomes of more than €115,000 for contributions made in respect of 2011. Others can still gain from full tax relief on pension contributions so, for the self-employed, a personal pension scheme offers a particularly favourable way of saving for the future although from 2011 onwards there is no relief from PRSI or the Universal Social Charge.

Workers can benefit by putting extra money into their own pension schemes while, for those not in pension schemes, Personal Retirement Savings Accounts (PRSAs) offer a relatively low-cost way of saving for retirement while qualifying for tax relief. That relief is particularly attractive for those paying tax at the top rate. The proposal to standardise the relllief at 20% seems to have been shelved for the foreseeable future. **For details see chapter 10 page 174.**

- Despite the recession, many firms are still making profits and it is possible to get some of your income tax free through an approved profit sharing scheme negotiated with your employer. Even if the business is not profitable but is expected to be in the future, you could help the firm's cash flow by accepting shares instead of pay. You can get €12,700 tax-free each year in the form of shares. **For details see page 290.**

- You can also get certain benefits from your employer tax free. They include a subsidised canteen, some leisure facilities, travel passes for a period of more than a month or a bicycle. You will find other ideas throughout this book.

Pay As You Earn

The vast majority of income tax payers come under the Pay As You Earn scheme (PAYE). They have no alternative. With very few exceptions, all employees come under the scheme which is designed to spread income tax liability over the year, thereby saving PAYE taxpayers from being faced with large bills once a year. The Exchequer benefits too, of course, from a nice even flow of revenue throughout the year.

For centuries, long before income tax was introduced, the financial year ran from April 6 to April 5. But since 2002, our tax year coincides with the calendar year and it is your income during the tax year that dictates your tax liability. With very few limited exceptions, it is not possible to carry forward reliefs or allowances from one year to another or to average your income over a number of years. PAYE is simply an administrative method of collecting that tax in easy stages during the year, once a week or once a month.

Employers have a legal obligation to stop tax on payments to employees and they do so on the basis of instructions given to them by the Revenue Commissioners. These in-

Making sense of your tax cert

■   Although tax allowances have been mostly replaced by tax credits, the few that remain create a complication in the system resulting in PAYE tax payers moving onto the top rate of tax at seemingly different levels depending on the allowances they have to claim against the top rate. The annual tax certificate known as 'Notification of determination of tax credits and standard rate cut-off point' provides PAYE taxpayers with details of their tax credits and also indicates the income level at which the higher rate of tax starts to apply. A tax credit is simply a deduction from your tax liability. The value of a tax allowance depends on whether you pay tax at the standard or at the top rate. A tax credit of €1,000 reduces your tax bill by €1,000 irrespective of what rate of tax you are on while a tax allowance of €1,000 is worth €200 (20% of €1,000) in saved tax for those on the standard rate and €410 (41% of €1,000) for those paying at the top rate.

A single taxpayer is liable for tax at 20% on the first €32,800 of income in 2012 and 41% on anything thereafter. The basic tax credits, personal and employee, amount to €3,300. So, on an income of €40,000, the tax liability works out like this:

Gross income	**€40,000**
€32,800 taxed at 20%	€6,560
€7,200 taxed at 41%	€2,952
Gross tax	**€9,512**
Less tax credit	€3,300
Tax liability	**€6,212**

If this taxpayer claimed approved expenses of €1,000 wholly, exclusively and necessarily incurred for the job, he or she would be given an extra tax credit of €200. That provides the necessary tax relief for someone paying tax at the standard rate. But relief may also be due at the top rate. To provide for that, the tax cert will raise the income level at which he or she moves onto the top rate of tax by €1,000. As a result, an extra €1,000 will be taxed at 20% rather than 41% and provide an extra tax saving of €210. So the person on the 41% rate of tax will save €410 in tax if they have allowable expenses of €1,000 – €200 of it will come by way of a tax credit and the other €210 by way of a raising of the pay level at which they move onto the top rate. The opposite happens in the case of a benefit-in-kind, for instance, where the threshold level is reduced to take account of the extra tax that needs to be stopped. Such items will also involve a deduction from tax credits. A benefit-in-kind worth €1,000, for instance, is shown on the certificate as a €200 deduction from tax credits. That's equivalent to taxing the benefit at 20%. To collect the extra tax payable by a top rate taxpayer, the certificate will also provide for a reduction of €1,000 in the level at which tax at 41% becomes payable.

structions are summarised on your 'Notification of determination of tax credits and standard rate cut-off point'.

Most tax changes unveiled in the annual Budget in December take effect from January 1 whether or not the Revenue has had time to issue new tax certificates. If necessary the changes are backdated

It's important to check your cert. It lists the tax reliefs you have been allowed. Do not ignore it. The taxman can make mistakes and so can you. You may not have claimed all your credits and reliefs. Some of them are given to you automatically but others you will not get unless you claim them. So check your certificate. The check list of tax credits and reliefs on page 330 contains most of the concessions applicable to the average taxpayer. A fuller list starts below. Check both.

It is all too easy for PAYE taxpayers to be overtaxed. It is important to check that you are claiming all your credits and reliefs. You will not get them all automatically

The table on page 259 is designed to help you work out your annual tax liability in exactly the same way the taxman would work it out. It is done on an annual basis whereas the PAYE system is geared to collecting the tax due from your pay packets over the course of the tax year. It should ensure that your tax payments over the year add up to your full liability and no more. But, in some circumstances, it may result in you paying too much or too little. If it has taken too much, then you are due a rebate. If it has taken too little you will get a demand for the difference if and when Revenue realises the error.

The tax on some income may not be collected under the PAYE system but total liability is calculated by charging your gross income to tax, so much at the standard rate and so much at the top rate if your income is high enough. That gives a gross tax figure from which is deducted your tax credits and reliefs to give your actual tax liability. Income includes all emoluments (pay) of any office or job including salaries; fees; wages; perquisites; profits; pensions; headage and other similar payments; most interest; and benefits-in-kind. Some of these may not be caught in the PAYE net but the tax liability is calculated in the same way.

People who are part-time self-employed, in addition to being in paid employment, may be liable to pay tax on their self-employed income under what is known as Schedule 'D' which allows for the tax to be paid in one annual instalment

— more about that later in the chapter. But the tax liability is calculated on the basis of your total income from all sources. So what credits and reliefs can be claimed? The following apply to the 2012 tax year.

PERSONAL CREDITS:

Single person	**€1,650**
Married couple	**€3,300**

■ **WIDOWED PERSON:**

Without dependant children	**€2,190**
Qualifying for one-parent credit	**€1,650**

■ **ONE PARENT FAMILY:** **€1,650**

■ **AGE CREDITS:**

If the taxpayer or his spouse is over, or will reach, the age of 65 during the tax year, the following extra credits apply:-

Single or widowed	**€245**
Married couple	**€490**

■ **CHILD CREDITS:** **€3,300**

There is a credit of €3,300 in respect of an incapacitated child, reduced if the amount spent in maintaining the child is actually less. The child must have become incapacitated before reaching 21 years of age, or while still receiving full-time education. There is no tax relief in respect of other children. But tax exemption limits are increased depending on the number of children in a family. This can be relevant to taxpayers who are over 65 — see page 332 for details.

■ **PAYE CREDIT:** **€1,650**

This credit is granted to all people liable to be taxed under the PAYE system. If a husband and wife are both wage-earning, there is a double credit. It is allowed to a child working full-time in a family firm but not to a spouse.

■ **DEPENDANT RELATIVE CREDIT:** **€70**

This credit is granted for each relative of the taxpayer, or spouse, who is incapacitated, and, even if not incapacitated, the widowed mother or mother-in-law of the taxpayer. The allowance is also granted in respect of a son or daughter of the taxpayer who is resident with him, and on whose services he or his wife depend because of old age or illness.

The Dependant Relative Credit is itself reduced by €1 for every €1 by which the dependant's income exceeds the maximum contributory old age pension rate for someone aged 80 or over — €240.30 in both 2011 and 2012.

■ **HEALTH INSURANCE:**

The allowance is granted on the amount paid in premiums during the previous year. It is granted in respect of insurance against the medical expenses of the taxpayer, spouse, child or other dependants. The relief is given at source. Insurers get the tax relief directly and reduce their premium levels to take account of it. As a result even those who are not liable for tax can benefit from the relief.

■ **BLIND PERSON'S CREDIT:**   **€1,650**

This credit can be claimed where either the taxpayer or the taxpayer's spouse is blind. If both are blind, the allowance is €3,300. A tax allowance of €825 can be claimed in respect of a registered guide dog.

■ **SPECIAL CARER'S ALLOWANCE: €50,000 — allowed at the top marginal rate of tax.**

This allowance is given to a totally incapacitated taxpayer who is employing a person to care for him or herself or for an incapacitated spouse. It is also allowed where a family employs a carer to look after a totally incapacitated person. Family members contributing to the cost of the carer can share the allowance between them. The requirement is for 'total' rather than 'permanent' incapacity.

■ **HOME CARER'S CREDIT €810**

Granted in respect of a taxpayer's spouse who works at home caring for children, the aged (defined as over 65) or the incapacitated. This allowance is not always given automatically. The Revenue does not have all the necessary information, so it may be necessary to claim it.

While it is aimed at stay-at-home spouses you can have an annual income of €5,080 and still get the full credit. Over €5,080 and the credit is reduced by €1 for every extra €2 of income. If the income goes above €6,880 there is no allowance left. The social welfare carer's allowance is not included in the definition of income for this purpose.

If you have failed to claim your full tax credits in the past, you can claim rebates for up to four years

The person being cared for need not live in the home so long as he or she lives close by — two kilometres is used as a rule of thumb for 'close by'. So even if the children are grown up you may qualify if you have an elderly parent living within two kilometres. Even if they still believe that they are looking after you, you can claim to be caring for them as long as either of them is over 65.

■ **PERMANENT HEALTH BENEFIT SCHEMES:**

The relief is allowed against premiums paid to insure income in the event of ill health or disability. It is limited to 10% of the taxpayer's income in the year of assessment. Benefits paid under the policy are taxed as income.

■ **MEDICAL EXPENSES:**

Full allowance is granted for most medical expenses paid by the taxpayer in respect of himself or anyone else. The relief is only granted at the standard rate in respect of medical expenses incurred after January 1, 2009 with the exception of nursing home charges which continue to be allowed at the claimant's top rate of tax.

Covenants can be used as an alternative way for an individual to get tax relief at the top rate in respect of contribution made towards the medical costs, including nursing home care, of someone over 65 — see page 297.

Medical expenses in respect of the following are not allowed: normal dental treatment, eye testing, or the supply of spectacles. Dental treatment which is not considered 'normal' in this context includes: crowns, veneers, tip replacing, gold posts, gold inlays, endodontics — root canal treatment, periodontal treatment, orthodontic treatment and the surgical extraction of impacted wisdom teeth. The tax relief is available on treatment performed outside the State.

In certain cases — kidney patients and child oncology patients — the Revenue Commissioners accept the cost of travelling to and from treatment centres as legitimate medical expenses for the purpose of this relief. Telephone

Income tax exemptions limits for over-65s

☐ People with incomes below certain exemption limits are not liable for income tax, although if tax calculations were done in the normal way they would be liable. It is important to remember that these are not allowances. Those with income above the threshold are taxed in the normal way with, some marginal relief granted by applying the rule that they pay no more than 40% tax on any income above the exemption limit. For example, a married man aged 66 with an income of €36,100 i.e. €100 above the exemption limit, will pay €40 in tax — 40% of the €100. The exemption limits shown below are increased by €575 for each of the first two dependent children and by €830 for each subsequent child. Since the tax authorities do not automatically know how many children a taxpayer has, since the general child tax allowance was abolished, it is important that taxpayers with children make a claim if their income is below or even marginally above the relevant limit.

	2010	2011	2012
Single and widowed 65 or over	€20,000	€18,000	€18,000
Married, either spouse over 65	€40,000	€36,000	€36,000

costs and certain costs involved in home dialysis treatment are also allowed. The claim is normally made at the end of the tax year on the form MED1 – or MED2 if in respect of dental treatment. Full details and forms can be requested from the Revenue on 1890 30 67 06. In the case of heavy or ongoing expenses, tax relief can be granted during the tax year.

■ **INTEREST PAYMENTS:**

Apart from the few exceptions mentioned below, relief is only allowed in respect of the interest on loans taken out to buy, maintain, or improve the taxpayer's principal residence, the residence of a former or separated spouse, or the residence of a dependant relative (other than a child) who is living in the house rent free.

A more detailed treatment of mortgage interest relief, with detailed examples and tables, is given in chapter 6 starting

Taxpayers can claim relief on their contributions to the medical costs for themselves or anyone else

on page 129. Where a loan is used to buy an investment residential property, tax relief at the taxpayer's marginal rate of tax is allowed on 75% of the interest.

This relief is normally granted at source i.e. by way of a reduction in the repayments to the mortgage lender so it is important to ensure that the lender has been authorised by the Revenue to provide the relief.

It is also important to ensure that your tax office has the full details of your mortgage account. Where a taxpayer moves house and there is a delay in selling the original house, both houses can be considered to be the sole or main residence for up to one year. And during that year, the interest on any loan taken out to buy the new house is allowed for tax relief in addition to the tax relief on the old loan — the limit is doubled. Interest on loans taken out to pay death duties is allowed for tax relief without any restriction. More information on this latter point is given in the section on reducing your tax bill on page 279.

■ RENT CREDIT:

This relief can be claimed by tenants living in private rented accommodation in respect of the rent paid. For those under 55 the maximum rent allowed for relief in 2012 is:

Married or widowed	**€2,400**
Single person	**€1,200**

A single taxpayer, over 55 years of age, living in rented accommodation can claim an allowance of up to €2,400 in respect of the rent paid. The maximum is €4,800 for a married couple or widowed person. These tax allowances cannot be claimed in respect of rent paid to local authorities or on tenancies of 50 years or more. The relief is only granted at the standard rate.

This relief is to be phased out by 2018. See page 133 for details.

■ PENSION CONTRIBUTIONS:

The contributions to an approved scheme are allowed in full, subject to the following maximum levels related to annual pay. Unused allowances in any one year can be carried forward.

Within those limits any allowances unused on retirement can be claimed as a relief against tax in any of the previous two years.

AGE	LIMIT
up to 30	15%
30 but under 40	20%
40 but under 50	25%
50 but under 55	30%
55 but under 60	35%
60 and over	40%

There was a cap of €150,000 in 2009 and 2010 on the income taken into account. That figure was reduced to €115,000 for contributions made in respect of 2011 which can be made until October 2012. The relief is not allowed on contributions that would bring the value of a pension fund to more than the equivalent of €2.3 million. That figure was set with effect from December 7, 2010. In certain circumstances a higher figure, up to €5.4 million, can apply to existing pension funds.

- **INVESTMENT IN IMPROVING HOME ENERGY EFFICIENCY**

There was a provision in the 2011 Finance Act for a scheme under which tax relief at the standard rate could be claimed on up to €10,000 invested on approved work to improve the efficiency of the home. It is to be commenced by Ministerial Order which had still not been made by the end of 2011.

- **EXPENSES:**

Allowances are also made for expenses incurred by the taxpayer in performing his job. In the case of a PAYE worker, the expenses must have been wholly, exclusively, and necessarily incurred. The 'necessarily' criterion does not apply to the self-employed taxpayer. PAYE workers may claim relief against the expense of buying tools and special work clothes, for instance.

Travelling expenses to and from work are not allowed. Very often, the tax inspector will agree a figure that can be claimed without any evidence of the expenses being incurred. But the taxpayer can claim more, provided he can justify the higher claim.

The table on page 243 provides an insight into the level of agreed rates which may find favour with the Revenue. They are the rates applicable to civil servants that came into effect from March 5, 2009.

■ YEAR OF MARRIAGE:

Married couples are taxed as single persons in the year that the marriage takes place. If they would have paid less tax as a married couple they can claim a rebate at the end of the tax year in respect of the proportion of the full tax year for which they were married. The various options facing married couples are considered in more detail in a separate section on page 285.

■ WIDOWS/WIDOWERS:

An extra credit of €3,600 is granted in the year following bereavement for widows and widowers with dependant children. It declines by €450 a year thereafter. So it is worth €3,150 in the second year, €2,700 in the third year, €2,250 in the fourth year and €1,800 in the fifth and final year.

■ TRADE UNION SUBSCRIPTIONS

A tax credit was given in respect of up to €350 paid in trade union subscriptions in 2010. It was €300 in 2007 but increased to €350 in 2008. It has been abolished and was no longer allowed in 2011. It was often given at source i.e. directly to the trade union who could pass it on in lower subscriptions. During 2011 it is still possible to make a back-claim in respect of 2007, 2008, 2009 and 2010.

■ SERVICE CHARGES Maximum €400 a year

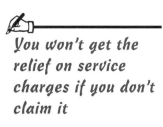

You won't get the relief on service charges if you don't claim it

This relief could be claimed in 2011 in respect of charges paid in 2010. It's no longer available so can't be claimed in 2012. Service charges included those imposed by local authorities for the provision of a domestic water supply, domestic refuse collection or domestic sewage disposal where, for instance, a house has its own septic tank. They also included payments made to group water schemes for domestic water supply and to independent contractors for domestic refuse collection or disposal.

Civil service subsistence rates

These rates have applied since March 5, 2009.
The normal overnight rate applies for the first 14 nights, the reduced rate for the next 14 and the detention rate for subsequent periods.

Rank	Night Allowances		Day allowances		
	Normal	Reduced	Full	10 hours or more	5 to 10 hours
Higher officials	€108.99	€100.48	€54.48	€33.61	€13.71
All others	€107.69	€92.11	€53.87	€33.61	€13.71

Usually the relief was claimed by the person liable to make the payments but it could be claimed by another person living in the home, for instance, a son or daughter living with an elderly parent who might not be liable for tax. The Revenue may ask for receipts but they don't have to be submitted with your claim.

■ **COLLEGE FEES:**

The relief is given in respect of tuition fees paid in publicly funded third-level colleges in the State and approved undergraduate and postgraduate courses in both private and publicly funded colleges both in the State and in other EU countries. It also applies to tuition fees for undergraduate and postgraduate distance education courses provided by colleges within the EU and for some postgraduate courses provided outside the EU.

The maximum relief is €5,000. Relief is also allowed on annual fees of up to €1,270 in respect of IT and foreign language courses that result in a certificate of competence rather than just a certificate of attendance.

The fees must not be recouped by grants or scholarships and the relief may not exceed the tax liability of the taxpayer. In the case of a married couple the relief may be claimed by either spouse provided they have not opted for separate assessment. The relief is given at the standard rate.

Tax on social welfare benefits

Many social welfare benefits are liable for tax if the recipient's income is sufficiently high to put them into the tax net. The Department of Social and Family Affairs does not operate the PAYE system under which tax would be stopped at source but the Revenue often arranges for the tax to be stopped out of any other income the recipient may have. Only the first four on the following list of taxable benefits is considered to qualify the recipient for PAYE tax credit. That means that a couple is entitled to the benefit of two PAYE tax credits if one is being taxed under PAYE on earnings and the other is in receipt of a contributory old age pension. The following are the taxable benefits:

- State pension, contributory and transition,
  Contributory survivor's and orphan's pensions,
  Invalidity pension,
  One parent family payment,
  Carers allowance,
  Jobseeker's benefit,
  Blind person's pension,
  Widow's pension, non-contributory
  Guardian's payment, non-contributory, and
  Social assistance for deserted or prisoners' wives.

A number of concessions apply:

- The first 36 days of illness benefit was not subject to tax in 2011 but the exemption no longer exists in 2012.

- Child dependant additions to illness and unemployment benefits are not taxed.

- The unemployment benefit payable to systematic short-term workers is not taxed.

- The first €12.70 a week of unemployment benefit is not liable for tax.

Benefits-in-kind are not all taxed

Since the introduction of the PAYE system many decades ago, most earnings have been taxed at source but this was only extended more recently to non-cash benefits such as company cars, cheap loans and lunch vouchers. Most of these benefits are, of course, taxable. They are considered by the Revenue to be every bit as much income as basic pay and are liable to tax as such. Employers are required to value the benefits and stop tax and PRSI at source through the PAYE system.

While most non-cash benefits provided by employers for individual workers or for employees in general are liable for tax, there are important exemptions that allow employers to provide some tax-free benefits to their workers. The exemptions are all subject to conditions that are strictly applied by the Revenue but if those conditions are met the employer can confer the benefit tax free and it remains tax free in the hands of the recipient.

One such exemption applies to small benefits worth no more than €250. Only one small benefit is exempt from tax in any tax year, so it may not sound like much but so long as the conditions are met, a €250 gift voucher, given as a bonus, costs an employer just that while providing the same benefit in cash can cost up to €532.45. That €532.45 would be subject to employer's PRSI of €51.67, employee's PRSI of €28.85 and, if the top rate applies, income tax of €201.92 leaving €250 for the worker.

The benefit doesn't have to be given in the form of a gift voucher of course so long as it isn't actual cash. However, since the vouchers can be used in a wide range of outlets they are nearly as good as cash to the recipients but in terms of euro for euro benefit, they are far less expensive for the employer. The €250 upper limit per year obviously limits the scope of this small benefit exemption for employers who genuinely want to provide workers with extra non-cash benefits at the smallest possible cost. But there are other non-cash benefits that employers can give their workers tax free. The following are some of the options:

- No benefit-in-kind tax is applied to meals, either free or subsidised, provided in a staff canteen. The facility has to be open to all employees so the exemption doesn't apply to a limited executive dining room. Neither is it extended to meal vouchers.

Workers can get some benefits tax free from their employers

- Sports and recreational facilities provided on an employer's own premises can be enjoyed tax free by workers. But the facilities must be open to all employees, not just a favoured few.

- Bus, train and Luas passes can also be provided tax free and they don't have to be used necessarily for work purposes. The main condition is that they are monthly or annual passes for use on a licensed passenger transport service. The Revenue allows employees to surrender pay to an employer in return for such a pass.

- Mobile phones can be provided to workers tax free but only if it can be justified on the basis of business use. The phone may be used for private use but it must be incidental to its use for business purposes. The same rules apply to the provision of computers or broadband access if they are to be provided completely tax free.

Monthly or annual bus, train and Luas tickets can be provided by employers tax free

- Employers can supply workers with a bicycle and associated safety equipment tax free to a value of €1,000 once in any five year period. The Revenue allows employees to take a pay cut in return for such a pass. The benefit in doing it is that, if the pay was taken through the payroll it would be subject to tax and PRSI, but the value of the bicycle is not.

- Fees paid in respect of courses of study relevant to the business of the employer can also be paid tax free. The employer can either reimburse the worker or pay the fees directly.

  A course is relevant, according to the Revenue, where it leads to the acquisition of knowledge or skills which are: necessary for the duties of the office or employment, or it facilitates the acquisition of knowledge which is necessary for or directly related to the performance of the employee's present duties or would be necessary for, or directly related to, the prospective duties of the employee with the employer.

- An award made to a worker in recognition of obtaining a qualification of some relevance to the job. The award must be no more than might reasonably be considered

PRSI and Social Charge in 2012

■ From 2011 the former Health and Income Levies were combined into a new Universal Social Charge and some income formally exempted is now subject to both PRSI and the new charge. The ceiling on private sector PRSI contributions was abolished and the self-employed rate raised from 3% to 4%. Public servants paying the reduced modified rate pay 4% PRSI on income above €75,036. Both PRSI and USC are charged on slices of income and there is a range of exemptions for those on lower incomes. Ignoring those exemptions, which are outlined below, the rates applicable to slices of incomes are as follows:

■ **PRIVATE SECTOR**

	USC	PRSI	Total
Up to €10,037	2%	4%	6%
€10,037 to €16,016	4%	4%	8%
Over €16,016	7%	4%	9%

■ **PUBLIC SECTOR (pre-1995 entrants)**

	USC	PRSI	Total
Up to €10,037	2%	0.9%	2.9%
€10,037 to €16,016	4%	0.9%	4.9%
€16,016 to €75,037	7%	0.9%	7.9%
Over €75,037	7%	4%	11%

■ **SELF-EMPLOYED**

	USC	PRSI	Total
Up to €10,037	2%	4%	6%
€10,037 to €16,016	4%	4%	8%
Over €16,016	7%	4%	11%

■ No USC is paid by those earning less than €10,036 a year but if income is above that, the charge is levied on all income. The exemption threshold was €4,004 in 2011.

■ No PRSI is payable on the first €127 a week earned by those paying the 4% rate. For those paying the lower public sector rate, the weekly exemption is €26 a week.

■ Those earning less than €352 a week are exempt from PRSI.

■ Both PRSI and USC are charged on pension contributions.

■ Those over 70 pay a maximum of 4% USC irrespective of income a reimbursement of the expenses incurred in studying for the qualification or sitting the exam.

- Workers can be provided with free living accommodation but only in very limited circumstances. The accommodation has to be in part of the employer's business premises and there has to be some work-related need for living there.

- The traditional Christmas party, celebrations for special occasions and events, such as sports days, are exempt from the benefit-in-kind rules provided the expenses are 'reasonable'.

- Subscriptions to professional bodies provided that membership is relevant to the business of the employer.

- Medical check-ups but only where they are required by the employer.

- Long service awards but not in the form of cash and only after at least 20 years service. The award must be a 'tangible article' costing no more than €50 for each year of service. No more than one award can be made every five years.

Tax and the company car

Some people need a company car, others get it as a perk. And given that it costs over €9,000 a year to run an average sized car, it could be a valuable perk if it wasn't taxed as a benefit in kind. The tax takes the gloss off the benefit particularly if the beneficiary doesn't actually do much business mileage. But it can still be worthwhile, and, for those who really do business mileage, there are ways of reducing the tax liability.

There are some benefits that an employer can provide tax-free to an employee but a car is not one of them. It is viewed as part of the recipient's salary - a benefit-in-kind (BIK) - and as such is subject to income tax. The benefit is also liable for PRSI and the Universal Social Charge. If you are a PAYE taxpayer the weekly or monthly value is included in your gross pay.

The tax charge is based on the car's original market value (OMV) and the business mileage undertaken during the year or pro-rata for periods of less than a year. The OMV is the price which the car might reasonably have been expected to fetch, if sold retail in Ireland on the open market, immediately before the date of its first registration either in Ireland or abroad in the case of an import.

There was provision in the 2008 Finance Act for the car's CO_2 emissions to be taken into account but it requires a Ministerial Order to introduce it and it has never been made.

The gross benefit-in-kind is taken as a percentage of the original market value that reduces as annual business mileage increases. The rates are as follows:

Business kms	% of original market value
Up to 24,135 kms	30%
24,136 to 32,180	24%
32,181 to 40,226	18%
40,227 to 48,271	12%
Over 48,272	6%

Some employees who do less than 24,135 in a company car can have their benefit-in-kind calculated at 24% of the OMV. To qualify they must work at least 20 hours a week, do at least 8,047 business kilometres a year and spend at least 70% of their working time away from their employer's premises. They must also keep a detailed log of their business travel and the reasons for it.

Company vans are treated in a different way. The benefit-in-kind is simply assessed at 5% of the original market value of the van. But that is not applied if certain conditions are met. To gain this exemption, the van must be used strictly for business purposes, the worker must be required by the employer to bring the van home, private use other than simply travelling to and from work must be prohibited and the worker must spend most of his or her working time away from the employer's workplace.

Company vans are assessed in a different way to cars

But there are ways of reducing the tax liability, or avoiding it altogether, by buying your own car and charging the company a mileage rate. Or if you don't claim a mileage rate you can claim tax relief on the expense of running the car including an allowance for the capital cost of buying it.

Let's have a look at an example of those calculations: Suppose you do 32,000 business kilometres a year in a company car that was bought new for €20,000. The taxable benefit in kind is assessed as 24% of that €20,000 or €4,800. The tax, at 41c in the euro, amounts to €1,968. If you manage to do an extra 180 business kilometres to bring you above the 32,180 kilometres threshold the taxable benefit would be a lower 18% of €20,000 or €3,600 and the tax liability would be reduced to €1,476.

Either way it's a painful tax but it may not be a high cost to pay for the benefit of a company car. Compare it with the depreciation costs on a €20,000 car you'd buy yourself. Without putting it on the road at all, it must be costing at least €2,500 a year in depreciation. Indeed in the early years of its life, it will lose far more than that in value.

Motorcycles weighing more than 410 kilograms are taxed on the same basis as cars. On motorcycles weighing less than that, the annual taxable benefit is calculated at 5% of the market value of the motorcycle when it was first provided.

In all cases allowance is made for any expenses borne by the employee and for any extra benefits provided by the employer.

eWorking from home

An increasing number of workers are operating from their homes using computers and telephone links to communicate with their employers or contractors. For tax purposes, many of them are self-employed but a large proportion are PAYE employees working for a single employer. The fact that they have control over where, and maybe even when, they work doesn't necessarily make them self-employed. They are taxable under the PAYE system and they and their employers are liable for PRSI. But the Revenue Commissioners recognise that there are some tax implications pecu-

Cutting the BIK on your company car

☐ The options available for reducing the tax liability on a company car fall into a number of fairly obvious categories.

Go green: Get a car with low CO_2 emissions. You may benefit if the long promised concession for low emission cars is introduced.

Reduce the price: The lower the original market price of the car, the smaller will be the benefit-in-kind assessment. That comes down to a choice over the type of car you want and the status you attach to it. There is, however, one way of having your cake and eating it i.e. having a high status car and at the same time reducing your tax liability. That's by buying an old but good second hand car. Such cars are also attractive to people who want to buy their own and charge the company for the business mileage done.

Do more mileage: If you're close to one of the thousand mile cut-off points it can obviously be worthwhile to move into the higher bracket. For instance, if you do 33,500 business kms rather than 30,000 you cut the assessment to 18% rather than 24% of its initial market value.

Use the car pool: There is no benefit-in-kind assessed if the company car you use is out of a car pool. But the Revenue apply very strict rules. The car must be made available to and used by more than one employee. The car must not normally be kept overnight at or close to any of the employees' homes. Any private use must be minimal and incidental to business use.

Charge mileage: If you use your own car for business use you can, of course, claim a mileage allowance from your employer. To escape Revenue displeasure, the payment must be based on actual mileage and an acceptable mileage rate. The employer has to get Revenue approval and while there is no definitive mileage rate, the Civil Service rates provide an indication of what may be appropriate.

Use a van: If you have a company van, rather than a company car, somewhat more favourable rules apply to the calculation of benefit-in-kind. Subject to certain conditions you may be able to take the van home and not be liable for BIK. But at worst, it's assessed as 5% of the original market value.

liar to these workers who are sometimes described as eWorkers.

It is not unusual, for instance, for employers to supply teleworkers with the computers, printers, scanners, modems, fax machines and software that they need to carry out their work. Normally when an employer gives such equipment to an employee and allows him or her to take it home it would be considered a benefit-in-kind.

Under the tax rules the employer would have to value such items and tax them under the PAYE system as if they were pay. But in the case of employees working from home, the equipment is obviously being supplied primarily for business purposes. The object is to enable the employee to do his or her work at home. In recognition of this, the Revenue is willing to bend the rules a little and ignore the fact that the computers are likely to be used occasionally for non-business purposes – anything from playing games to helping the children with their homework.

The same liberal approach is taken to the provision of a telephone line for business use or the supply of other items such as stationery and office furniture. So long as the items are supplied 'primarily' for business use, the Revenue doesn't make any benefit-in-kind assessment. The employer can supply them tax-free and can claim the costs involved as a business expense.

There are other tax implications as well. While employees working from home can save a lot in travel expenses they do incur some costs in heating and lighting their home office. They are quite entitled to claim this as an expense in their own personal tax return. Self-employed workers operating from home often claim tax relief in respect of a sixth or seventh of their household heating and lighting bills to cover that portion of the expense relating to the part of the house used for business purposes. The proportion depends on the size of the home and the proportion used for business. An employee can make a similar claim but, as with the self-employed taxpayer, they may be asked to justify it and supply receipts.

A good employer may agree to reimburse a worker for these incidental expenses that arise from working at home. And, of course, such expense payments can be made tax-free. The Revenue will allow a payment of up to €3.20 a day tax free without question. Up to that maximum, payment for expenses can be made without deduction of PAYE or PRSI and are tax free in the hands of the employee. Payments above that level require justification and receipts.

It is also possible to claim tax relief in respect of a notional rent paid for the home office but it's generally not worthwhile. Making such a claim effectively means designating part of the home as a business premises and that has all sorts of potentially nasty implications. It could create a liability for Capital Gains Tax if the home was sold. No Capital Gains Tax liability arises from the sale of a principal private residence but there is no such exemption for business premises so a pro-rata tax liability could arise.

There might also be a liability for local authority rates. The rules with regard to company cars and motoring expenses apply equally to all employees whether they work from home or at the employer's place of business. A company car is treated as a benefit-in-kind but mileage expenses can be paid tax free so long as they can be justified and don't exceed the rates paid to civil servants. Complications can arise, however, in determining the employee's normal place of work.

Tax-free mileage expenses can only be paid in respect of business journeys. Travel to and from work is not included. But if someone normally works from home, can they be given tax-free mileage expenses in respect of the occasional journey to head office? The answer is possibly "yes" although the Revenue will look at each case on its own merits. They do say that where employees work part-time from home and part-time at the employer's place of business, their base is considered to be the employer's place of business. But what's the definition of part-time? Would a brief visit every week or month constitute part-time work? The Revenue's view is far from clear.

Even where a business journey starts at the worker's home, tax-free mileage expenses may only be paid in respect of the mileage from the normal place of employment if that happens to be shorter. There is nothing to prevent employees who pay their own motoring expenses from claiming tax

Special rules with regard to benefits-in-kind are applied to items supplied for the business use of eWorkers

Claiming an income tax rebate

☐ The Revenue Commissioners estimate that as much as €100 million of tax relief is going unclaimed each year. If you have missed out it is possible to make a back claim for up to four years so the sooner you act the better. Claims can be made until the end of 2011 in respect of 2007. If you have a claim all you have to do is get some tax return forms at your tax office or by phoning 1890 30 67 06. They are easy to fill out. Each year is treated separately so get enough forms.

Rent Allowance: A taxpayer over 55 years of age, living in private rented accommodation, can claim an allowance of up to €3,200 in respect of the rent paid — €6,400 for a married couple or widowed person. The credit is half that for those under 55. Those are the 2011 allowances. They were higher in 2010 and will be phased out by 2018. See page 133.

Medical expenses: Full allowance is granted for most medical expenses at the standard rate of tax. On expenses incurred up to and including 2008 it's allowed at the taxpayer's top tax rate.

Expenses: Allowance is also made for expenses incurred by the taxpayer in doing his job. In the case of a PAYE worker, the expenses must have been wholly, exclusively, and necessarily incurred. The 'necessarily' criterion does not apply to the self-employed. The allowance can be given for tools and special work clothes.

Local authority charges: The tax relief on service charges is being abolished from 2012 but can still be claimed for earlier years. See page 242.

Union dues: This is no longer available but a back claim can still be made. The credit has been €70 since 2008.

Medical insurance: If your employer pays your medical insurance you may be entitled to the tax relief on it. But you do have to claim it.

DIRT: Those over 65, or permanently incapacitated, who are not liable for tax can claim back any DIRT stopped on deposit interest. Such people can have their interest paid DIRT-free by simply informing the bank or other deposit taker of their status.

relief on the actual cost of any business journeys. That includes fuel and also a proportion of the motor tax, insurance costs and wear and tear on the vehicle. The calculations are a bit complicated but the claim is effectively granted at the employee's top rate of tax since it is actually a deduction from taxable income. See page 266.

Calculating your tax liability

Calculating your total tax liability became easier with the introduction of tax credits although some reliefs, such as those on medical expenses and on the employment of a carer for an incapacitated spouse or relative, are still available. A full explanation of tax credits is given on page 234. The basic point is that an allowance of €1,000 is equivalent to a tax credit of €200 since each euro of standard rated allowance is worth so many times 20c in saved tax.

To calculate your annual tax liability, you first calculate a gross tax liability by applying the 20% tax rate to the first band of your income and the 41% rate to the remainder. From that gross tax liability you then deduct your tax credits to arrive at a figure for your actual liability. The size of your standard rate tax band differs according to your personal circumstances.

In 2012 a single person will pay tax at 20% on the first €32,800 of income and anything above that at 41%. A very simple example would be a single taxpayer on €40,000 a year entitled to only the personal and PAYE allowances. First of all we ignore the tax credits and calculate the tax due on the full €40,000. The sums work out like this:

€32,800 at 20c	€6,560
€7,200 at 41c	€2,952
Total	**€9,512**

From that is deducted the tax credits, in this case the personal credit of €1,650 and the PAYE tax credit of €1,650. That's a total of €3,300 which when deducted from €9,512 leaves a tax liability of €6,212. Of course, there is also the USC to pay charged on slices of income and PRSI charged at 4% on everything above €127 a week.

Standard rate tax bands

☐ The first slice of income up to these levels is charged at the standard rate of tax. Income above these levels is liable for tax at the higher rate

Category of taxpayer	2012	2011	2010
Married, one income	€41,800	€41,800	€45,400
Married, two incomes	€65,600	€65,600	€72,600
Single parents	€36,800	€36,800	€40,400
Single	€32,800	€32,800	€36,400

Let's have a look at a more detailed example. Mr. Murphy is married with two children — both still at school. He is going to earn €70,000 during 2012. In addition his company supplies him with a car which is valued as a benefit-in-kind.

Mr. Murphy will pay €4,500 in interest on a house mortgage, and will be allowed that in full since it is below the upper limit of €6,000 for non-first time buyers. It comes by way of reduced repayments since it goes directly to the building society.

His employer paid €1,000 to a health insurer last year to provide cover for the Murphys and Mr Murphy is entitled to claim the tax relief on that. He has put in the claim for the relief which is allowed on the previous year's premiums. He paid €2,000 into the company pension scheme. He claims a tax credit of €400 in respect of a local service charge. The calculations are shown in the table. In doing your own calculations, you can use the form provided on page 259.

With the exception of an agreed expenses allowance of €150, all of Mr Murphy's tax allowances are standard rated. Since his wife has no income, he is only allowed a standard rate band of €41,800. But they do benefit from the €810 home carer's credit. Mr. Murphy's total income tax liability is €13,862 while the USC takes €6,686 and PRSI another

How the Murphys' tax is calculated

☐ Tax liability is based on annual income. The PAYE administrative system tries to ensure that the tax is collected in instalments during the year. But it can result in you being over-or under-taxed. To check, you have to calculate the liability on the basis of your annual income. Here's an example of how it is done:

GROSS PAY	€70,000
Plus Benefit-in-kind (company car)	€4,500
Less Pension contributions	€2,000
TOTAL liable to PRSI and Social Charge	€74,500
TOTAL taxable	€72,500
Allowances at marginal rate i.e. agreed expenses	€150
Income after marginal rate allowances	**€72,350**
First €41,800 at 20c in euro	€8,360
Remainder (€30,700) at 41c in euro	€12,587
Tax before deductions for tax credits	**€20,947**
TAX CREDITS	
Personal credit	€3,300	
Home carers credit	€810	
Allowable interest (€4,500 @ 15c)	€675	
Healthcare premiums (€1,000 @ 20c)	€200	
Employee credit (PAYE)	€1,650	
Service charges	€400	
Total credits	**€7,085**
TOTAL INCOME TAX	**€13,862**
Plus USC (€10,036@2%, €5,980@4%, €58,484@7%)	**€4,534**
Plus PRSI (€74,500@4%)	€2,715
TOTAL TAX, PRSI and USC	**€21,111**

€2,715. Both of these charges apply to gross pay the pension contributions and benefits-in-kind. The PAYE system will ensure that the tax liability is paid in either weekly or monthly instalments over the period. If there is any under- or over-payment of tax it can be sorted out in a balancing statement at the end of the year. These are not always issued so if you think you have been overtaxed it is important for you to claim.

Doing your own sums

The pro-forma table opposite and the Murphy example can help you to do your own sums. Even if you don't feel like getting the calculator out, at least have a look at the list in the panel on page 254 of some allowances and reliefs which are commonly missed. All the figures for your own calculations can be obtained earlier in this chapter and/or by reference to Appendix 1 on page 330.

Don't forget to include taxable benefits-in-kind. The private use of a car is not the only benefit-in-kind which may be valued and assessed as part of the taxpayer's income. Other such items include the provision of accommodation, entertainment, services or indeed any benefits or facilities supplied by the employer and not paid for by the employee. There are some notable exceptions, however. Childcare facilities supplied by an employer and at least partially managed by him are not treated as a taxable benefit.

Payments towards childcare expenses are taxable, however, although legitimate expenses wholly, exclusively and necessarily incurred in the performance of one's duties are not assessed for tax. Neither is the benefit of subsidised canteen meals.

Calculating your own tax liability

☐ The pro-forma table below can help you work out your liability in the same way as the Murphys' liability is calculated in the table on page 257. There is a list of tax credits and bands in Appendix 1 on page 328 and there are more details of the credits earlier in this chapter starting on page 236.

GROSS PAY		
Plus Benefit-in-kind (company car etc.)		
Less Pension contributions		
TOTAL (a)		
Less	Allowances at marginal rate	
Total allowances at marginal rate (b)		
Income after marginal rate allowances (a minus b)		
First €41,800[1] (€32,800 single) at 20c in the euro		
Remainder at 41c in the euro		
Tax before deduction of tax credits (c)		
Tax credits		
Personal		
Allowable interest		
Local authority charges		
PAYE		
Total credits (d)		
TOTAL TAX (c minus d)		
Plus Universal Social Charge (€10,036@2%, €5,980@4%, and anything above €16,016@7%)		

Note: 1. A two income married couple has a standard rate band of at least €41,800 but where both spouses have incomes of at least €23,800 the band is widened to €65,600. The band is calculated at €41,800 plus the income of the lower earner up to a maximum of €65,600. The band is €36,800 for one parent families.

Self-employed income

A growing proportion of the workforce is self-employed. Before the recession it was about one in six and the proportion is possibly higher now. For some it's a matter of choice. For others, who might prefer the security of a permanent and pensionable job, it's simply a matter of circumstance. There are advantages and disadvantages either way. What some people view as an advantage can seem a disadvantage to others. For instance, the ability of the self-employed to delay the payments of income tax may seem attractive to the worker whose tax is stopped each week or month under the PAYE system. But the self-employed may not see it quite the same way when the tax bill has to be met each October.

By the end of October 2012, for instance, the self-employed taxpayers will have to make the following returns and payments:

- Make a final income tax return for 2011 and pay any additional tax due for that year.

- Calculate and pay preliminary tax for 2012. To avoid penalties the amount paid must be at least equal to 90% of the total tax that is eventually found to be due or be 100% of the tax actually assessed for 2011.

The self-employed don't have to prepare accounts on a calendar year basis. The accounting period taken into account by the Revenue is that which ended during the relevant tax year. So while, for instance, the 2011 tax return mentioned above might be in respect of the calendar year 2011, it might just as easily be in respect of a 12-month period ending January 31, 2011. It's up to the self-employed person to pick their own accounting period although once picked, changing it can lead to complications.

Any delay in making the necessary returns and paying the tax due can be costly. A surcharge of 5% of any tax due can be imposed if the return is anything up to two months late. If you are more than two months late in making your return the surcharge goes up to 10%. In addition to the surcharge, interest at the rate of 0.0322% a day (about 1% a month) is charged on any outstanding tax. Apart from paying the tax the self-employed are required to estimate their own tax liability. They either have to pay an accountant to do the job or do it themselves. The DIY route has been made a lot simpler in recent years through the Revenue's Online Service (ROS). It provides online versions of the tax forms that enable you to easily skip irrelevant portions of the lengthy tax returns.

While the ongoing computerisation of tax returns enables the Revenue to do much more sophisticated cross-checks, they have assured taxpayers that filing returns early or on the internet makes no difference to the compliance procedures applied. There is no greater chance of being chosen for an audit, for instance. Late returns on the other hand undergo a screening process that can increase the risk of being selected for audit. All returns made on paper are entered into the same computer programmes as those made on the internet.

The Revenue's Online Service (ROS) makes it a lot easier to file returns

Apart from the greater ease in making returns, other benefits include an ongoing facility of accessing your own tax data, and provision for filing early but not making payments until the final due date. Another plus-point is that any refunds due are likely to be processed more speedily. If you have access to the internet you can try it out for yourself without any commitment. You can access the Revenue website at www.revenue.ie. Just click on the Revenue Online Service (ROS) option towards the top left-hand corner of the screen. That brings you into the service and you can opt to have a demonstration including a trial filling in of forms. If you like what you see, you can immediately register to become a 'ROS customer'.

There are concessions for those who have recently become self-employed. The first deadline for those who became self-employed in 2011 is October 31, 2012. That's the date by which they have to pay preliminary tax for 2012 and any tax due for 2011. Once that tax is paid they have until October 31, 2013 to make a final tax return in respect of 2012. So in October 2012, they need to pay tax in respect of 2011 and preliminary tax in respect of 2012. In October 2013, they'll have to make their actual tax returns for 2011 and 2012 and pay any remaining tax due in respect of 2012 together with preliminary tax for 2013.

As mentioned above, the self-employed don't have to make up their accounts for the actual tax year i.e. the calendar year. That's something for those starting off to bear in mind. They can start their accounting year in whatever month they like. Someone starting up in business in July, for instance, may decide to operate an accounting year from August to July. Alternatively they may do their first accounts for the period from July to December and thereafter do accounts on a calendar year basis.

The cost of capital items can be written off against profits over eight years

The choice depends on a number of factors. It's often simpler to have an accounting year-end during a traditionally slack period of the year. But having the accounting year coincide with the tax year and VAT accounting year can also have significant administrative advantages. Another important factor is that the choice of year-end can help delay the payment of tax. But remember some of the cash flow benefits would be offset by delays in claiming allowances. And if you change your end of year accounting date, the Revenue will go back a year and calculate what your liability would have been had you used the new accounting period during the previous year.

You'll get an extra tax bill if the profits in that accounting period were in excess of the actual profits assessed. That doesn't mean that it can't be worthwhile changing your accounting year or picking a favourable starting date for the business. But there's likely to be many other factors involved in that decision and the cash flow benefits may not accrue for a few years in any case because the tax liability during the early years of the business are subject to special rules.

The profits assessed for the first tax year are the actual taxable income from the date of commencement to the following December 31. The profits assessed in the second year are those for the first 12 months of the business. It is only in the third year that the normal ongoing system starts to operate.

There are, of course, additional allowances which can be claimed by the self-employed. These are basically the costs of running the business. To be allowed as a tax deduction an employee must show that any expenses were incurred wholly, exclusively and necessarily for trade or professional purposes. The self-employed taxpayer has only to meet the 'wholly and exclusively' requirements. He does not have to show that the expenses were necessarily incurred. That makes more expenses allowable.

The following are some of the more general possibilities.

- Wages paid to employees. See page 280 for the benefits of formally paying wages to a spouse, or children, who are helping in the business.

- Rent paid for business premises is allowed but it may not be worthwhile claiming a notional rent allowance for a room in your private home even if it is used as an office. Instead you can claim for the cost of heating and lighting that room. Claiming for rent could result in part of your house being considered to be a commercial premises. That can have implications for local authority rates and Capital Gains Tax. There is no Capital Gains Tax on a principal residence but there could be a liability on a business premises. If it is only a matter of using one room as an office it is probably best just to claim tax relief on the 'running cost' of the room — perhaps, in the case of a four bedroomed house, one seventh of your total household outgoings on heat and light.

- Repairs to premises and repairs to plant and machinery are allowable costs but not the cost of improvements or additions.

- Interest paid on business loans. Restrictions of the type applicable to mortgage interest relief on a home do not, of course, apply.

- The cost of advertising.

- Other business costs include travelling, stationery, telecommunications, postage etc. Receipts should, of course, be kept. Motoring expenses are considered in more detail on page 266.

- Bad debts are also an allowable expense. That includes doubtful debts but the expense must relate to specific debts. It cannot simply be a global provision in the ex-

How to avoid a tax audit

☐ Most revenue audits are targeted. Some taxpayers are picked at random but the vast bulk – perhaps over 90% – are picked because of their past record or because their tax returns trigger some alarm bells in the Revenue computers or the tax inspector's mind. It is not too difficult to imagine the type of return which might trigger an audit. All you have to do is put yourself in the tax inspector's shoes and consider what he or she might be looking for. An irregular trading pattern, for instance, might be considered a bit strange and worthy of investigation. It might reflect tax evasion but it might also be due to the nature of the business, lost contracts, illness of key workers – any number of possible explanations.

☐ If there is an explanation like that, it is better to add a note to your tax return. It might just offset an audit. The same is true of the other possible factors which might put a tax inspector wondering – factors like the following:

☐ Low drawings: Where the amount of money drawn out of a business by the proprietor seems unduly low by reference to previous periods or by reference to realistic spending needs the inspector may wonder what is sustaining the taxpayer's lifestyle. If there is a legitimate explanation, make it in an addendum to your tax return.

☐ Fluctuating turnover: This may, of itself, raise questions in a tax inspector's mind unless the business is of an obvious seasonal nature. A change in the pattern is, of course, just as likely to prompt questions.

☐ VAT: Discrepancies between VAT and income or corporation tax returns are very easily spotted now that the Revenue has encouraged a standardisation of tax periods. In small businesses, particularly, there can be a legitimate explanation. If there is, it is better to make it known before an audit is prompted than during the audit.

☐ Careless returns: Sloppy VAT and PAYE returns will obviously raise a suspicion that accounting procedures are not all they should be.

pectation that a certain proportion of bills will be unpaid.

■ Allowances can also be claimed in respect of capital expenditure on plant and machinery used in the business.

Since December 4, 2002 the write off is extended over eight years at a rate of 12.5% a year. So if you buy a computer worth €1,000 you can write off €125 as a cost against your income for eight years. There are limits on the amount of allowances that can be claimed in respect of cars. There is more detail on this later in this section.

- In addition to these business expenses, the self-employed taxpayer, who has no other income, can also deduct the same personal allowances outlined above for the PAYE payer. The only exception is the PAYE allowance which the self-employed person cannot claim. The PAYE allowance is not available either in respect of a spouse working for a self-employed taxpayer. But it may be worthwhile formally employing a spouse in a family business to make use of the new wider lower-rate tax band available to two income couples. The pros and cons are examined on page 280.

Rental income

Income from the letting of flats, houses or other property is treated in the same way as the self-employed income mentioned above. It is added to the taxpayer's other income in arriving at his overall tax liability but it is not, of course, paid under the PAYE system. The one exception, is that up to €10,000 in rent can be received tax free from the letting of a room in one's principal private residence. That was increased in 2008 from the €7,620 that applied in 2007. This exemption is not available where the tenant is a 'connected' person, a child who is claiming tax relief on the rent paid.

In assessing the taxable income from rents, the normal personal allowances are available if they have not already been offset against other income and, in addition, the cost of the following may be deducted from the gross income before arriving at taxable income.

- Any rent payable by the taxpayer himself — i.e. ground rent on the premises.

- Any rates on the premises.

- 75% of the interest on borrowing used to acquire or improve the premises. This interest relief is unlimited — not subject to the upper limit which applies to mortgage interest relief on a principal residence.

- The cost of any goods or services which he provides to the tenants and which are not paid for separately from the rent. An example might be providing light in the hallways of flats.

- The cost of maintenance, repairs, insurance etc.

- Management costs i.e. cost of collecting rents, advertising for tenants etc.

- Wear and tear allowances on the cost of furniture and fittings at the rate of 12.5% of the cost over eight years. Different rules apply to expenditure incurred before December 4, 2002. See page 264. Where the costs exceed the income from the rental property, that loss is only allowed as an offset against future rental income. It cannot be used to reduce the tax due on PAYE earnings for instance.

Motor vehicles

Taxpayers, whether employed or self-employed, who use their own motor cars for business can claim for wear and tear on the car in addition to running expenses. It doesn't arise too often in the case of an employee since he or she is normally either supplied with a company cars or has the expenses reimbursed by the employer. But self-employed taxpayers very often use their own cars.

There are restrictions on the amount which can be claimed and a new system, which applies to cars bought after July 2008, precludes any claim being made in respect of cars rated for carbon emissions of more than 191 grams per kilometre. For those with emission ratings between 156 and 170 grams per kilometre the allowances and leasing expenses are based on 50% of the value of the car at the time of purchase subject to a maximum cost of €24,000. For cars with lower emissions the allowances are calculated on the value of the car subject to a maximum of €24,000.

Capital allowances on a car

Cost	€32,000
Restricted to 50% of €24,000[1]	€12,000
Allowance at 12.5% (12.5% of €12,000)	€1,500
Restricted for business use (2/3rds of €1,250)	€1,000
Allowance for year one	**€1,000**
Written down value for year two (€12,000 minus €1,000)	€11,000
Allowance at 12.5% (12.5% of €11,000)	€1,375
Restricted for business use (2/3rds of €1,833)	€917
Allowance for year two	**€917**

1. Since July 2008 assuming the car meets the middle range emission criteria. Lower emission cars would be restricted to 50% of the actual cost subject to a maximum writeoff of €24,000.

The wear and tear allowed each year is calculated at 12.5% of the declining value of the car restricted by that initial maximum value. It is also reduced to allow for any private use of the car. A one-third private to two-thirds business is a generally accepted norm.

The table above provides an example of the calculation.

No overall restriction applies to the running costs of a car used for business purposes. Where a car is used for both private and business use, the allowable business costs are apportioned generally in the ratio that business use bears to private use.

Working outside Ireland

To be liable for tax in Ireland you need to be resident in Ireland or, in some cases, to have been recently resident in Ireland. The definition of 'resident' is strictly defined in this context but it is a fairly liberal definition. A person is considered to be resident in Ireland for tax purposes if he or she is in the country for 183 days or more in a tax year; or is in the country for more than 30 days in that year and 280 days or more during that and the previous tax year.

You are counted as having spent a day in Ireland if you are in the country at the end of the day so you could, in fact, spend every day in Ireland provided you left the country every night. As a non-resident you are not liable for income tax on earnings you make abroad. But for three years after becoming non-resident, you are liable for tax on income arising in Ireland and on investment income from any source. You may also be liable for Capital Gains Tax. See page 271.

Rental income is taxable irrespective of where the landlord lives

Rental income from Irish property is taxable in Ireland even if the recipient is non-resident. If the rent is paid to an Irish-based agent he or she is liable for the tax. Otherwise the tenant is required to stop tax at 20c in the euro on the rent and pay it directly to the Revenue Commissioners. For example if the rent is €1,000 a month the tenant pays €800 to the non-resident landlord and the other €200 to the Revenue Commissioners.

Tax rebates for emigrants

An estimated 76,000 people emigrated from Ireland in 2011. About 40,000 of those were Irish, the rest foreign nationals. Emigration in not a new phenomenon. It has been a fact of Irish life for centuries. Even in the best of years the number of people leaving the country never dipped below 25,000 but the trend has been markedly upwards since early 2008. PAYE workers who emigrate having left, or lost, a job may be entitled to a tax rebate. But it has to be claimed. Such claims can be backdated for up to four years - back to and including 2008 for claims made in 2012 - so it's still not too late for those who left in recent years to put in a claim. The size of the rebate depends on a number of factors - most notably the date of leaving or losing the Irish job. The potential refund is highest for those who leave jobs a few months into the tax year. It is lowest for those who leave towards the very end of a tax year. If you leave just prior to December 31 there is unlikely to be any rebate entitlement at all.

The potential rebate can be sizeable where the emigrant spends at least a full tax year abroad. Provided that condition is met, the Irish and overseas earnings of the emigrant are effectively ignored for Irish tax purposes. Occasional visits home, of course, don't affect the entitlement.

A tax rebate may be due both in the year you leave and in the year you return

Normally an Irish resident is liable for tax in Ireland on their worldwide income and most emigrants would be considered to be resident during the year they emigrated. So technically, they should be liable for Irish tax not only on their earnings in Ireland before they leave but also on their earnings abroad during the remainder of the tax year while also paying tax in their new home. They might, of course, be able to get some relief under a double taxation agreement between Ireland and their new host country. But that's complicated to say the least. What's known as 'The Split Year Rule' allows eligible emigrants to ignore that.

If you leave Ireland to work abroad and you stay abroad for at least the following tax year, then you are only liable to pay Irish tax on income earned in Ireland before you left. There can be no disputing your claim if you have already stayed abroad for the full tax year. But you can make the claim even before you emigrate. The Revenue Commissioners may accept that you intend staying abroad if you have sold your house, for instance, or if you have evidence of taking a long-term job abroad. So, how does the rebate arise?

Under the PAYE system, your tax allowances are spread out equally over the full year. You are allowed a proportion of them for each week or month, depending on how you're paid. So if you leave a job and emigrate, after say six months, you will only have got the benefit of half of your tax allowances for the year. It's the other half that entitles you to the rebate.

Don't forget, of course, that there is the overriding condition that you are going to work outside the country for the whole of the following tax year.

The claim should be made to whatever tax office you dealt with prior to leaving Ireland. You will need to fill out a tax return for the year you left the country. Ideally you would have a copy of the P45 form you got from your Irish employer on leaving which would show your earnings up to the date you left and details of the tax stopped.

The size of a possible tax rebate is obviously not the only thing to be considered when planning a date for either emigrating from or returning to Ireland. But it's a factor to be taken into account.

The point to remember is that you can earn up to your annual tax free allowance level without any liability for income tax. Since the basic annual tax credits this year for a single individual who is paying PAYE amount to €3,300 it follows that if a single person earns less than about €16,500 in Ireland from the beginning of the tax year before he or she emigrates there is an entitlement to a full rebate of all the tax paid in that tax year i.e since January 1. The tax on €16,500 at 20% would be €3,300 but the credit offsets that, so no tax is actually payable although the PAYE system will have collected some.

A single person returning to Ireland this year can earn up to about €16,500 between the date they return and December 31 and pay no tax on it. For example, if you returned this month, get a job and decide to stay, you can earn up to €16,500 between now and December 31 without incurring any tax liability. Remember though, that this only applies to those who have spent at least a full tax year abroad. Otherwise income that you earned abroad may be taken into account.

Capital Gains Tax

If you acquire an asset at one price and sell it at a higher price or even give it away, you have made a capital gain and may be liable for tax. Some gains are exempt and gains made during any period up to January 1, 2003 are adjusted downwards to take account of inflation. For that period, you are assumed to have made a taxable gain only if the value of the asset has gone up by more than the rate of inflation.

Gains are liable for tax at the flat rate of 30% since December 6, 2011. Prior to that the rate was 25% which applied to gains made on or after April 8, 2009. The following are some of the more important exemptions:

- The first €1,270 made in each tax year.

- Gains from the sale of your principal residence including up to one acre of land. If the price you get is based on the development value of the land then you are liable for tax on the gain attributed to that value.

- Gains on the sale of a residence, also including up to an acre of land, which you have been providing for the sole occupation of a dependant relative as his or her sole residence. Dependant relative, in this regard, includes any relative who because of incapacity or infirmity is not able to maintain him or herself. Also included is the widowed mother of either spouse.

- The notional gain on the gift of a house site worth less than €500,000 to a child who builds his or her principal private residence on it. The tax becomes due if the child subsequently disposes of the site to anyone other than a spouse without having built a dwelling and lived in it for three years.

  If the site is very valuable or if there have been previous substantial gifts the child may be liable for Capital Acquisitions Tax on the gift — see page 274. But where a liability to both Capital Gains and Capital Acquisitions

Tax arise on the same transaction, one is offset against the other.

- Bonuses on Post Office or State savings schemes and gains from the disposal of Government stocks.

- Gains from life assurance policies or deferred annuities.

- Gains from the disposal of a movable tangible asset worth €2,540 or less when sold.

- Gains on assets with a predictable life of under 50 years.

- Gains from the disposal on retirement of a farm or business to a member of one's family — see below.

- Winnings from lotteries, betting etc.

Business assets

There are also special concessions for business assets passing to a child on the retirement of a parent. Business assets which have been held for 10 years by an individual aged over 55 may be passed to a natural or adopted child without any liability for Capital Gains Tax. Child, in this case, includes not only sons and daughters but also nephews or nieces who have worked full-time in the business for at least the previous five years. The child has to retain ownership of the assets for at least six years. Shares in a family company may also qualify for this concession if the person selling them or passing them on was a full-time director for at least 10 years including five years as a full-time working director.

Capital Gains Tax is payable on a self-assessment basis. The payment dates are January 1 and mid-December

Where the transfer is to someone other than a child the concessions are less generous. The seller has to be over 55 and no tax is payable provided the consideration is less than €750,000. Where the sale is for more than €750,000, the maximum tax payable is set at half the proceeds from the sale minus €750,000. There is no Capital Gains Tax payable on transfers between spouses. The transfer of assets on the death of the owner is not a disposal for tax purposes so no Capital Gains Tax liability arises. The person inheriting the assets is deemed to have acquired them at their market value on the date of the inheritance. Payment of Capital Gains Tax is made on a self assessment basis. The tax on gains made

Calculating capital gains tax liability

☐ The following is based on an asset acquired for the £ equivalent of €4,000 during the tax year 1979/80 and sold in July, 2010 for €30,000. There were selling expenses of €600. Indexation relief applies only up until December 31, 2002. The purchase price is adjusted upwards to take account of inflation between 1979 and that date. The relevant Revenue index number is 3.742. There is a list of index numbers on page 336. It is assumed that no other capital gains were made in the year.

Selling price	€30,000	
Value on 31/12/2002	€24,000	
Gain since 31/12/2002		**€6,000**
Adjusted purchase price (€4,000 x 3.742)	€14,968	
Capital gain from 1979 to 31/12/2002 (€24,000-€14,968)		**€9,032**
Total capital gain		**€15,032**
Less selling expenses		€600
Less annual exemption		€1,270
Taxable gain		**€13,162**

between January 1 and November 30 are paid in mid December while tax on gains made during December is due before the end of January. Late payments can attract interest and penalties.

Leaving the country

An anti-avoidance measure applies to the sale of business assets where the individual owns at least a 5% stake in the company. If, in those circumstances, the individual leaves Ireland but becomes resident here again within five years, the disposal of the assets is deemed to have taken place before he or she left the country and the proceeds are liable for tax in Ireland.

Inheritance and gift taxes

Capital Acquisitions Tax is charged on the value of gifts and inheritances but only if the value goes above certain thresholds. It is the recipient who is liable for the tax and the threshold applied depends on his or her relationship with the donor. There are three thresholds. All gifts and inheritances taken after December 5, 1991 are added together to decide whether one or other of the threshold levels has been reached. The thresholds were reduced with effect from November 20, 2009 and the rate increased from 20% to 22%. It was subsequently increased to 25% in respect of gifts or inheritances taken on or after April 8, 2009 and to 30% from December 6, 2011.

A foster child is entitled to the benefit of the same tax-free threshold as natural or adopted children provided he or she has been cared for, maintained by and resided with the foster parent for a successive period of five years while under the age of 18. In recent years the tax thresholds have been progressively reduced, the latest change, which applied only to the Class A threshold, taking effect from December 6, 2011.

For details of earlier thresholds and rates see page 334. In deciding whether or not a threshold has been reached, only those gifts and inheritance from the relevant class of donor are taken into account. So a person can receive €250,000 from a parent, a total of €33,208 from uncles and aunts and a further €16,604 from more distant relatives before becoming liable for tax. As outlined above all gifts and inheritances taken after December 5, 1991 are taken into account. Gifts of up to €3,000 a year from any single donor are ignored for tax purposes.

CAT on family businesses

There is a major concession on the transfer of agricultural and business assets, by way of gift or inheritance in that the value of such assets is reduced by 90% for tax purposes subject to certain conditions. It's a very valuable concession. The main condition with regard to business assets is that

Capital Acquisition Tax thresholds

☐ Capital Acquisition Tax is charged on inheritances and gifts at a standard rate of 30% since December 6, 2011. The threshold below which no tax is payable depends on the relationship of the donor to the recipient. Gifts and inheritance received after December 5, 1991 are combined in calculating whether a threshold has been breached. The rate was 25% from April 7, 2009, 22% between November 11, 2008 and April 7, 2009 and 20% before November 2008.

☐ RELATIONSHIP TO DONOR	2011 (From 8/12/2010)	2012 (from 6/12/2011)
Child, or the minor child of a deceased child. Also from child to parent but only for inheritance tax.	€332,084	€250,000
Brother, sister, child of brother or sister or lineal descendant other than a child, or the minor child of a deceased child.	€33,208	€33,208
If none of the above.	€16,604	€16,604

they are held by the recipient for at least 10 years after the transfer. If this requirement is breached within six years all of the tax concession is clawed back. If it is breached between six and 10 years the relief is reduced and the difference clawed back. But the clawback is limited to the additional relief granted under the 2007 and 2008 budgets.

The business concerned must be carried on wholly or mainly within the State but the definition of business assets is quite wide ranging. It includes property consisting of a business or an interest in a business; unquoted shares or securities of an Irish company subject to some restrictions; quoted shares or securities in an Irish company which were owned by the disponer before they became quoted; buildings, land and machinery owned by the disponer but used by a company controlled by him or her, or else used by a partnership in which he or she was a partner. Businesses whose sole or main business is dealing in land, shares, securities etc. are not covered by the concession.

The business assets on which the concession is claimed must have been owned by the disponer or his/her spouse for at least five years prior to the transfer in the case of a gift, or for at least two years where the transfer results from the death of the disponer. So the business assets don't need to have been in the family for very long to qualify for the relief.

Agricultural assets

Concessions on the valuation of agricultural assets have been a feature of Capital Acquisitions Tax since it was first introduced. They have been greatly extended in recent years in line with similar concessions which now apply to business assets outside of farming. Subject, as always, to some conditions, agricultural assets are valued at only 10% of their true market value in calculating liability for Capital Acquisitions Tax.

The reduction applies to farm assets transferred to a 'farmer'. The definition of farmer is important as is the definition of farm assets. Another important factor may be the 'valuation date' for an inheritance i.e. the date on which the transfer is deemed to take place and on which the assets are valued.

Farm assets include: farm land, buildings and woodland, machinery, livestock and bloodstock. The value of Single Farm Payment entitlements are included. Money may also qualify so long as the transfer is conditional on it being invested into qualifying agricultural property and that condition is met within two years.

That latter concession widens the availability of the relief considerably. The recipient doesn't have to have ever been a real farmer or even to have owned farm assets.

A 'farmer' in this context doesn't even have to know the difference between a bull and a cow or be able to tell the difference between wheat and barley or silage and slurry. The sole requirement is that at least 80% of his or her assets are farm assets. That requirement is measured after getting the inheritance or gift, or after complying with a requirement to buy such assets. Since 2007 the value of an off-farm residence is calculated net of any outstanding borrowings on the property.

It is not too difficult to ensure that all the necessary conditions are complied with. But it is also all too easy to fail some of the tests through a lack of adequate planning. However farmers may opt to be assessed for the tax either under the business relief rules or the agricultural relief rules whichever is more beneficial.

As with business assets the agricultural assets transferred must be held for at least six years to avoid a claw back of the concessions. If the assets are disposed of, and not replaced, after six but before 10 years there is a partial clawback. After 10 years there is no clawback.

Tax can also be reduced by ensuring that the maximum possible proportion of the assets being transferred consist of farm assets at the time of the gift or on the valuation date used for inheritance tax purposes. Crops in the ground are farm assets. Crops lifted are not. In the same way livestock are farm assets. The cash from their sale is not. Other factors to consider are outlined on page 274. There are such a wide range of factors involved that careful planning is essential and professional advice is advisable.

There is a further concession in respect of business property or shares in a company left or given to the child of a brother or sister. If the nephew or niece has spent five years working in the donor's business, the tax liability is calculated as if he or she were a child of the donor. The requirement is that the nephew or niece have worked at least 24 hours a week at a place where the business is carried out, or a lower 15 hours a week where there are no employees other than the person leaving the inheritance, or making the gift (the disponer), his or her spouse, and the recipient.

Private residences are exempt from CAT subject to certain conditions. It must be the principal private residence of the disponer and/or the recipient and the recipient must have been living there for the three years prior to the transfer and not have an interest in any other residential property. The recipient must continue to live in the property for six years after the transfer.

A 'farmer' in this context doesn't even have to know the difference between a bull and a cow

Other exemptions

The owners of heritage houses or gardens can avoid Capital Acquisitions Tax liability on a transfer by gift or inheritance by allowing limited public access. The house has to be open for 60 days a year including a minimum of 40 days during the summer. Full details of opening hours and admission prices must be notified to Fáilte Ireland before January 1 each year.

A similar exemption from CAT applies to other assets of national, scientific, historic or artistic interest. This includes works of art, scientific collections, and libraries. In all cases the tax exemption may be lost if the assets are disposed of within six years of being transferred.

Homes are exempt provided the recipient has lived in it for the previous three years and doesn't own any other residential property

Other assets which are exempt from CAT include: the first €3,000 received by way of a gift from any one disponer in any tax year; charitable gifts or inheritance; pension and death benefits payable to an employee; certain compensation payments; reasonable payments received from a family member and used for support, maintenance or education; prizes and lottery winnings; and, of course, the proceeds of qualifying insurance policies taken out with a view to paying eventual CAT liabilities.

14 Reducing your tax liability

There is nothing that can be done to alter your basic tax credits and reliefs but it is possible to reduce your tax bill by making use of those concessions and incentives that still remain even after the 2012 Budget cutbacks. Tax evasion is illegal but there is nothing wrong in knowing your entitlements and making use of them. It is not only the self-employed and high-earners who can make use of these legal tax avoidance measures. At least some of them are available to the ordinary PAYE payer as well.

The most obvious way to reduce your tax bill is to ensure that you are claiming all the reliefs to which you are entitled A lot of reliefs go unclaimed. Have a look at the panel on page 254. You may also be able to get some of your income tax free. Options range from subsidised canteen meals, leisure facilities, bus and rail passes, or even a bicycle provided by an employer. Those are outlined on page 244.

This chapter details a number of other ways of reducing your tax liability in addition to detailing the tax position for some specific groups — such as separated couples — where good management can reduce your tax liability.

Many tax reliefs go unclaimed either because of a lack of knowledge or just plain inertia

Employing your child or spouse

Self-employed people may be able to cut their family tax bills by formally paying their children and/or a spouse for work done in the business. In small family businesses it is not unusual for children and a spouse to do a significant amount of work. This is particularly true of retail businesses or farms. But the type of business does not matter.

The tax saving in the case of a child arises from the fact that any individual can earn up to €16,500 a year free of tax. The annual figure takes account of only the personal and employee tax credits. In the case of a spouse the saving can arise from the fact that a two income couple benefits from an extra €23,800 standard rate tax band – €65,600 instead of the €41,800 that applies to a single income couple. So a self-employed couple with an income of over €41,800 can benefit from having two earnings. More about that later but first the potential tax saving from employing a child.

Employing your child

A child can be paid up to €16,500 a year from the family business and not be liable for tax. If that payment reduces the parent's taxable income by that amount, the family's overall position has improved. The child can get the money free of tax while the parent would have had to pay tax at his or her highest marginal rate.

A child who works in a family firm is entitled to get a wage from it and can earn up to €16,500 tax free

That is how the tax advantage arises, but remember that the child must be genuinely doing the work for which he or she is paid. And there are other factors to be considered. It is necessary for the proprietor of the business — the father or mother in this case — to register as an employer for PAYE and PRSI purposes. And it may be necessary to pay PRSI on the wages paid to the child — even though the income is too small to be liable for tax.

These requirements need not be as onerous as they might

seem. In most cases, there will be very little paperwork after the initial registration.

There is no clear cut guideline on liability for PRSI payments. In some cases, PRSI may be payable on the money paid to the child but, if it is, there could be an eventual benefit in the form of unemployment and pay related payments if you cease employing the child.

The final decision rests with the Department of Social Welfare but it does not spell out in detail just who is liable for PRSI at the various rates. The following, however, is an outline of the factors it takes into account in making its decisions.

If the work is full time and there is a written or implied contract of employment, then the employee is liable for PRSI at the full rate. In deciding whether an implied contract exists, the Department will take account of whether there are fixed hours involved and whether there is a fixed wage or salary.

A son living on a farm and helping his father is unlikely to be considered to have a contract of employment for instance. In this case the son would be classified as a Class K contributor. If his income is more than €10,036 he will be liable for the Universal Social Charge but at a lower rate than his father would have to pay. It's payable on slices of income — 2% on the first €10,036, 4% on the next €5,979 and 7% on income above €16,016.

The Universal Social Charge would be payable on the income whether it was kept by the parent or paid to the child. Indeed, depending on the level of income, the child might be exempt or, in any case, the parent would be paying it at a higher rate.

Where a child is employed in a family business, the work is likely to be part-time and the question of whether there is a contract of employment or not may not be relevant. There are two classes of PRSI which may apply. Class M applies to employees under 16 years of age — they pay no PRSI. Close relatives working in a family business or farm are exempt from the requirements of the Protection of Young Persons (Employment) Act 1996 provided the health and safety of the young person is not put at risk.

That exception apart, the general minimum age for a regular job is 16 but a 14-year-old may be employed on light work outside of school term-time subject to a maximum of 35 hours a week on holiday work or 40 hours on work experience. A 15-year-old may be employed for eight hours a week during school-term. Class J may apply to children over 16 earning less than €38 a week. In this case, the employer pays 0.5 per cent on all income.

Anyone intending to employ someone at more than €8 a week or €36 a month must register as an employer. You write to your local tax office for a form CC151. Once completed, the taxman will take it from there. It is not too complicated and the savings can be worthwhile.

Employing a spouse

Many married couples have been forced to live on a single income in recent times and not by choice. Not only do they lose an income but they may also lose some tax benefits in the form of a wider standard rate tax band and the PAYE tax credit. The self-employed have more ways of avoiding those tax losses. If a wife of a self-employed farmer, for instance, loses an off-farm job, the couple remain a two-income couple for the remainder of that tax year enjoying both the broader tax band and the €1,650 Employee Tax Credit that the wife is entitled to by virtue of being a PAYE worker. But in the subsequent tax year, both of those benefits are lost unless the wife takes up some employment.

By formally employing her on the farm the couple can regain their two-income couple status with regard to the tax bands but to regain the Employee (PAYE) Credit the wife would need to get an off-farm PAYE job for at least some portion of the year.

There is no tax advantage in a PAYE taxpayer employing a spouse, as a housekeeper for instance. Indeed as a couple they could end up paying more tax. Take for instance the case of a wage-earning husband whose wife works at home looking after the children. If the husband were to formally pay his wife a wage he would have to pay it out of his take home pay and he wouldn't be given any tax relief on it.

Technically the Revenue might decide that the money paid to the spouse should be treated as taxable income. If you employ a tradesman to do a job around the house you have to pay him out of your after-tax income. A PAYE worker can't normally claim any relief for that but that doesn't prevent the payment being taxable in the hands of the tradesman.

In the same way a PAYE worker who formally employed his or her spouse as a housekeeper couldn't claim any relief on the payment but it would become taxable as either the spouses income or, if they opt for joint assessment, as part of the couple's joint income. There's no tax saving to be made by opting for anything other than joint assessment so the exercise is of no more than academic interest.

The only additional allowance available to the stay-at-home spouse of a PAYE worker is the special €810 tax credit for those caring for a child, elderly or permanently incapacitated person.

The situation is different for the self-employed or those involved in family businesses. Before the introduction of individualisation there was no financial sense in formally employing a spouse in a family business although many spouses actually do a significant amount of work in such businesses. The farmer's wife is an obvious example. There was no sense in a farmer putting his wife on the payroll since her income would simply be jointly assessed with his. She could benefit from no extra tax credits in her own right. She couldn't and, indeed, still can't benefit from the employee (PAYE) tax credit.

The individualisation of tax bands changed all that. It created a situation where a two income couple could end up paying significantly less tax than a single income couple. So it can be very worthwhile spreading the income from a family business between the two spouses rather than having it all going to one spouse. That can be achieved by formally employing the spouse and paying him or her an income.

The spouse must, of course, be actually working in the business and if he or she has an existing income, it must be less than €23,800, if there is to be any tax benefit. The joint income of the couple needs to be at least €41,800. The maximum tax saving is €4,998.

This potential saving arises from the fact that a two income family can benefit from a €65,600 standard rate band as opposed to the €41,800 band available to a single income family. To benefit from the full €65,600 band each spouse needs to have incomes of at least €23,800 since no one spouse can benefit from a standard rate band in excess of €41,800.

Let's have a look at an example. Tom is a self-employed businessman earning €60,000 a year. His wife is not formally employed but she does a fair amount of office work, keeping books, answering phones etc. If Tom doesn't employ his wife his income tax liability works out as follows:

Taxable Income	€60,000
€41,800 at 20c in €	€8,360
€18,000 at 41c in €	€7,462
Total Tax	**€15,822**

That liability will be reduced as a result of personal tax credits etc. but they are the same in each case so they can be ignored for the sake of the example.

So what is the situation if Tom formally employs his wife and pays her €20,000. That reduces his income - the income from the business - to €40,000. So he has now taxable income of €40,000 while Mary has taxable income of €20,000.

Tom		**Mary**	
Taxable income €40,000		Taxable income	€20,000
€40,000 at 20c	€8,000	€20,000 at 20c	€4,000
Total Tax	**€8,000**		**€4,000**

That's a grand total of €12,000 - a saving of €3,822 on the tax that would be payable if Mary wasn't formally employed. That saving would be partially eroded - to the tune of €810 - if Tom and Mary were entitled to home carer's tax credit.

They'd be entitled to the full €810 tax credit if Mary has an income of less than €5,880 and cares for a child, a person over 65 or a person who is permanently incapacitated. A dependent relative needs to live within two kilometres of Tom and Mary's home.

Tax and marriage

Married couples can opt to be taxed as two single people, but unfortunately there is seldom, if ever, any monetary advantage in so doing unless they are legally separated. There are, in fact, three options facing two income married couples. If they do nothing, they will be automatically taken to have opted for Joint Assessment. They are treated as a single unit for income tax. The second alternative, Separate Assessment, is a variant of that. The couple is still treated as a single taxable unit but is able to arrange a more equal sharing of their joint tax burden. The third alternative, Single Assessment, is to opt to be treated as two single individuals.

Let's look at each of the options in more detail.

Joint assessment

This is how most married couples are taxed. The highest earner will automatically get the benefit of the bulk of the couple's joint tax free allowances. The lower earning spouse will normally only get his or her own PAYE credit - €1,830. That only applies, of course, if the lower earning spouse is wage earning and not working in the family company.

Under joint assessment, the couple is still legally taxed as one unit. And indeed either spouse can be nominated as the accountable person for tax purposes. The important point is that concessions not used by one spouse can be transferred to the other. This is the important point. The true legal liability for tax is worked out at the end of a tax year by way of a balancing statement which combines the two incomes.

If there is a wide difference between the two incomes it is possible that the PAYE system will result in too much tax being collected during the year. But it will be refunded at the end of the year, when the balancing statement is made out. The refunds are allocated between the spouses in proportion to the tax paid by each.

Balancing statements are not prepared automatically so two income families, in particular, should do a rough calculation each year to see that they are not being overtaxed. If they are, tax returns should be speedily prepared and a balancing statement asked for.

Separate assessment

This is only a variation on the joint assessment option. Either spouse can opt for it provided they notify the tax office before April 1, in the year of assessment. Separate assessment then continues until the tax office is told otherwise by the spouse who first opted for it.

The total tax liability of the couple is not reduced in any way by separate assessment but most credits are evenly split between them. Personal, age and blind persons' credits are evenly divided while other credits may be granted to the individual bearing the cost.

The important point is that any credits unused by one person can be passed back to the other. And the same is true for unused tax bands. So if the husband has moved into the 41c tax band while the wife still has not used up all of her 20c band, there is no loss. It will be sorted out when a balancing statement is prepared at the end of the year and a refund given. But it should be possible to avoid being overtaxed during the year by dividing the credits up broadly in proportion to each person's income.

This transferability does not apply to the income levy thresholds. A couple's liability is the same no matter what form of income tax assessment they opt for.

Separate assessment is the ideal option for couples on dissimilar incomes since it allows them to split their tax credits fairly between them. Under ordinary joint assessment, a low earner can very often find his or her income very heavily taxed since the higher-earning spouse is getting the benefit of most of the tax credits. Separate assessment will not reduce their joint tax bill but it can ensure that the tax burden is more proportional to the couple's individual income levels during the year.

Single assessment

This is where the couple decide to be treated exactly as if they were two single people for tax purposes. Their tax liabilities are kept entirely separate. In general, there is no financial advantage to be gained by opting for single assessment. If their incomes are about equal, the joint tax bill of a couple opting for single assessment may be no higher than if they opted for joint or separate assessment. But if one of their incomes is considerably higher than the other, they could end up with a higher tax bill because one spouse cannot pass on the benefit of unused credits or standard rate band to the other. Either spouse can serve notice on the taxman for single assessment at any time during the tax year. Once served, the notice is applied to that year and all subsequent years until it is withdrawn. Only the person who served the notice can withdraw it.

Separated couples

Undoubtedly reflecting the growing number of couples who are separating or getting divorced, the Revenue Commissioners has an explanatory booklet on "What to do about tax when you separate". It's a complicated area and there are plenty of choices to make. Agreeing on the right one can leave the couple jointly better off. It can be well worthwhile doing the sums, getting advice if necessary and then reaching agreement with your estranged spouse.

The Revenue have adopted a broad definition of separation. A couple is deemed to have separated if they are divorced, legally separated or even if they have separated in what the Revenue describe as "such circumstances that the separation is likely to be permanent." Exactly what that means is not clear but presumably decisions are made on a case-by-case basis.

Also described as separated are couples who have obtained a civil annulment but, unlike other separated couples, they cannot opt to continue being treated as a married couple for tax purposes. Legally separated and even divorced couples can. Indeed the option is available to any separated couple who are both resident in the country provided neither has remarried or has to make legally binding maintenance payments. There can be an advantage in being taxed as a married couple but both spouses must agree to adopt that option. There are other options and unfortunately there can be no hard and fast rule as to which is best. What is best for one couple may not be for another. It depends on individual circumstances. It can also depend on the couple jointly opting for the best alternative. It's not good enough for one to make the choice. They both have to.

Even divorced couples can opt to be treated as married for tax purposes

Continuing to be taxed as a married couple may be as good an option as any if one spouse has no earnings. The earning spouse gets the benefit of all the tax allowances and rate bands available to a married couple and simply makes maintenance payments out of net income. The non-earning spouse has no tax liability on those maintenance payments.

A separated couple can, in some circumstances, qualify for more tax reliefs than a couple living together.

If both spouses are earning, the situation is a bit more complicated. Normally in such a case the spouse earning the most money enjoys the bulk of the tax allowances so the lower earning spouse can lose out if nothing is done. The ideal first step would be to split the tax allowances and bands in a more equitable manner between the two. Provided that they are both resident in the State they can agree to opt for separate assessment. They are still considered to be a married couple for tax purposes but the tax allowances and low rate tax band are split more equitably between them.

Separated couples may both be able to claim one-parent family tax credits

Any couple can have that done. It's generally a good idea since it means that the lower earning spouse isn't left paying an unequal share of the couple's tax burden. Since they are still a married couple, for tax purposes, there are no tax implications for any payments such as maintenance from one to the other. More commonly, a separated couple will opt to be treated as two single individuals for tax purposes. This is also an option for any married couple but there is no benefit for a couple living together and there may, indeed, be extra tax to pay because a low-earning spouse cannot then pass unused allowances or tax bands over to a higher earning spouse.

For a separated couple, however, it can make sense and be financially beneficial to be treated as two single individuals i.e. opting for single tax assessment. Their tax affairs become completely separated in line with the reality of their situation and legally enforceable maintenance payments become taxable in the hands of the recipient.

Let's suppose that under a court settlement a husband has to pay his wife €5,000 a year. He is allowed to deduct that €5,000 from his income for tax purposes. If he is paying tax at 41c in the euro that could save him €2,050 (5,000 times 41c). The money becomes taxable in the hands of the wife but depending on circumstances she may not be liable for tax. This doesn't apply to payments in respect of children.

A husband making maintenance payments may calculate that he would be better off foregoing the tax relief on the maintenance payments and getting the full married allowances instead. On single assessment he is only getting the benefit of a single person's tax allowances and bands. So he can gain but there are potential gains and losses for his wife. She would no longer be taxed on the maintenance payment but if she is getting a single parent's allowance she would lose it. Whether the gains outweigh the losses depend on each individual case.

Separated individuals may both be entitled to claim a one-parent family tax credit in respect of dependant children. The child must reside with the claimant for at least part of the tax year. But that could be as short as one night. To be eligible, the couple cannot be living together as man and wife.

There are extra tax benefits to be claimed in the year of separation provided the couple had not previously opted to be taxed as two single individuals. Once they meet that condition one spouse can claim the full married tax credit and tax band for the year while the other spouse gets the benefit of a single person's tax credit and tax band.

Share incentives

Profit sharing schemes are hardly at the top of anybody's agenda at the moment but, when the inevitable recovery takes hold, they could afford many businesses an opportunity to reward continuing productivity gains while maintaining competitiveness. The attraction for workers is that bonuses paid under approved profit sharing schemes can be received tax-free.

Tax-free profit sharing

Workers have few opportunities of getting tax-free income. Wages are automatically taxed and the tax definition of wages is wide. It includes practically all monies paid by an employer to an employee. Most non-cash benefits are taxable too. They are treated as benefits-in-kind and their cash value is liable for income tax. Examples are company cars and loans at preferential interest rates.

But there are some benefits that can be provided tax-free by an employer including subsidised canteen meals and sporting facilities — see page 244 — and certain bonus payments paid under an approved profits sharing scheme.

It is possible to get up to €12,700 of your income tax free each year through an approved profit-sharing scheme

There has been no tax relief on approved share option schemes since November 2010 but the tax relief on other schemes remain. Companies can still give tax-free bonuses in the form of shares up to an annual value of €12,700 provided certain other conditions are met. This is a benefit-in-kind which is not taxable although since January 1, 2011, the benefit is subject to PRSI and the Universal Social Charge (USC). It was also intended to make such bonuses liable to employers' PRSI but that was subsequently resinded as part of the new Government's jobs initiative.

Shares, of course, are only really valuable if they can be sold. So ideally the company should be quoted on the stock exchange or be tradable in some other way. Many such schemes are operated by companies whose shares are quoted abroad. To qualify for the tax relief they have to be held for three years.

The rules of the scheme must apply equally to all workers. The level of bonuses may be related to salary or years of service or both but those are the only criteria that can be used. Blue-eyed boys or green-eyed girls cannot get special treatment. The total amount to be given out in shares may be linked in some way to profitability or productivity in the same way as any other bonus scheme. From the employer's point of view the bonus is expected to provide an incentive which, when, given in the form of shares is worth significantly more to the recipient than a similar amount of taxable cash.

At least during the required three years, and subsequently if they hold onto the shares, the workers have a direct interest in the performance of those shares on the stock exchange. So the employer has built in an initial incentive of a bonus scheme and an ongoing incentive in the form of share ownership.

During those three years, and subsequently if they keep the shares, the workers have a direct interest in the performance of those shares on the stock exchange. So the employer has built in an initial incentive of a bonus scheme and an ongoing incentive in the form of share ownership. Obviously this type of profit-sharing scheme is of particular interest in companies whose shares are listed on the stock exchange, although many of those schemes are, in fact, operated by firms whose shares are quoted abroad rather than in Ireland.

SAYE

Save As You Earn (SAYE) schemes have been operated in Ireland for some years. A tax concession applies where workers are given options to buy shares at a discounted price and the money required to eventually exercise the options is saved over a three or five year period. That may sound a bit complicated but it isn't. It works like this. The workers are given options to buy shares in the company at a fixed price. That price can be up to 25% below the current value of the shares. Those options can be exercised in three, five, or seven years time when, hopefully, the shares will be worth a lot more than the price fixed at the time that the option was given. If the shares haven't risen in price, then there is no need to exercise the option. So there is no chance of incurring a loss.

As an adjunct to the share options, the workers involved agree to save a fixed amount each week or month out of their pay packages. That money comes out of their net pay i.e. after tax, and goes into a special fund. The only tax concession on the savings part of the deal is that the money in the fund grows tax-free – any interest or bonus earned is free of income tax and DIRT. SAYE schemes are obviously less attractive to workers than the bonus type scheme where up to €12,700 worth of shares a year can be given tax-free. Under the SAYE scheme, the shares have to be paid for albeit at what may be a bargain basement price. But they are likely to be more favoured by employers for the very reason that the shares aren't entirely free. The company should also benefit from a more motivated and involved workforce. To get Revenue approval, schemes must comply with a number of requirements.

■   All workers with more than a minimum service must be invited to participate. Workers with more than three years service can't be excluded.

■   The same rules must apply to all but they may provide for the level of share option granted to vary according to pay levels and/or length of service.

■   The workers must contract to save at least €12 and at most €500 a month over a three or five-year period. The actual amount saved should be geared to provide about the right amount to pay for the shares when the options are exercised.

No income tax is payable either when the option is granted or when the shares are actually purchased. That might not seem like a concession at all, but remember that the worker will be getting shares worth more than the price paid. That's a benefit he's getting from his employer. Normally the difference between the price paid for the shares and their actual value would be treated as a benefit-in-kind and taxed as such. Suppose the worker has an option to buy 1,000 shares at €2 each. That was the price fixed at the time the options were granted. It is now three or five years later and the shares have trebled in value to €6. In exercising his option the worker will be paying €2,000 for the 1,000 shares that are now worth €6,000 on the stock market. He'll be making €4,000 on the deal. And that's tax free since it is not considered to be a benefit-in-kind although it is subject to PRSI and the Universal Social Charge.

But although there is no income tax liability, the worker may be liable for Capital Gains Tax when the shares are sold. The gain is calculated as the difference between the price the shares are sold for and the price actually paid. The first €1,270 of gain in any tax year is exempt. For details of Capital Gains Tax, see page 271.

If this worker sold his shares immediately after buying them he would be liable for tax on €2,730 (€4,000 minus the exemption of €1,270. The standard rate of Capital Gains Tax is 25% so the tax payable would be €682. Of course if the sale was spread over a number of years the tax could be avoided entirely. But tax or no tax, SAYE schemes effectively allow workers to share in any growth in their company's fortunes without taking any risk themselves. They have to save a regular amount but the savings are kept in a risk-free account and the option to buy the shares doesn't have to be exercised if the share price has gone down. The Revenue has specimen rules and forms for use in these schemes. Copies can be obtained from your local tax office.

Employment and Investment Incentive

The Employment and Investment Incentive Scheme (EII) came into operation on November 25, 2011 replacing the old Business Expansion Scheme which continues to be open for new applicants until December 31, 2011. The changes include a significant increase in the maximum amount of investment that qualifies for tax relief and, perhaps more significantly an major extension in the type of projects that qualify. The Business Expansion Scheme allowed an individual to claim tax relief on up to €150,000 invested in shares in certain qualified companies. There was an overall cap of €2 million on the qualifying investments of which no more than €1.5 million could be raised in any one year. Under the EII scheme the maximum individual investment remains at €150,000 a year but the cap on total investment has been raised to €10 million of which a maximum of €2.5 million can be raised in any one year.

Investments in many service type businesses not covered by the BES scheme can qualify under the EII scheme. BES tax relief was limited to manufacturing, traded services and certain tourism, horticulture and music projects. Traded services are ventures which have to compete in the international market place. But those restrictions don't apply to EII which is open to trade generally with some stated exceptions.

Excluded activities include:

- Share, commodity dealing etc.
- Financing activities
- Professional services
- Dealing in or developing land
- Occupying woodlands
- Operating nursing and care homes
- Coal, steel and shipping
- Operating or managing hotels, guesthouses and self-catering accommodation.

The project must be based in Ireland and larger projects with more than 250 employees or with a turnover of more than €50 million must be located outside of Counties Dublin, Meath, Kildare, Wicklow and Cork City with the exception of Cork Docklands.

To qualify for the tax relief the investment must be made in the purchase of ordinary unquoted shares. They have to be held for three years. The investor can claim tax relief at the rate of 30% in the year the investment is made and gets tax relief at the rate of 11% at the end of the three years provided the project has resulted in increased employment and increased payroll costs or the company has increased its research and development spending.

Investors do need to take care. If you want to make use of them you have three options.

- Invest in a fund that will in turn invest your money in a number of EII projects thereby spreading the risk.

- Invest in a single project run by someone else.

- Invest in your own project.

The second option is obviously the most risky. The shares you buy, either directly or through an investment fund, cannot be quoted on any stock exchange. So you have no easy way of judging exactly what they are worth. There is no market price. Neither will you have any great idea of future prospects. And, most importantly, there may be no guarantee that you will be able to dispose of the shares in the future.

You may get some basic accounts, or you may not. Either way you will not be able to do the type of detailed analysis necessary to really value the shares or to evaluate the prospects of the venture during the five years for which you have to hold the shares if the tax relief is not to be clawed back. The trick is to reduce the risk as much as possible.

Investing in a fund rather than a single project helps to spread the risk. But up-front charges of about 3% are common and fund managers may have a conflict of interest since they collect fees from the companies in which they invest. Also not all funds have guaranteed exit mechanisms.

As well as the commission there is another initial cost in that it may take up to a year to get the tax rebate. The investor who puts up €10,000 may have to wait to get the initial €3,000 rebate or reduction in his or her tax bill. So there is a loss of interest on that money. The shares bought have, by the nature of the scheme, to be in relatively small enterprises. While they have the potential to grow rapidly, they also have the potential to fail miserably.

If things go well, and the return is big enough, there may be a liability for Capital Gains Tax but it is the full investment, before tax relief, which is taken into account as the purchase price of the shares. So, in our example, the purchase price is €10,000 not the actual post tax relief cost of €5,900. The

The best use of the EII scheme is to invest in your own project

first €1,270 of capital gains realised by an individual in any one year is tax free so providing the net return on the investment does not exceed €11,270 on the initial real investment of €5,900, there would be no liability for Capital Gains Tax on present rules. Indeed a larger tax free gain would be possible given that the initial purchase price is adjusted upwards in line with inflation.

Seed Capital Scheme

A variant of the EII scheme, known as the Seed Capital Scheme, allows for tax relief on up to €600,000 invested in a new project. The relief can be claimed against tax paid during the previous six years at a maximum rate of €100,000 a year thereby giving the claimant a refund of tax previously paid. The basic requirement is that the would-be entrepreneur is setting up a new business having been employed. The claimant has to take up full-time work with the new company and needs to have been paying a lot of tax over the previous six years to qualify for the maximum rebate. You can only reclaim tax that you have actually paid.

The incentive isn't available to an existing businessman moving into a new venture. To ensure that this requirement is met, the condition is that no more than half of the claimant's income, subject to a maximum of €50,000, should have come from non-employment sources during the three years prior to the year preceding that in which the first investment is made. Each claimant must own at least 15% of the venture.

Tax breaks for relatives and carers

Many elderly people are not liable for tax simply because their incomes are too small. The tax exemption limits that apply to the over 65s were reduced in 2011 but were left unchanged in 2012. A couple, either of whom is over 65, can have an income of up to €36,000 before coming into the tax net. While in general it is good to be exempt from tax, there are drawbacks such as not being able to claim tax reliefs such as those on medical expenses.

Those over 70 are no longer automatically entitled to a medical card but even if they have medical cards they can be faced with nursing care expenses that are not covered and anyone can incur very heavy medical expenses. If the pensioners involved are not liable for tax, they obviously can't claim back the tax relief. But there are other ways in which tax relief, at the top rate, can be effectively transferred to children or other relatives who provide some financial help to the elderly people.

- Making use of special carer's tax allowance.

- Making payments under a deed of covenant.

The Special Carer's Allowance provides tax relief on the cost of employing a carer to look after a person who is permanently incapacitated by old age or infirmity. Subject to a maximum of €50,000 a year, it can be claimed by the taxpayer, his or her spouse or by other family members who contribute to the cost.

The relief can be spread among a number of claimants and is allowed at the claimant's top rate of tax so it can be worth up to €20,500 (41% of €50,000) a year in saved tax. It can be claimed in respect of wages and other costs such as expenses and employer's PRSI. It may not be necessary to register as an employer but, if it is, the Revenue will let you know. It's an easy enough process. Tax relief is, of course, allowed on medical expenses including nursing home costs but the relief is only available at the standard rate except on nursing home costs. The relief can be claimed by the person availing

Wording for a tax-saving covenant

☐ **There is no need to get a solicitor to draw up a covenant. Simply copy the wording below and adjust it as appropriate with the relevant details.**

☐ I...(name)

of...(address)

covenant to pay my father/mother

....(name)

of...(address)

an amount which after the deduction of

standard rate tax amounts to €.........(sum) each year for

seven years or during our joint lives or until (name of third

party) says the covenant should end the first payment to be

made during December 2012.

Signed, sealed and delivered by

.................................(name)

in the present of.................................

(witness's name, address and occupation)

.............(Date)

of the care or by any relative who is paying or contributing to the cost. See page 238.

Making a covenant

Another way for children to get tax relief on contributions made to a parent's healthcare, is by making the payments under covenant. In this way, it may be possible to get tax relief at the top rate. These can be used irrespective of what the money is finally used for. And can provide some tax relief where anyone makes a regular payment to a person over 65 or to an incapacitated person of any age provided the recipient has unused tax credits. A covenant is simply a legal undertaking to make payments to someone else. In order to qualify for tax relief, the payments must be capable of lasting for at least six years.

Let's assume, for example, that a son wants to give €1,000 a year to a parent. Other brothers and sisters could, of course, do the same thing providing the total transfer doesn't push the parent into the tax net. The son makes out a covenant and pays €800 to the parent. The parent gets the other €200 by way of a tax rebate while the son also gets an additional tax relief of €210. The cost to the son is only €590 while his parent gets the benefit of €1,000. The logic behind this is relatively simple although you do not have to understand it to benefit from it. Because the son has entered into a legal undertaking to pass the money to the parent, the taxman considers the €1,000 to be the parent's rather than his. But he has already paid €410 tax on the €1,000. That tax is returned. The mechanics of the process dictate that €210 goes back to the son and €200 to the parent.

There are some points to watch. Covenants may provide no saving if a parent is in receipt of some means-tested benefit since the covenanted income will be treated as means. The covenant should include a clause allowing it to be ended on the say so of a third party e.g. a trusted friend. This is just a precaution. A covenant can always be ended by the mutual consent of the parties but circumstances could arise where it is desirable to end it for one reason or another and the mutual consent cannot be obtained. For instance, the covenant could, in some circumstances, prevent the parent from claiming some means-tested benefit. There is nothing to stop the parent making gifts of money to his or her children, even returning the covenanted money provided that there is no prior understanding that that would be done.

The covenant can be drawn up using the wording above. You don't need a solicitor. You can get the wording typed out or even write it out filling in the blanks as appropriate. The person making the covenant should also get a tax form

A child can give a parent €1,000 at an cost of only €590

R185 from his or her local tax office. It is a single page requiring very little information such as PPS number and place of employment or source of income. That completed form together with the signed covenant and, of course, the money is given to the parent. The parent can get a tax reclaim form from a local tax office or by phoning the special Revenue Commissioner's 24 hour phone number at LoCall 1890 306706. That form together with a copy of the covenant, form R185 and some evidence of the payment (a photocopy of the cheque or a bank statement showing the deposit) is then returned to the tax office.

Your shortcut to a quick & easy money makeover

This isn't a book designed to be read from cover to cover. It's for dipping into for information and advice on personal finance matters that can save, or make, you money. This section is an exception. It is designed to be read from start to finish to help you undertake a money makeover, reviewing past financial decisions, setting goals and mapping out the path towards achieving them. Financial decisions, once made, are all too seldom reviewed, yet the financial environment is constantly evolving while personal circumstances change. Ideally you should be constantly evaluating the appropriateness of past decisions in the light of these changes. But an occasional review is better than nothing. Remember that even if you initially picked the right bank, mortgage lender, insurance company or investment outlets, they may no longer be the best choice.

There's money to be made, or saved, by sitting down and reading this section on your own or with a partner. It suggests the questions that you should be asking yourself and the courses of action you should be taking. You'll find more information on the various topics in the main body of the book.

In this section you'll find advice on

- **Quick fixes if your budget has become unbalanced**
- **Planning for the future**

> — Identifying your goals,
>
> — assessing where you are, and
>
> — mapping a route to where you want to be.

Getting started

Financial planning has become an essential part of modern living and it shouldn't be a daunting prospect. It's simply a matter of ensuring that you make the best use of your resources to achieve your personal goals. It's an on-going process that needs to take into account, not only changing personal circumstances, but also the ever-evolving financial environment. The need for such a review is not confined to those facing some financial difficulty. Everyone is likely to benefit from a money makeover.

It's basically a matter of evaluating past decisions in light of current circumstances and future prospects and then taking fresh decisions taking account of where you are and where you want to be.

The first steps

- ☐ **Identify your goals.**

- ☐ **Assess your current financial position.**

- ☐ **Map a route from where you are to where you want to be.**

Set your own objectives depending on your personal circumstances and make-up.

There's a list of suggestions on the next page. The choice is yours. Take your pick but be as specific as possible.

Once you have set your goals you need to assess how realistic they are and how best to achieve them. Your objectives don't exist in isolation. Their achievement depends partly on the resources you can muster and partly on the decisions you make. In all cases, of course, you have to start from where you are now.

Setting out your goals

When setting objectives, it's important to be as specific as possible. It's not enough to simply decide that you should put some money aside for retirement. That's not a bad objective but it's likely to remain just that unless you put some flesh on the bones by outlining the sort of pension you would like to have and how much you are prepared to put aside. You need to go beyond drawing up a simple wish list.

The following are some possible goals that you might consider setting for yourself.

Short-term

- ☐ Manage your day-to-day finances to better effect. You must start by drawing up a budget. When are you going to do it?

- ☐ Pay off short-term debt. How much and when?

- ☐ Save for a holiday or a special occasion. Set a target amount, for instance how much on each pay day?

- ☐ Provide adequate insurance cover for the family. Preview your existing cover and detail your requirements.

- ☐ Build up an emergency fund. Outline exactly how much and how you intend doing it.

- ☐ Make a will. Set a firm date for doing it.

Medium-term

- ☐ Buy a house. Save how much by when?

- ☐ Build up an investment fund. For what purpose? What's your target?

- ☐ Save for future needs, children's education etc. Set a target amount and a time scale.

Long-term

- ☐ Provide for retirement. Set a pension target and detail any shortcomings in your existing entitlements.

ℰℭ Where are you now?

Informed decisions can only be made on the basis of adequate information. So there is no alternative to drawing up a personal statement of affairs. That statement of affairs should include a balance sheet of assets and liabilities and also as detailed an income and expenditure budget as you can prepare. That may seem like a chore but it is one that can yield high dividends. The worksheets, starting on page 318 can be used as a guide.

Your balance sheet

List all your assets itemising the value of each and the income it is generating. Include items such as your house which could yield an income if you decided, for instance, to trade down to a smaller home.

It's nice listing your assets but it's just as important to list your liabilities. Include details of all outstanding loans, the repayments, interest rates and any early repayment penalties that may be applicable. Just gathering that information will help you pinpoint those loans that should get first priority, if and when you have any spare cash.

Planning is about making choices which should only be made on the basis of good information

Your income and expenditure budget

Detailing your income is easy enough. It's harder to itemise your spending. But you do really need to get an idea of where the money goes. You can adjust the worksheets to suit your own circumstances. The more detail you include, the easier it is to pinpoint those areas where spending patterns can be changed to best suit your goals. Once you have gathered the data, you can carry out your own financial audit covering:

- ☐ Savings and investments
- ☐ Borrowings
- ☐ Family protection
- ☐ Retirement planning
- ☐ Wills and inheritance planning

So let's look at the questions you need to ask yourself in each of these areas and the actions you may need to take.

෫ Savings and investments

Saving is an essential element in achieving many financial goals. At its simplest, it only involves holding onto some money to meet the occasional expense that arises less regularly than pay days – a holiday, car insurance, even ESB or gas bills. That type of saving has more to do with the day-to-day management of money. The money is normally not at any risk and since the amounts are small, the rate of return doesn't really matter.

That's not the case, of course, with savings aimed at some longer-term objective such as providing a pension in retirement, saving the deposit for a house or paying for a child's education. Rates of return and risk are important considerations and there is a wide range of options from basic deposit accounts to investment funds. There is no definitive correct choice. It depends on individual circumstances, attitudes to risk and personal goals.

Saving is an essential element in achieving many financial goals including the ability to borrow

Whatever the goals, there is a need to consider:

? Questions you should be asking yourself

- [ ] the provision of emergency funds,
- [ ] the scope for saving, and
- [ ] **whether existing investments are yielding the best possible returns.**

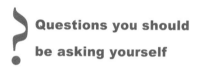 Savings and investments 2

Ensuring that you have speedy access to financial resources is a reasonable first goal to have in the area of saving and investment. The need is to provide flexibility to take advantage of opportunities that may arise and it also provides security against running into financial difficulties in an emergency. Emergencies come in all shapes and sizes. There are the joyful ones like being invited to a wedding abroad or having your favourite team qualify for international competition. But there can be less happy events such as unexpected medical expenses, a cut in income or an unforeseen bill for major car repairs. This goal of having access to money when needed can be satisfied, to some extent, by having the ability to borrow by way of overdraft, term loan or by having a sufficiently flexible credit card limit.

? Questions you should be asking yourself

- ☐ Have you got an overdraft permission?

- ☐ Have you a good enough relationship with a bank or credit union to be able to borrow at short notice in an emergency?

- ☐ Is your credit card limit adequate?

Actions to take

✔ Save to build up an emergency fund.

✔ Ensure that some of your savings can be accessed reasonably quickly without penalty.

✔ Develop a good relationship with a bank to ensure speedy access to overdrafts and/or term loans.

✔ Get an increase in your credit card limit if you can be sure of using it only for short-term needs and not for getting into long-term debt.

Savings and investments 3

Y ou can think of saving as the actual act of accumulating money. In the short term, you may simply be building up a surplus in your bank account when your income exceeds your spending needs. Or you may be putting regular amounts into a formal savings plan such as an investment fund. There is a wide range of options and the boundary between saving and investment is far from clear cut.

Questions you should be asking yourself

- ☐ What are you saving for?
- ☐ How much can you afford to save?
- ☐ Do you need access to your money?
- ☐ Are you getting the best rate of return consistent with your need for access?
- ☐ Have you too much, or not enough money, in relatively low yielding short-term savings?

Actions to take

- ✔ Specify targets for your savings in terms of amounts and time scales.
- ✔ Undertake regular reviews to ensure that you are getting the best rate of return.

ℰℴ Savings and investments 4

Your current mix of investments reflects a series of past decisions. They may have been the right decisions at the time but they need to be assessed in the light of your present circumstances, your future needs and changes in the financial environment. There is a need to regularly review your investments to ensure that you are getting the best possible return. If you have completed the worksheets starting on page 318 you have a list of investments, rates of return and some measure of the degree of risk involved in each.

Part of your assessment involves balancing your attitude to risk with the riskiness of your investments. It's important to consider both when making a decision on any investment option. It is very much an individual decision but it's a decision that should be taken in a considered way and not just left to a gut feeling.

In assessing each investment, the starting point has to be the present, not sometime in the past. In the case of a share, all that counts is the current price and future prospects. The price you bought at should have no place in the decision making. The share is currently worth a certain amount of money. If that money can yield a better return elsewhere then it should be switched. The loss has already been incurred even if it hasn't been realised.

If one of your objectives is saving for retirement then investing in a pension fund offers very distinct advantages, in particular the tax relief on contributions. So investing in a pension fund must be considered as one of your options. The restrictions on what can be done with the money built up in a personal pension fund or through additional voluntary contributions (AVCs) to a pension scheme have been greatly eased in recent years, adding to the attractions of such investments.

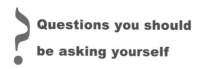

Questions you should be asking yourself

☐ **Examine each investment in the light of**

— **what you want from it,**

— **when you might have to cash it in,**

— **the prospects over that time frame,**

— **its riskiness in the light of your current attitude to risk, and**

— **the alternatives.**

□ Is your mix of personal use assets (house, holiday home, boat, caravan etc.) appropriate to your needs? Should you be thinking of converting them into investment assets by, for instance, selling or renting them?

□ Are you making the best possible use of investment tax incentives such as those on pensions contributions?

Actions to take

✔ List all your investments.

✔ Assess each one as outlined above.

✔ Make the appropriate adjustments. If in doubt, take professional advice.

✔ Read Chapter 3, Page 43.

Borrowing

Sensible borrowing can play a beneficial role in your financial planning. It's not a case of saving being good and borrowing being bad. Both have a part to play in managing your finances over time. There is a cost involved in borrowing, of course, but that can often be justified. The benefits can outweigh those costs. Borrowing can enable you to buy something now rather than having to wait until you have saved up the money. Whether or not that benefit offsets the interest paid on the loan is a matter of personal judgement. In some cases such as borrowing to buy a home, tax relief can reduce the real rate of interest payable.

Interest is not the only cost, of course. There is a reduction in financial flexibility if only because of the need to meet the repayments on the loan. But also if you have borrowed for one purpose, it reduces your ability to borrow for something else. There is a tendency not to review financial decisions once made. This can be particularly true of borrowing. Yet personal circumstances change, interest rates vary and the need for debt may diminish as other assets become available. So it is worthwhile doing an occasional check of outstanding loans.

The following are some of the factors you should consider:

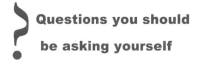

Questions you should be asking yourself

☐ **Are you paying over the odds on any of your loans? Are there savings to be made by switching lenders?**

☐ **Have you got the optimum mix of loans in terms of interest payable and risk? Could you increase your mortgage, for instance, and pay off some more expensive loans. That's not a decision to be taken lightly since you are increasing the risk of losing your home in the event of default.**

☐ **Are you relying too much on expensive credit card debt?**

☐ Have you spare cash that would be better used in reducing your debt?

☐ What capacity have you got to borrow more? Could you use extra money to finance projects that would yield benefits more than enough to offset the cost?

Actions to take

✔ List details of all your loans.

✔ Check out the interest rates being charged by the competition.

✔ Work out the savings that could be achieved by switching, taking into account any penalties for early repayment. The bigger the loan the greater the potential. Switch if the savings justify it.

✔ If you are constantly in debt on your credit card get a term loan to pay it off. If you go into long-term credit card debt again take the scissors to your card.

✔ Work out the cost/benefits of borrowing to finance new projects where you think the benefits may outweigh the costs.

✔ Read Chapter 5 page 98.

✍ Family protection

Every financial plan should contain some provision for insurance against the unexpected and the unpredictable. That includes protection against the financial loss that you and/or your dependants would suffer as a result of serious illness, disability or untimely death. It should also include some general insurance against other losses, house insurance, for instance.

With life insurance policies, it is important not to confuse saving for the future with actual life insurance which only pays a benefit in the event of death. Many policies include elements of both although that is not the case with what is known as term insurance which simply provides a guaranteed benefit, either a lump sum or an income, if death occurs within a fixed term of years. If the insured person is still alive at the end of the term, then no benefit is paid and it may seem like a waste of money. But the premiums have provided a very real benefit by way of peace of mind in much the same way as house or car insurance. People are generally pleased if they never have to make a claim on their house or car policies. They certainly have no reason to believe that the policies represented bad value just because they didn't have to claim. The same principle applies to term life insurance.

If the aim is to provide the maximum financial cushion for dependants in the event of your untimely death, then term insurance is the cheapest option. For the same death cover the premiums are significantly lower than for policies that do include a savings element. There is a trade off between the ideal level of protection and the premiums payable. But meaningful decisions on the balance to be taken must be based on a consideration of all the information. Having decided what you need, it can be well worthwhile shopping around for the best deal.

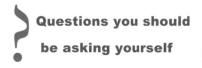
Questions you should be asking yourself

☐ What events, over which I have no control, could cause me or my family to suffer significant financial loss? Which of them can I reasonably insure against?

☐ What financial loss would I or my family suffer in the event of my partner or I suffering illness, disability or death?

☐ How much of that potential loss should I insure against?

☐ What cover have I already got, including cover through company schemes?

☐ If my partner or I were to lose our jobs, would the impact be sufficiently severe to justify taking out some insurance protection for the repayment of loans?

☐ Have I sufficient cover on my house and other assets?

Actions to take

✔ Gather the information on the work sheet on page 326. Compare the cover you have with what you think you need.

✔ If you need additional cover, shop around for the cheapest option. Term insurance rates differ greatly from company to company for exactly the same cover. Take advice.

✔ Check out your general insurance policies. Shop around when they come up for renewal.

✔ Read chapter 4, page 79.

❧ Planning for retirement

There's a lot more to planning for retirement than simply ensuring an adequate income. But it's a good place to start. People are living longer and hoping to retire earlier. The income you'll have in retirement will generally depend on how much you have saved during your working life, either in a pension scheme or otherwise.

Saving through a pension fund makes good sense if only because of the generous tax relief available on contributions. The tax concession is available on up to 40% of income put into a pension fund and effectively means a State top-up of 41c for every 59c contributed by a top income tax payer. Given that from 2011 there is no relief from PRSI or the new Universal Social Charge there is very little incentive for those paying tax at the standard rate to save for retirement through a pension fund given that the money cannot be accessed until retirement.

Pension entitlements can be enhanced if you take action early enough. It's too late to start planning when you reach retirement age. Some pension schemes are better than others. If your scheme is not one of the best or if you are not going to have enough service to qualify for the maximum pension, there's undoubtedly scope for improving your entitlements and getting some tax relief in the process.

With many newer occupational pension schemes, the pension is determined by the amount of contributions made and the investment return on the fund. The same is true, of course, of personal pension plans taken out by the self-employed and by those not in occupational pension schemes. It is particularly important with such schemes to regularly assess the likely future benefits since the outlook can change significantly with changing interest rates and stock market trends. You may want to increase your contributions if investment returns are not coming up to expectations.

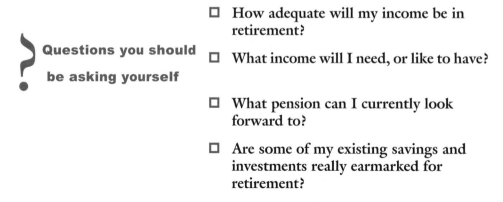

Questions you should be asking yourself

- ☐ How adequate will my income be in retirement?

- ☐ What income will I need, or like to have?

- ☐ What pension can I currently look forward to?

- ☐ Are some of my existing savings and investments really earmarked for retirement?

PLANNING FOR RETIREMENT

Actions to take

✔ Calculate how much it costs you to live now and how much you would ideally like to be able to spend in the future.

✔ Detail the income you can expect to have in retirement from existing entitlements.

✔ Do the calculations as accurately as you can. If you are in a company scheme, find out in detail how your pension is calculated. If it is based on 'final pay' how is that defined? Is there provision for post-retirement increases? Will some pension continue to be paid to your spouse should you die?

✔ If you have your own personal pension plan or if you are in a defined contribution scheme that doesn't guarantee a pension based on final salary, what pension can you expect on current projections? How confident are you that those projections can be achieved?

✔ Check your entitlement to a State pension.

✔ If there is a shortfall between your potential income and your lifestyle aspirations then you should take advice on increasing your pension entitlement.

✔ If you are in an occupational scheme, examine the possibility of making additional voluntary contributions (AVCs) or opening an additional personal pension plan of your own.

✔ Look at the possibility of speeding up contributions, if you are a top-rate taxpayer.

✔ If you are self-employed, you need to look at improving your personal pension scheme or starting one if you haven't already done so.

✔ Read chapter 10, page 174.

ℰ Wills, inheritances

Everyone over 18 years of age, or younger if married, should have a will drawn up. It's particularly important, of course, where there are dependants. A will ensures that your estate is distributed in accordance with your plans. Once drawn up, wills should not just be put away and forgotten. They need to be reviewed from time to time. Personal circumstances change and so too does the tax code.

Inheritance tax isn't going to be a problem for most people inheriting from parents. But there are situations where a little advance planning can significantly reduce the tax payable. Wills must be in writing. While a simple will can be drawn up at home, it is well worthwhile getting a solicitor to oversee the task. The few euro it costs can save a lot of trouble in the long run. Tax advice is also advisable where the estate is large or some of it is going to people other than a spouse or children. Conferring an enduring power of attorney on a person of your choice allows him or her to look after your affairs in the event of you becoming unable to because of illness or disability. The role can be shared. It can also be limited and there is a range of legal protections. A living will, while of no legal import, can provide family and friends with an insight into your wishes should you lose the ability to make them known yourself.

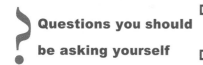
Questions you should be asking yourself

☐ **Have I drawn up a will and, if so, does it still reflect my wishes?**

☐ **Do I need to change the executor?**

☐ **Have I considered the inheritance tax implications? If one person is to inherit the family home will he or she be able to benefit from the tax exemption on homes?**

☐ **Have I drawn up an enduring power of attorney? Should I draw up a living will?**

Actions to take

✔ Consider all the questions above and take the appropriate actions as soon as possible, seeking professional advice if you have any doubts over the impact of what you are doing.

✔ Read chapter 7 page 134.

Get a clearer view of your family's finances.

FOOD & CLOTHING
25%

HEALTH & EDUCATION
15%

HOME REPAYMENTS
30%

ENTERTAINMENT & LEISURE
10%

SAVING & PENSIONS
10%

UTILITIES
10%

We've a range of tools and brochures to help you keep your finances on track.

Drop into any branch

Try our Family Finance Budgeting Tool.
Go to aib.ie/family

1890 724 724

www.aib.ie

be with AIB

The above percentages are for indication purposes only and do not constitute financial advice. Terms and conditions apply. Allied Irish Banks, p.l.c. is regulated by the Central Bank of Ireland.

Gathering information for your financial makeover

The first step in any financial review is to marshal the facts. You don't necessarily have to put them down in writing but it helps if you do. A little time spent filling in the worksheets on the following pages can help to concentrate the mind and aid the decision-making process. The worksheets provide only a suggested format. You may find it simpler to jot down the information on a separate sheet of paper.

These worksheets can be useful in assessing how best to achieve your financial goals

But whether you do it in your mind or on paper, any financial review entails much the same approach. It involves a consideration of all your assets itemising the current value and the income it is currently generating and/or may generate in the future. You should include items like your house that could free up money if you decided, for instance to trade down to a smaller home. Everything that could yield an income is relevant. It is worth ranking each investment according to risk.

You could allocate a score between one and five – the higher the score the greater the risk that the value of your investment could go down. You might allocate a score of one to bank deposits, three to a broadly based managed fund and five to speculative shares. Liabilities, mainly borrowings, are the other side of the balance sheet. They need to be listed and assessed too. It can often make financial sense to borrow, while, at other times, it may make sense to use spare resources to pay off borrowings. Keeping an eye on income and expenditure trends can also be useful particularly if they start getting out of balance. Preparing a list of your insurance policies, such as suggested on the next page, may encourage you to review your needs and your existing cover from time to time. That can save you money so it's well worthwhile.

Assets	Current value	Income	Rate of return	Risk rating
Savings accounts				
Investment funds				
Shares				
Business assets				
Family home				
Holiday home				
Boat, caravan				
Other				
Pension entitlements				
Total				

Liabilities	Amount due	Interest rate	Repayments
Mortgage			
Car loan			
Credit card debt			
Term loans			
Other loans			
Total			

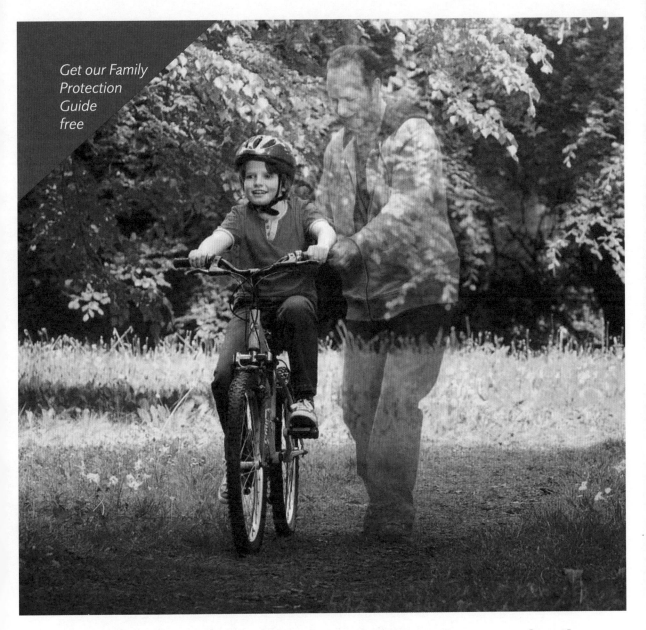

Get our Family
Protection
Guide
free

You don't have to be there, to be there for your family

It is the instinct of every parent to protect their children. And you can give your family the protection they deserve from as little as €15 a month with an Irish Life protection plan. To find out more, or for your free copy of our guide to protecting your family, talk to your broker, your financial adviser or go to **irishlife.ie**

Protect what's important to you.

The cost of cover depends on your age, gender and health. Terms and conditions apply.
Irish Life Assurance plc is regulated by the Central Bank of Ireland.

Income		Notes
Salaries – net		
Child benefit		
Interest, dividends from savings and investments		
Other, self-employed income, asset sales etc.		
Occupational pension		
Social welfare pension		
Other		
Total income		

One of the golden rules of finance is that the demands on a family budget tend to exceed the amount of money available. The solutions fall into two categories. You can reduce spending demands or you can increase the supply of money. Neither option is easy.

If the money supply is fixed, then budgeting is going to involve economising and there are two approaches to that. You can zone in on the big items of spending and try to save on those or you can try to penny-pinch right across the board. Your personal make-up has a lot to do with which approach you adopt. But, in every case, it makes some sense to put a little structure on your budget.

Don't let the word 'budget' put you off. Drawing up a budget can be as simple, or as complicated, as you like. The amount of detail is up to yourself. But even the simplest budget will help you to get the most from your spending.

Expenditure		Notes
Mortgage/rent		
Loan repayments		
Electricity/gas		
Fuel/heating oil		
Telephone/internet		
Life/medical insurance		
Car insurance/tax		
Household insurance		
TV – cable and licence		
Housekeeping		
Newspapers		
Petrol/public transport		
Meals out		
Entertainment/sport/hobbies		
Personal grooming		
Alcohol and tobacco		
Books, stationery etc.		
Medical expenses		
Clothing		
House maintenance		
Car maintenance		
Garden		
Donations etc.		
Holidays/Christmas		
Total expenditure		
Total income		From previous page
Surplus or shortfall		

Life insurance Company	Policy number	Person insured	Purpose, cover and maturity date

General insurance Type	Company	Policy number	Amount insured
House			
Car			
All risks			
Medical			
Disability			
Travel			

Other

Will – date when last reviewed where it can be found	
PPS Number	
Employer's tax number	
Credit card numbers	

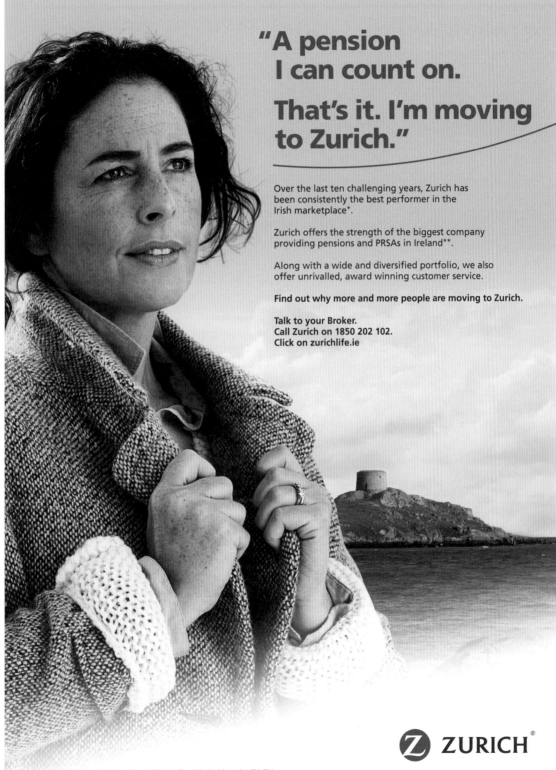

"A pension I can count on. That's it. I'm moving to Zurich."

Over the last ten challenging years, Zurich has been consistently the best performer in the Irish marketplace*.

Zurich offers the strength of the biggest company providing pensions and PRSAs in Ireland**.

Along with a wide and diversified portfolio, we also offer unrivalled, award winning customer service.

Find out why more and more people are moving to Zurich.

**Talk to your Broker.
Call Zurich on 1850 202 102.
Click on zurichlife.ie**

ZURICH®

Source: Bloomberg (market capitalisation) and Standard & Poor's (financial ratings) September 20th 2011.
*Returns based on an independent survey September 2011. **Biggest refers to market capitalisation.
Zurich Life Assurance plc is regulated by the Central Bank of Ireland.

Income tax rate bands

2009

SINGLE
| First €36,400 | 20% |
| Balance | 41% |

MARRIED (one income)
| First €45,400 | 20% |
| Balance | 41% |

SINGLE PARENT
| First €40,400 | 20% |
| Balance | 41% |

MARRIED (two income)
| Up to €72,800 | 20% |
| Balance | 41% |

2010

SINGLE
| First €36,400 | 20% |
| Balance | 41% |

MARRIED (one income)
| First €45,400 | 20% |
| Balance | 41% |

SINGLE PARENT
| First €40,400 | 20% |
| Balance | 41% |

MARRIED (two income)
| Up to €72,800 | 20% |
| Balance | 41% |

2011

SINGLE
| First €32,800 | 20% |
| Balance | 41% |

MARRIED (one income)
| First €41,800 | 20% |
| Balance | 41% |

SINGLE PARENT
| First €36,800 | 20% |
| Balance | 41% |

MARRIED (two income)
| Up to €65,600 | 20% |
| Balance | 41% |

2012

SINGLE
| First €32,800 | 20% |
| Balance | 41% |

MARRIED (one income)
| First €41,800 | 20% |
| Balance | 41% |

SINGLE PARENT
| First €36,800 | 20% |
| Balance | 41% |

MARRIED (two income)
| Up to €65,600 | 20% |
| Balance | 41% |

Some treat pensions as savings, others as investments.

At Friends First, we have pensions for both.

Putting away money for your retirement is the sensible thing to do. Therefore it's only fair that you decide on the level of risk involved.

Are you a saver who likes to watch your funds grow steadily? Or an investor who is comfortable playing the markets?

For over 175 years Friends First have been helping both types of customer - and everyone in between - to successfully meet their retirement needs.

So whether you prefer safe protected options or you like to speculate on the currency and equity markets, contact your Independent Financial Adviser today for a Friends First pension that will work for you.

Friends First
Part of the EUREKO Group

Looking forward to your future

Warning :	The value of your investment may go down as well as up.
Warning :	This product may be affected by changes in currency exchange rates.
Warning :	If you invest in this product you may lose some or all of the money you invest.

Friends First Life Assurance Company Limited is regulated by the Central Bank of Ireland.

Basic tax credits

	2008	2009	2010	2011	2012
Single	€1,830	€1,830	€1,830	€1,650	€1,650
Married	€3,660	€3,660	€3,660	€3,300	€3,300
Widowed	€1,830	€1,830	€1,830	€1,650	€1,650
– without dependent children	€2,430	€2,430	€2,430	€2,190	€2190
Additional one-parent family	€1,830	€1,830	€1,830	€1,650	€1,650
Widowed parent – bereaved in					
2011	—	—	—	—	€3,600
2010	—	—	—	€4,000	€3,150
2009	—	—	€4,000	€3,500	€2,700
2008	—	€4,000	€3,500	€3,000	€2,250
2007	€3,500	€3,250	€3,000	€2,500	€2,800
2006	€3,250	€3,000	€2,500	€2,000	—
Home carers	€900	€900	€900	€810	€810
Employee credit	€1,830	€1,830	€1,830	€1,650	€1,650
Age single/widowed	€325	€325	€325	€245	€245
– married	€650	€650	€650	€490	€490
Blind – one spouse blind	€1,830	€1,830	€1,830	€1,650	€1,650
– both spouses blind	€3,660	€3,660	€3,660	€3,300	€3,300
Incapacitated child	€3,660	€3,660	€3,660	€3,300	€3,300
Dependant relative	€80	€80	€80	€70	€70
Carer for incapacitated person[1]	€10,000	€10,000	€10,000	€10,000	€10,000
Rent credit for under 55s (maximum)					
– single	€400	€400	€400	€320	€320
– married/widowed	€800	€800	€800	€640	€640
Rent credit for over 55s (maximum)					
– single	€800	€800	€800	€640	€640
– married/widowed	€1,600	€1,600	€1,600	€1,280	€1,280
Trade union subs	€70	€70	€70	nil	nil

(1) This allowance is allowed at the taxpayer's top rate of tax. The tax credits shown, only reflect the relief at the standard rate. Those paying tax at the top rate get additional relief.

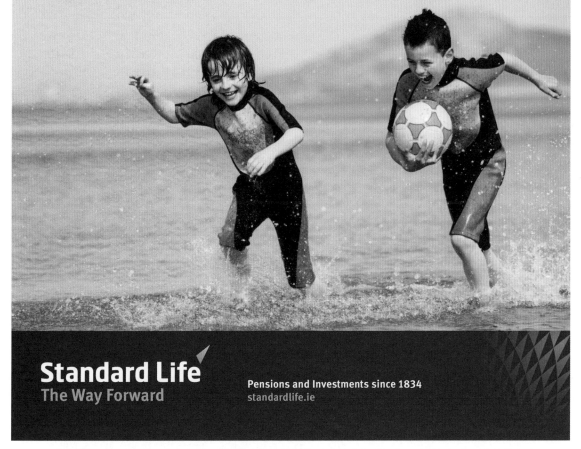

You like flexibility.
So do we.

With our pensions you can choose to start, stop, increase
and reduce your payments to suit your changing needs.
Talk to your financial adviser or visit standardlife.ie

Standard Life
The Way Forward

Pensions and Investments since 1834
standardlife.ie

Exemption limits

Persons whose income is below these limits are exempt from income tax.

	2008	2009	2010	2011	2012
Single/w'ed over 65	€20,000	€20,000	€20,000	€18,000	€18,000
Married over 65	€40,000	€40,000	€40,000	€36,000	€36,000

The limits increase by €571 for the first and second child and €825 for each subsequent child. Persons earning more than these exemption limits are entitled to marginal relief. Their total tax liability can be no more than 40% of the income above the threshold.

PRSI and health levy

See page 247 for full details of the PRSI and the new Universal Social Charge for 2012.

PRSI rates (including the health levy up until its abolition in 2011) applicable to most private sector and State employees, are as follows.

		Private Sector	State Sector	Self Employed
2009				
To April 30	First €52,000	6%	3.15%	5%
	Next €48,100	2%	2%	5%
	Remainder	2.5%	2.5%	5.5%
From May 1	First €75,036	8%	5.15%	7%
	Next €48,100	2%	2%	5%
	Remainder	2.5%	2.5%	5%
2011				
From July 2	First €75,036	4%	0.9%	4%
	Remainder	4%	4%	4%

No PRSI is payable on the first €127 weekly earned by those paying the 6% rate. For those paying the lower rate the first €26 is exempt. Those earning less than €500 in any week were exempt from the health levy. Those earning less than €352 are exempt from PRSI.

Where Family Counts

Financial Review

Whatever your plans are for the future

Come in and talk to us

Whether it's setting off on a trip of a lifetime, providing for your children's education or saving for retirement – taking time out to review your plans is always worthwhile.

That's why we'd like to invite you for a free review of your finances, to help you get on with your life plans.

It costs nothing and we think you'll find it's time well spent.

Drop into your local EBS or call us on 1850 654321.

Capital Acquisitions Tax

Threshold Levels

Relationship to donor	2010[1]	2011[2]	2012[3]
Child, or the minor child of a deceased child. Also from child to parent but only for inheritance tax. Since December 6, 2000 foster children enjoy the same tax threshold as natural and adopted children.	€414,799	€332,084	€250,000
Brother, sister, child of brother or sister or lineal descendant other than a child, or the minor child of a deceased child	€41,481	€33,208	€33,208
If none of the above	€20,740	€16,604	€16,604

1. From 1/1/10 to 8/12/10. **2**. From 8/12/10. **3**. From 6/12/2011

For gifts and inheritances received between December 1, 1999 and November 20, 2008 the tax was charged at a rate of 20%. It was increased to 22% from November 20, 2008 and to 25% in respect of gifts and inheritances received on or after April 8, 2009. The rate was raised to 30% from December 6, 2011.

There are major concessions for agricultural land passing to a farmer; for business assets, and for businesses or farms passing to a nephew or niece who has worked on the farm or in the business for at least five years. Since December 1999, a house left to someone who has been living in it for at least three years is exempt from the tax, subject to certain conditions— **see page 274**.

An Bord Pinsean
The Pensions Board

Pension
Calculator

Information
Booklets

Pension
Checklist

ENGAGE WITH YOUR

PENSION

www.pensionsboard.ie

Capital Gains Tax

The first €1,270 of gains made by an individual (€2,540 for a married couple) in any one tax year are exempt from the tax. A flat rate of 30% applies to disposals made after December 6, 2011. Prior to that the rate was 25%. The rate was 20% up to October 15, 2008 and 22% between then and April 7, 2009. For periods up to the end of 2003, the acquisition price of assets other than development land, is multiplied by an index number which adjusts it for inflation in the intervening period. The index numbers are as follows:-

Assets bought in	And sold during						from
	1998/99	*1999/00*	*2000/01*	*2001**	*2002*	*2003*	*2004 on*
1974/75	6.215	6.313	6.582	6.930	7.180	7.528	7.528
1975/76	5.020	5.099	5.316	5.597	5.799	6.080	6.080
1976/77	4.325	4.393	4.580	4.822	4.996	5.238	5.238
1977/78	3.707	3.766	3.926	4.133	4.283	4.490	4.490
1978/79	3.425	3.479	3.627	3.819	3.956	4.148	4.148
1979/80	3.090	3.139	3.272	3.445	3.570	3.742	3.742
1980/81	2.675	2.718	2.833	2.983	3.091	3.240	3.240
1981/82	2.211	2.246	2.342	2.465	2.554	2.678	2.678
1982/83	1.860	1.890	1.970	2.074	2.149	2.253	2.253
1983/84	1.654	1.680	1.752	1.844	1.911	2.003	2.003
1984/85	1.502	1.525	1.590	1.674	1.735	1.819	1.819
1985/86	1.414	1.436	1.497	1.577	1.633	1.713	1.713
1986/87	1.352	1.373	1.432	1.507	1.562	1.637	1.637
1987/88	1.307	1.328	1.384	1.457	1.510	1.583	1.583
1988/89	1.282	1.303	1.358	1.430	1.481	1.553	1.553
1989/90	1.241	1.261	1.314	1.384	1.434	1.503	1.503
1990/91	1.191	1.210	1.261	1.328	1.376	1.442	1.442
1991/92	1.161	1.179	1.229	1.294	1.341	1.406	1.406
1992/93	1.120	1.138	1.186	1.249	1.294	1.356	1.356
1993/94	1.099	1.117	1.164	1.226	1.270	1.331	1.331
1994/95	1.081	1.098	1.144	1.205	1.248	1.309	1.309
1995/96	1.054	1.071	1.116	1.175	1.218	1.277	1.277
1996/97	1.033	1.050	1.094	1.152	1.194	1.251	1.251
1997/98	1.017	1.033	1.077	1.134	1.175	1.232	1.232
1998/99	—	1.016	1.059	1.115	1.156	1.212	1.212
1999/00	—	—	1.043	1.098	1.138	1.193	1.193
2000/01	—	—	—	1.053	1.091	1.144	1.144
2001	—	—	—	—	1.037	1.087	1.087
2002	—	—	—	—	—	1.049	1.049
from 2003 on	—	—	—	—	—	—	1.000

* period from 6/4/2001 to 31/12/2001

CARRY ALL YOUR
CASH IN A CARD

FAST · HANDY · SAFE

Civil Service Mileage

Per mile

Official travel in a calendar year	Under 1200cc	1,201cc to 1,500cc	1,501cc and over
Up to 4,000 miles	62.94c	74.42c	95.05c
4,001 miles and over	34.13c	38.00c	45.79c
Reduced rate	23.55c	26.76c	31.36c

Per kilometre

Official travel in a calendar year	Under 1200cc	1,201cc to 1,500cc	1,501cc and over
Up to 6,437km	39.12c	46.25c	59.07c
6,438km and over	21.22c	23.62c	28.46c
Reduced rate	14.65c	16.64c	19.49c

The reduced rate applies where the journey is connected with official business but not actually in the discharge of that business. These rates apply from March 5, 2009.

Motoring benefit-in-kind

The use of a company car is assessed for tax as a benefit-in-kind. The assessment is based on a percentage of the original market value of the car, depending on the business mileage done during the year.

Business miles	CO_2 emissions		
	up to 155g/km	156g/km 190g/km	over 191g/km
Under 24,000	30%	35%	40%
24,001 to 32,000	24%	28%	32%
32,001 to 40,000	18%	21%	24%
40,001 to 48,000	12%	14%	16%
Above 48,000	6%	7%	8%

Social Insurance

Maximum rates of benefit	*2011*	*2012*[1]
State pension (contributory)/(transition)		
Under 80		
— Personal rate	€230.30	€230.30
— Person with qualified adult under 66	€383.80	€383.80
— Person with qualified adult over 66	€436.60	€436.60
80 or over		
— Personal rate	€240.30	€240.30
— Person with qualified adult under 66	€393.80	€393.80
— Person with qualified adult over 66	€446.60	€446.60
Widow's/Widower's Contributory Pension		
— Under 66	€193.50	€193.50
— 66 and under 80	€230.30	€230.30
— 80 or over	€240.30	€240.30
Invalidity Pension		
Personal rate under 65	€193.50	€193.50
Personal rate 65 to 80	€230.30	€230.30
Personal rate 80 or over	€240.30	€240.30
Person under 65 with qualified adult	€331.60	€331.60
Person 65 to 80 with qualified adult [2]	€436.60	€436.60
Person over 80 with qualified adult [2]	€446.60	€446.60
Jobseeker's/Illness Benefit[3]		
Personal rate	€188.00	€188.00
Person with qualified adult	€312.10	€312.10
Guardian's payment (contributory)	€161.00	€161.10
Payments for child dependants		
All schemes — Each qualified child	€29.80	€29.80

Note: *1. From January 1, 2012. 2. Over 66. 3. Lower rates apply to new claimants under 25.*

Social Assistance

Maximum weekly rates of social assistance	*2011*	*2012*[1]
State pension (non-contributory)		
Under 80		
— Personal rate	€219.00	€219.00
— Person with qualified adult	€363.70	€363.70
80 or over		
— Personal rate	€229.00	€229.00
— Person with qualified adult	€373.70	€373.70
Widow's/Widower's non-contributory pension		
— Under 66	€188.00	€188.00
— 66 and under 80	€219.00	€219.00
— 80 or over	€229.00	€229.00
Disability allowance		
— Personal rate	€188.00	€188.00
— Person with qualified adult	€312.80	€312.80
Jobseeker's allowance [2]		
— Personal rate	€196.00	€196.00
— Person with qualified adult	€326.10	€326.10
Supplementary welfare allowance		
— Personal rate	€186.00	€186.00
— Person with qualified adult	€310.80	€310.80
One-parent family payment *(including one child)*		
— Under 66	€217.80	€217.80
Carer's allowance		
— Under 66	€204.00	€204.00
— 66 years and over	€239.00	€239.00
Increases for child dependants		
— All schemes	€29.80	€29.80
Child Benefit		
— For first and second child	€140.00	€140.00
— For third child	€167.00	€148.00
— For fourth child onwards	€177.00	€160.00

Note: *1. From January 1, 2012.* **2.** *Lower rates apply to new claimants under 25.*

Index

A

APR   100

Annuities   **58**

Assurance

     see life insurance   79

B

Bank deposit guarantees   **53**

Benefits in kind

     taxed and tax free   244

Borrowing   **98**

     APR   100

     Finance houses   106

     Pawnbrokers   109

     Term loans   103

     Top-up mortgages   106

Budget accounts   **103**

Building societies

     Personal loans   106

Business expansion scheme   **293**

C

Capital Gains Tax   **271**

Capital allowances   **264**

     Motor cars   266

Charge cards   **26, 32**

Consumer Protection Act   **193**

Consumer protection   **193**

     European union   209

     Financial advisers   198

     Financial services ombudsman   197

     Goods and services   209

     Insurance   93

     Investor Compensation Fund   70

     Life insurance   92

     Pensions ombudsman   180

     Solicitors   198

     Unfair contracts   211

     Using your rights   212

Credit Cards   **26**

     Insurance   170

     The rules   34

     borrowing   109

Credit Unions   **54, 108**

Credit ratings   **205**

D

DIRT

     Rate of tax   54

     Reclaiming   54

     Tax free accounts for over 65s   54

Data Protection Act   **199**

Debit cards   **26, 32**

Debt, tackling problems   **112**

Deposit account

     As an investment   51

Deposit accounts

     Government guarantees   53

Divorce   **139**

E

Employment and Investment Incentive Scheme   **293**

Employment legislation   **144**

     Emergency time off   159

     Equality rights   157

     Holiday entitlements   149, 151

     Maternity leave   159

     Minimum notice   156

     Minimum wage   153

     Parental leave   159

     Redundancy entitlements   146, 148, 150

     Unfair dismissal   155

Equality rights   **157**

Executors   **140**

F

Fair deal nursing home subvention   **224, 226**

Family home

     Rights to   138

Farmers

     Capital acquisitions tax   276

Freedom of information act   **204**

H

Health insurance   **95, 97**

Hire purchase   **109**

Holiday Money   **37**

House insurance

     All risks   173

Buildings   167
Contents   169
Switching   208
House purchase   118
Costs   124
Mortgage tax relief   129

I

Impaired life annutities   59
Inheritance
Capital Acquisition Tax   274
Joint bank accounts   21
Interest rates
APR   100
Investment funds   63
Switching   69

J

Job Assist tax relief   15
Judicial separation   139

L

Laser cards   26
Life insurance   79
Borrowing against   109
Buying   89, 91
Critical illness   87
Disability   86
Endowment   84
Income protection   86
Term   81
Whole of life   84

M

Marital breakdown
Pension rights   192
Medical expenses
Tax relief   238
Medical insurance   95
Minimum notice   156
Minimum wage   153
Mobile phone insurance   170
Money makeover
Worksheets   318
Your guide   301
Mortgages
Dealing with arrears   114
Endowment versus annuity   122
Home Choice Loan   122
Local Authority loans   122

Tax relief   129
Top-up mortgages   106

N

National Consumer Agency   193
Nursing home fair deal   224, 226

P

Part-time workers
Social welfare   216
Pensions   174
ARFs and AMRFs   191
AVCs   149
Changes proposed   176
Defined benefit   181
Defined contribution   181
Last minute AVCs   183
Legal rights of members   180
Marital breakdown   192
Maximum contributions   241
Occupational schemes   179, 183
Options on retirement   189
Social welfare   217
Personal liability insurance   172
Post Office Investment Schemes
Instalment Saving   55
Saving Certificates   55
Savings Bonds   55
Solidarity Bond   56
Postbank   54
Power of attorney   136
Probate, taking out   141

Q

Quinn Health Care   96

R

Redundancy entitlements
Tax   147
Rental income
Rent a room tax relief   133
Tax treatment   265
payable to non-residents   268
Revenue online service ROS   261

S

Same-sex couples
Emergency time off work   159
Saving
Regular Saving Accounts   52
Small Claims Court   201

Social welfare

Budget changes 2012   215
Child Benefit   218
Contributory old age pension   217
Family Income Supplement   219
Free TV licence   229
Free telephone rental   229
Free travel   227
Homemakers Scheme   219
Medical cards   221, 223
Part-time workers   216
Rates of payment   340
Transitional State Pension   219

Stock Exchange

stocks and shares   60

Store Cards   35

Store budget accounts   107

Sunday work

Entitlement to pay   155

T

Tax

Benefits in kind   244
Calculating liability   255, 257
Company cars   248
Income tax certs   234
Income tax credits   236
Job Assist relief   15

On inheritances and gifts   274
On investment funds   65
On rental income   265
PAYE   233
Personal allowances   236
Reducing your bill   230, 232
Rent a room tax relief   133
Rent relief   133
Summary of rates   328
eWorkers   250

Tracker bonds   57

Travel insurance   40

U

Unfair dismissal   155

Unit funds   65, 67

Unit trusts   67

V

VHI   95

W

Wills   134

Duties of executors   140
Living will   138
Taking out probate   141

Working hours   152

NOTES